I S S H O N I

Book 2

• Margaret Lee •

An introductory course in Japanese

Illustrated by Junko Fukuoka

MORETON BAY PUBLISHING

Moreton Bay Publishing
102 Dodds St
South Melbourne 3205

Moreton Bay Publishing is an imprint of **Nelson I⊤P®**

Nelson I⊤P® *an International Thomson Publishing company*

First Published 1991 by Moreton Bay Publishing
10 9 8 7 6
05 04 03 02 01 00 99 98 97

Copyright © M. Lee 1991

National Library of Australia
Cataloguing-in-Publication data

Lee, Margaret.
    Isshoni. Book 2.
    ISBN 0 949199 39 7.
    1. Japanese language – Textbooks for foreign speakers –
English. I Fukuoka, Junko. II. Title.
495.682421

Cover designed by Concept Communications Pty Ltd, Brisbane
Printed in Australia by Merino Lithographics Pty Ltd, Brisbane

Nelson Australia Pty Limited ACN 004 603 454 (incorporated in
Victoria) trading as Nelson ITP.

The 46 mnemonic aids to the katakana script employed in
Isshoni have been reproduced from the *Gold Coast Lanuage
Centre Katakana Kit* developed by L. Kirwan. The author
wishes to express her gratitude for permission to re-use these
aids. Copies of the kits are available from:

Gold Coast Language Centre
P.O. Box 7229
Gold Coast Mail Centre, QLD 4217

Contents

Acknowledgements

I offer my sincere thanks to my many teaching colleagues and students of Japanese who encouraged and supported me throughout this project. I also wish to acknowledge the invaluable help and expertise offered by the following people:

Kerry and Yasushi Ikei
Yoshiyuki Setoguchi
Toshiaki and Masami Kashihara
Nobuyoshi, Yuriko and Aiko Nakayama

Particular thanks go to Kyoko Seo, Lecturer, Division of Asian and International Studies, Griffith University, who provided much invaluable help in the final stages of editing and checking.

To my children, Andrew and Mariana

Unit 13

My Japanese family
私の日本の家族
（わたし　にほん　かぞく）

A

アンドルーさんは　日本の　かぞくと　すんでいます。
マシューさんは　オーストラリアの　がっこうで　日本ごを　べんきょう　しています。

...アンドルーさん、ホスト　ファミリーは
どうですか。おとうさんは　かいしゃで　はたら
いていますか。おかあさんも　はたらいています
か。らいねん　ぼくは　日本へ　いきたいです。
でも　たかいですね！...

...おとうさんは　かいしゃで　はたらいていま
せん。おいしゃさん　です。おかあさんは
はたらいていません。でも　PTAいいんです。
よく　がっこうに　いきます。おかあさんは
とても　しんせつです。...

マリアさんも　日本に　すんでいます。　マリアさんも　エリザベスさんに　日本ごで　かきます。

...ほんとうに　オーストラリアへ　かえりたく
ないです。　かぞくは　五人　です。こどもは
二人　います。おにいさんは　二十二さいです。
いもうとさんは　十三さい　です。いもうとさん
の　なまえは　えみこです。えみこさんは
ちゅうがっこうの　せいとです。おばあさんも
かぞくと　すんでいます。...

...わたしの　あにも　二十二さいです。まだ
だいがくで　べんきょうしています。おにい
さんの　ごしょくぎょうは　何ですか。...

B

Age is very important to one's status or position in Japanese society. Siblings therefore are referred to as either *younger* or *older* brothers or sisters:

おとうと is "my younger brother" and あに is "my older brother";

あね is "my older sister" and いもうと is "my younger sister".

The words for members of families vary depending on whether the person is related to you or to the person to whom you are speaking. They can also vary depending on whether you are speaking *to* the person or *about* that person. For example, when speaking to your mother you would always call her おかあさん but when speaking about her it is acceptable to use はは. This applies to all the asterisked terms in the table below. When speaking directly to these members of your own family, use the asterisked expression.

A wife may refer to her own husband as おっと while the husband may call his wife つま. These terms denote more equality between the sexes and apart from meaning "husband" or "wife" can also be translated as "my spouse".

	Used when speaking about your own relatives	Used when speaking about other people's relatives
Family	かぞく	ごかぞく
Parents	りょうしん	ごりょうしん
Brothers and sisters	きょうだい	ごきょうだい
Older brother	あに	おにいさん*
Older sister	あね	おねえさん*
Younger brother	おとうと	おとうとさん
Younger sister	いもうと	いもうとさん
Father	ちち	おとうさん*
Mother	はは	おかあさん*
Grandfather	そふ	おじいさん*
Grandmother	そぼ	おばあさん*
Uncle	おじ	おじさん*
Aunt	おば	おばさん*
Cousin	いとこ	おいとこさん
Husband	しゅじん or おっと	ごしゅじん
Wife	かない or つま	おくさん
Son	むすこ	むすこさん
Daughter	むすめ	むすめさん
Child	こども	こどもさん

C

While you are staying in Japan there will be many occasions when you have to say who you are and give the names of the various members of your family. You have already learnt how to say "I am ..." and "He/She is ..." 「... (さん) です。」

Study Sentence Patterns 37a and 37b to see how else this information could be given.

Sentence Pattern 37a

わたしは　アンドルー　リーと　もうします。　　　My name is Andrew Lee.

This sentence is very humble and is commonly used when introducing yourself.

Sentence Pattern 37b

おとうとさんは　何^{なん}と　いいますか。　　　What is your brother's name?
おとうとは　トニーと　いいます。　　　My younger brother is called Tony.

ほんだ
けんすけ

はなこ
(68 yrs)

たかの
しゅじ
(73 yrs)

ひろこ

けんたろう
(39 yrs)

ゆきこ
(45 yrs)

ゆきお
(50 yrs)

まきこ
(46 yrs)

ゆうこ (20 yrs)

さだこ (14 yrs)

たけし (16 yrs)

としあき (12 yrs)

Use the family tree on page 3 to answer the following questions in Japanese.

Example:

さだこさんの　おとうさんは　なんと　いいますか。
さだこさんの　おとうさんは　たかの　ゆきおと　いいます。

1. さだこさんの　おねえさんは　なんと　いいますか。
2. としあきさんの　おにいさんは　なんと　いいますか。
3. ゆうこさんの　おかあさんは　なんと　いいますか。
4. ほんだ　はなこさんは　なんさいですか。
5. たけしさんの　おじさんは　なんと　いいますか。
6. ゆうこさんの　ごりょうしんは　なんと　いいますか。
7. ゆきこさんの　おとうとさんは　なんと　いいますか。
8. たかの　ひろこさんの　ごしゅじんは　なんさいですか。
9. たかの　ゆきおさんの　おくさんは　なんと　いいますか。
10. さだこさんの　おとうとさんは　なんと　いいますか。
11. たかの　しゅじさんの　むすこさんは　なんと　いいますか。
12. ほんだ　けんすけさんの　おくさんは　なんと　いいますか。

D₂ On the copy of this exercise that your teacher will give you, fill in the squares with the word describing the relationship between each of these people and あやの. (See the example given.)

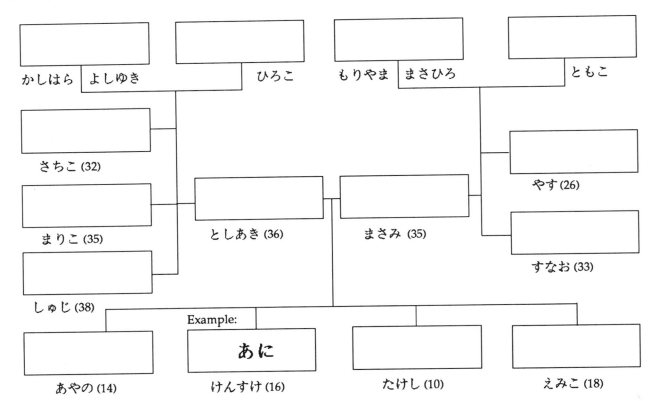

D₃ Draw your family tree. Illustrate it with sketches of each family member, or from magazines cut out pictures to represent each member. Name each person in terms of how he or she is related to you. For example:

おばあさん   おじいさん

D₄ In complete sentences, give the name of each of your own relatives, as shown in the example. Try to write ten sentences. (If you don't have that many relatives, use fictitious characters!)

Example:

おとうさんは　*Bill*　と　いいます。

D₅ ブレーンティーザ　　**Brain teaser**

Who am I?

1. わたしは　わたしの　おとうさんの　おじいさんの　むすこ　です。
2. わたしは　いもうとの　おとうとの　おばさん　です。
3. わたしは　おかあさんの　いもうとさんの　おにいさん　です。

E 書きましょう・漢字
　　　かき　　　　　かんじ

Kanji — the Chinese ideograms which the Japanese use in their writing — often reflect some aspect of Chinese society or its beliefs. Usually, the simple story of how such kanji were first written, and what was meant by each part (or "radical") of the character, makes remembering each kanji quite a simple procedure. Try to visualise the character and remember the stories that go with each one.

The one kanji can be pronounced in more than one way, depending on the word itself and on the other character or characters in the word. Most kanji have both a くん or Japanese pronunciation and an おん or Chinese pronunciation.

Example:

Look at the following ways of reading the kanji 一, meaning "one".

one	one person	one thing	one year old
いち	ひ と り	ひ と	いっ
一	一人	一つ	一さい

In this example there are two completely different sounds for the one kanji and then the pronunciation of one of the readings differs slightly (いち andいっ).

★習い方　**How to learn**
なら　かた

1. *Look* at the story and *learn* a simple way of remembering the kanji.
2. As you are *writing* the kanji, *think* of the story as you go and *say* the sound.
3. *Write* out each kanji 10–15 times until you are sure of the stroke order, the pronunciation and its meaning.
4. When you have practised each new kanji separately, write out all the new kanji one after the other and check that you can still remember how to write and read each one.
5. Practise all kanji daily.

1.　一　One

When you are pointing to *one* person, it is easy to see how the kanji for "one" evolved.

くん　ひと(つ)　おん　いち、いつ　いみ　一つ、一、一じ
　　　　　　　　　　　　　　　　　　　　　ひと　　いち　いち

かきじゅん　一
(Stroke order)

1かく

2.　二　Two

In indicating two things, we can still see the kanji for *two*.

くん　ふた(つ)　おん　に　いみ　二、二つ、二ひゃく 200
　　　　　　　　　　　　　　　　　に　　ふた　　に
　　　　　　　　　　　　　　　　　二人 two people
　　　　　　　　　　　　　　　　　ふた り

かきじゅん　一　二

2かく

3.　三　Three

You can still see the kanji when indicating *three* objects.

くん　みっ(つ)　おん　さん　いみ　三、三<ruby>三<rt>さん</rt></ruby>つ、<ruby>三<rt>さん</rt></ruby>じ

かきじゅん　｜ー｜二｜三｜

3かく

4.　四　Four

A simple way to remember this one is that a window with a curtain in it has *four* sides.

くん　よっ(つ)、よん　おん　し　いみ　<ruby>四<rt>よん</rt></ruby>、<ruby>四<rt>よっ</rt></ruby>つ、<ruby>四<rt>し</rt></ruby>、<ruby>四<rt>よ</rt></ruby>じ

かきじゅん　｜丨｜冂｜𠃌｜四｜四｜

5かく

5.　五　Five

The number *five* began in a similar way to one, two and three, with each line representing one unit. But as there were too many horizontal lines, the Chinese eventually turned two of the lines vertically and chopped off a corner so that it looked balanced.

くん　いつ(つ)　おん　ご　いみ　五、<ruby>五<rt>いつ</rt></ruby>つ、<ruby>五<rt>ご</rt></ruby><ruby>人<rt>にん</rt></ruby>

かきじゅん　｜ー｜丁｜五｜五｜

4かく

6. 六 Six

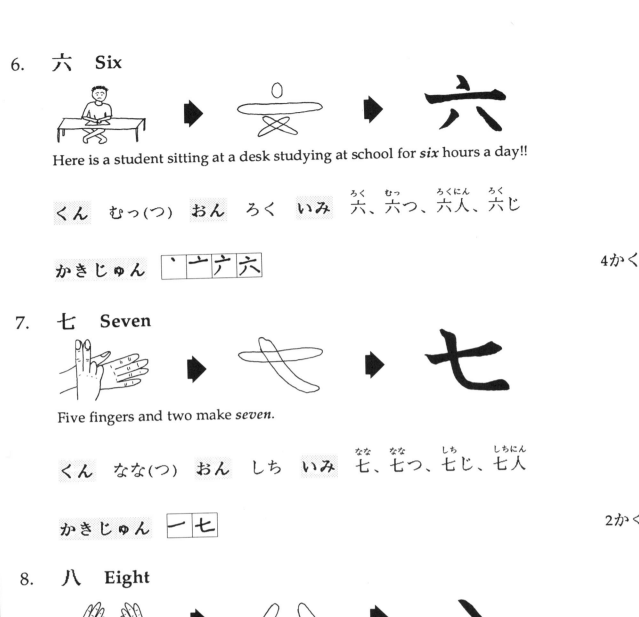

Here is a student sitting at a desk studying at school for *six* hours a day!!

くん むっ(つ)　**おん** ろく　**いみ** 六、六^{むっ}つ、六人、六じ

かきじゅん 丶　亠　六　六　　　　　　　　4かく

7. 七 Seven

Five fingers and two make *seven*.

くん なな(つ)　**おん** しち　**いみ** 七、七つ、七じ、七人

かきじゅん 一　七　　　　　　　　2かく

8. 八 Eight

Four plus four is *eight* (4 + 4 = 8).

くん やっ(つ)、よう　**おん** はち　**いみ** 八、八つ、八人

かきじゅん ノ　八　　　　　　　　2かく

9. 九 Nine

After practising the kanji for the numbers one to *nine* you will have developed great strength. You'll need it for all the other kanji and katakana that you will learn this year!

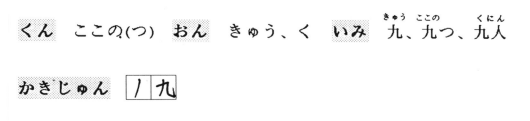

かきじゅん ｜ノ｜九｜

2かく

10. 十　Ten

Ten fingers of two crossed hands.

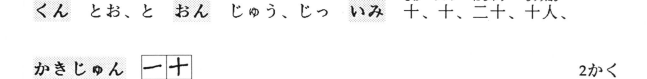

かきじゅん ｜一｜十｜

2かく

11. 人　Person

It is easy to see that this character represents a *person*.

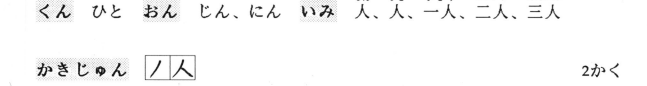

かきじゅん ｜ノ｜人｜

2かく

12. 何　What

Two people are carrying a bucket of something. *What* is in the bucket?

| くん | なに、なん | おん | か | いみ | 何、何人 |

かきじゅん　| ⼃ | ⼫ | ⼬ | ⼭ | 佰 | 佰 | 何 |　　　　7かく

F₁ 覚えましょう

> ### Sentence Pattern 38
>
> *ごかぞくは　何人　ですか。　　How many people are there in your family?
> （かぞくは）　五人　です。　　There are five people (in our family).

*Notice the use of ご in ごかぞく when asking about someone else's family.

F₂

Just as there is a set of "counters" used when counting bowls of things, so too there is a special set of counters used when counting people.

Counting people

何人	なんにん	How many people?
1	一人	ひとり
2	二人	ふたり
3	三人	さんにん
4	四人	よにん
5	五人	ごにん
6	六人	ろくにん
7	七人	しちにん、ななにん
8	八人	はちにん
9	九人	くにん、きゅうにん
10	十人	じゅうにん
11	十一人	じゅういちにん
12	十二人	じゅうににん

何人ですか。

F₃

Answer the following questions in Japanese, using clues if given. Where there are no clues, give your own answer. If you don't have a particular relative, for example あに, write あには います ん. Remember to use the correct form of the word for your own relatives.

1. ごかぞくは　何人　ですか。
2. ごきょうだいは　何人　ですか。(Remember to include yourself.)

3. おいとこさんは　何人　いますか。

4. いもうとさんは　何人　いますか。

5. おにいさんは　何人　いますか。

6. この　えに　人は　何人　いますか。

7. 何人　テレビを　みて　いますか。

8. 日本ごの　クラスに　せいとは　何人　いますか。

9. あなたの　がっこうに　日本ごの　せんせいは　何人　いますか。

10. かぞくは　六人　です。　あなたの　ごかぞくは？ (What about yours?)

Sentence Pattern 39

Q. *ごしょくぎょうは　何(なん)ですか。 — What's your occupation?

Q. おとうさんの　ごしょくぎょうは　何(なん)ですか。 — What does your father do?　(What is your father's occupation?)

A. てんいん　です。 — I am/He is a shop assistant.

*Notice how you add the honorific ご when talking about someone else's occupation.

At some stage, your Japanese host family will want to know the occupations of your parents and your older brothers and sisters.

Find out the words for the occupation of each member of your family and add them to your vocabulary list for this unit.

You have already learnt how certain verbs take particular particles or signposts. For example, we usually say それ　**が**　わかります。 ("I understand that.")

Look at the two verbs つとめています and はたらいています in these two dialogues concerning employment and note which particles each verb takes.

1.

ははは　びょういんに　つとめています。

おいしゃさん　ですか。

いいえ、かんごふ　です。

2. おとうさんは　どこで　はたらいていますか。

おとうさんは　ぎんこうで*　はたらいています。

*It makes sense to use で anyway because the bank is a place of action, isn't it.

G₃ What is the occupation of each of these people? Give your answers in English.

1. さとう　みちこと　もうします。
   びょういんで　はたらいています。
   いしゃ　じゃないです。

2. ぎんこうに　つとめています。
   八じから　六じまで　はたらきます。

3. ほんが　すきです。
   まいにち　ほんを　たくさん　よみます。

4. せいとに　おしえます。
   げつようびから　どようびまで
   がっこうへ　いきます。

5.

H Imagine that you are each of these people. Introduce yourself to a new acquaintance, giving *all* the information shown.

Watanabe (41 yrs)

Tanaka Yukari (16 yrs)

Satoo (35 yrs)

Setoguchi Hiroko (26 yrs)

I₁ When talking about yourself, it is useful to be able to tell your Japanese friends what you want to do when you leave school.

Look at how easy this is in Sentence Pattern 40.

Sentence Pattern 40

Q. そつぎょうごは¹ 何に なりたい
ですか。   What do you want to become after you graduate?

A. きょうし²に なりたいです。   I want to become a teacher.

¹ そつぎょうご literally means "after graduation". It can also be translated as "after graduating", or "after you graduate".

² Notice that it is more humble (and therefore more polite) to refer to yourself as a きょうし rather than as a せんせい.

Extension

To express what you want to become even more politely, use 「と おもいます」
instead of 「です」.

For example:

わたしは きょうしに なりたいと おもいます。

I think I want to become a teacher.

I₂ Write out what your friends say when they are telling you what they want to become.

1. さとうさん   2. いしかわさん   3. たかはしさん

4. わたなべさん   5. こんどうさん   6. こばやしさん

7. ますださん　　　　8. たなかさん　　　　9. やまもとさん

J

When Maria applied to become an exchange student, she had to fill in many forms that asked questions about her and her family. When she got to Japan, she had to answer similar questions but in Japanese. Using the information in the following document, work out the answers that she could give to the questions below which could be asked of her in Japan.

Application for Exchange

1. **Name:** *Maria Thompson*

2. **Age:** *13*

3. **Family members** (give names, ages, occupations, place of employment):

Mother	*Helen*	*47*	*Teacher*	*Primary school*
Father	*Michael*	*48*	*Lawyer*	*Company*
Older sister	*Lauren*	*24*	*Nurse*	*Hospital*
Older brother	*Nicholas*	*20*	*Shop assistant*	*Department store*
Self — student (I want to become a doctor and work in a hospital)				

---

1. そつぎょうごは　何に　なりたいですか。
   (or そつぎょうごは　何に　なりたいと　おもいますか。)

2. おとうさんは　どこで　はたらいていますか。

3. おかあさんは　どこに　つとめていますか。

4. おとうさんの　ごしょくぎょうは　何ですか。

5. ごきょうだいは　何人　ですか。

6. おにいさんが　いますか。　（何人　いますか。）
7. おにいさんの　ごしょくぎょうは　何ですか。
8. トムソンさんは　いもうとさん　ですか。
^{To mu so n}
9. トムソンさんの　ごしょくぎょうは　何ですか。
^{To mu so n}
10. ニコラスさんは　何さい　ですか。
^{Ni ko ra su}
11. おとうさんは　何さいですか。
12. おかあさんは　何さいですか。
13. おかあさんの　ごしょくぎょうは　何ですか。
14. ごかぞくは　何人ですか。

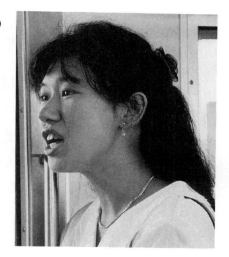

K₁ By now you have probably worked out a simple rule for expressing the idea that you want to do something. You know the ます ending of many verbs. For example:

いきます   I go

なります   I become

たべます   I eat

かえります   I return

In each case, to express the idea "I want to ..." just replace ます with たいです. So:

いき   →   いきたいです   ＝   I want to go

なり   →   なりたいです   ＝   I want to become

たべ   →   たべたいです   ＝   I want to eat

かえります   →   かえりたいです   ＝   I want to return

This pattern is usually only used when talking about *yourself* or when asking other people a question about *themselves*.

You are already familiar with two uses of this pattern:

Q. どこへ　いきたい　ですか。   Where do you want to go?

A. とうきょうへ　いきたいです。   I want to go to Tokyo. (Sentence Pattern 5)

Q. そつぎょうごは　何に
　なりたいですか。   What do you want to become after you graduate? (Sentence Pattern 40)

A. きょうしに　なりたいです。   I want to become a teacher.

Sentence Pattern 41 provides some other examples of how this ending could be used.

Sentence Pattern 41

Q. そつぎょうごは どこで
はたらきたいですか。

After you graduate, where do you want to work?

A. トヨタで はたらきたいです。

I want to work at Toyota.

Q. 何を たべたいですか。

What would you like to eat?

A. チキンを たべたいです。

I would like to eat chicken.

Q. 何を したいですか。

What do you want to do?

A. 何でも いいです。

Anything would be good.

A. あきはばらへ かいものに いき
たいですが...*

I would like to go to Akihabara to do some shopping, but ...

* The が makes the sentence sound not so demanding. It could be interpreted as "I'd like to go to Akihabara to do some shopping but ... I don't wish to impose on you!"

K₂ 日本語で つぎの しつもんに こたえてください。

1. そつぎょうごは どこで はたらきたいですか。
2. いま、おかあさんに でんわしたいですか。(Yes)
3. そつぎょうごは 何に なりたいですか。
4. あした どこへ いきたいですか。
5. あさくさへ いきたいですか。(Yes)
6. まんがを よみたいですか。(Yes)
7. 何を かいたいですか。
8. どこで べんきょうしたいですか。
9. 何で うちへ かえりたいですか。
10. ばんごはんは 何を たべたいですか。

The Kaminarimon at the entrance to a street lined with little shops in front of the Sensoji Temple, Asakusa

K₃ Find in magazines (or draw) ten pictures of famous people. Imagine that you are each one of them and write out your wish. Try to be as creative as possible!

Example:

オーストラリアへ いきたいです。

I want to go to Australia.

L While lying awake on your first night in Japan you undoubtedly will be thinking about what you want to do in Japan or what you already miss about home. Write down at least ten of your wishes, using this illustration for inspiration.

M 新しいことば　New expressions

Now that you can say what you *want* to do, what about expressing the idea that you *don't* want to do something?

Remember, you can only use this sentence pattern when talking about yourself because it is expressing a very personal feeling.

Sentence Pattern 42

Q. かずおさんは　くつやで　はたらき
たい　ですか。

Kazuo, do you want to work in a shoe shop?

A. いいえ、くつやで　はたらきたくない
です。やおやで　はたらきたいです。

No, I don't want to work in a shoe shop.
I want to work in a vegetable shop.

Q. マリアさんは　ミルクを　のみたい
ですか。

Maria, would you like some milk to drink?

A. いいえ、ミルクを　のみたくないです。
ジュースを　のみたいです。

No, I don't want to drink any milk.
I want to drink juice.

Q. ケーキを　たべたいですか。

Would you like some cake?

A. いいえ、けっこうです。

No thanks, I'm right.

A. ええ、すこし　たべたいです。

Yes, I'd like a little, please.

A. ケーキを　たべたくないですが
サンドイッチを　たべたいです。

I don't want any cake, but I would like a sandwich.

Explanation

When たい is added to any verb, it changes the word from being a verb to a kind of adjective.

In the sentences:

- I am **hungry**

  "Hungry" is an *adjective (i.e. a describing word)*

- I **eat**

  "Eat" is a *verb (i.e. an action word)*

But in the sentence:

- I **want to eat** (or I am in the state of wanting to eat)

  "Want to eat" *(in Japanese) is like an adjective because it describes the state that you are in.*

So the good news is that once you've mastered the pattern "I want" and "I don't want", you've also gone a long way towards mastering expressions in the next unit concerning adjectives — and aren't these really what you want to use when describing your new friends to others?

Let's get started by studying how this new ending works with a selection of verbs.

★ 習い方

When learning a new ending it is very important to

(a) Say the new ending with as many words as you can.

(b) Say it loudly if you can when you are at home.

(c) Say it over and over again until in the end only the correct form sounds right and you can easily recognise a mistake.

I/you …	I want to …	I don't want to …
たべます	たべたいです	たべたくないです
いきます	いきたいです	いきたくないです
みます	みたいです	みたくないです
ならいます	ならいたいです	ならいたくないです
はたらきます	はたらきたいです	はたらきたくないです
でんわします	でんわしたいです	でんわしたくないです
まちます	まちたいです	まちたくないです
かきます	かきたいです	かきたくないです

★ Do you remember what all of the above words mean? If not, ask your teacher or look them up.

N3 See if you can make up your own list of ten more verbs and their adjectival forms. Remember — say them to yourself as you work and always check that you know what they mean.

N4 Answer each of these questions, using the clues given and following the example below.

Example:

Q. まさよしちゃんは　ごはんを　たべたいですか。 (No, bread)

A. いいえ、ごはんを　たべたくないです。パンを　たべたいです。

1. マリアさんは　いま　がっこうへ　いきたいですか。 (No, later)
2. すなおさんは　2じに　でたいですか。 (No, at 3 o'clock)
3. アンドルーさんは　ぎんざへ　かいものに
   いきたいですか。 (No, at Akihabara)
4. じろうさんに　あいたいですか。 (No, Mariko)
5. としょかんで　べんきょうしたいですか。 (No, at home)

6. あいこさんの　うちへ　いきたいですか。 (No, Jiroo's)

7. がっこうの　プールへ　いきたいですか。 (No, the town pool)

8. えいがを　みたいですか。 (No, read a book)

9. あさくさから　うえのまで　あるいて　いきたいですか。 (No, by subway)

10. いぬと　あそびたいですか。 (No, with the cat)

It would certainly not be appropriate to speak to your host family using lots of statements such as "I don't want to do this" and "I don't want to do that". But amongst friends (and even in your own home, in the right circumstances) it would not be inappropriate to use these sentence patterns.

Look at the scene below. You are feeling particularly homesick and you don't want to do anything that you know you are supposed to do. If you had to write down your thoughts about what you don't want to do, what would they be? Use the clues given!

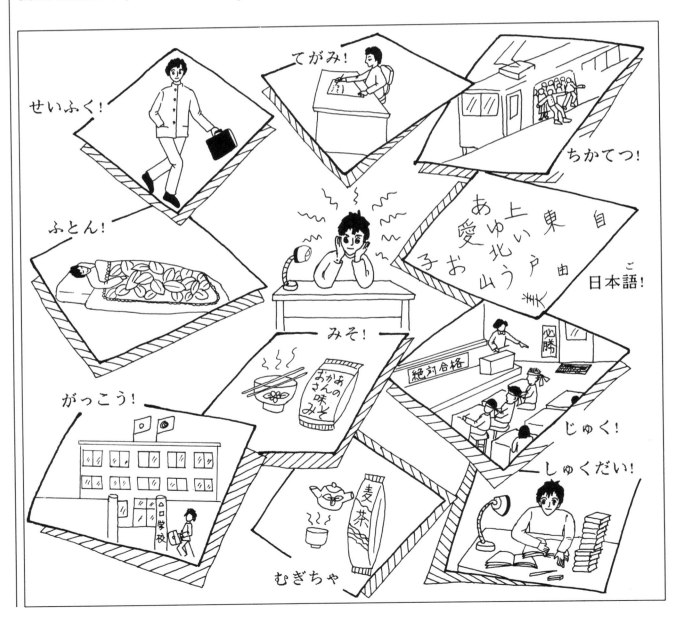

N₆ Now try a variation on the previous exercise. What do you think a Japanese person living in Australia might say to himself/herself if feeling homesick? See if you can find at least five things he or she would *want* to do and at least five things he or she might *not* want to do.

O Try this quiz. (Your teacher will give you a copy that you can write on.)

わたしは だれですか。

↓

1. おかあさんの　いもうと

2. Younger sister

3. いもうと、おとうと、あに

4. こうばんで　はたらきます

5. みせで　はたらきます

6. "Possessive" particle

7. ちちの　はは

8. おとうさんの　いもうと

9. My older brother

10. はは

11. びょういんで　はたらきます

12. I drink

13. Daughter

14. Son

15. Child

16. Anything

17. I disagree

Tick the correct box. ☐ おかあさん ☐ おじいさん ☐ おじさん ☐ むすこ

P What are you like at maths?

You already know most of the words used in these maths problems and you should be able to work out the meaning of any other words from the context.

ア あいこさんの　おうちの　人は　ぜんぶで　6人　です。
こどもは　3人　です。
おとなは　何人　ですか。 ＿＿＿＿ こたえ

イ こどもが　5人　います。
おんなのこは　2人　です。
おとこのこは　何人　ですか。 ＿＿＿＿ こたえ

ウ おんなのこは　16人、おとこのこが　2人　います。
おとこのこが　1人　かえりました。
おとこのこの　のこりは　何人　でしょうか。 ＿＿＿＿ こたえ

エ 54人と　35人の　ちがいは　何人　でしょうか！ ＿＿＿＿ こたえ

オ ほんを　よみました。
せんしゅう … 17ページ
きのう … 6ページ
きょう … 3ページ
あわせて　何　ページ　よみましたか！ ＿＿＿＿ こたえ

Q ## NEW EXPRESSIONS
Occupations

Bengoshi	べんごし	Lawyer
Daiku	だいく	Carpenter
Enjinia	エンジニア	Engineer
Fukukoochoo (sensei)	ふくこうちょう(せんせい)	Vice (Deputy) principal
Gishi	ぎし	Engineer
Hisho	ひしょ	(Private) secretary (to Director)
Hyakushoo	ひゃくしょう	Farmer
Isha	いしゃ	Doctor
Jimuin	じむいん	Clerk, office worker
Kaishain	かいしゃいん	Company employee
Kangofu	かんごふ	Nurse
Koochoo (sensei)	こうちょう (せんせい)	Principal
Kusuriyasan	くすりやさん	Chemist (person)
Kyooshi	きょうし	Teacher (used when talking about self)

Kyootoo (sensei)	きょうとう（せんせい）	Deputy principal/Head teacher
Maneejaa	マネージャー	Manager
Oishasan *or* Isha	おいしゃさん，いしゃ	Doctor
Roodoosha	ろうどうしゃ	Labourer
Shachoo	しゃちょう	Company director, head of a firm
Shufu	しゅふ	Housewife
Tenin	てんいん	Shop assistant, salesperson
Toshokanin	としょかんいん	Librarian
Tsuuyaku	つうやく	Interpreter
Ueetoresu	ウエートレス	Waitress
Uketsuke	うけつけ	Receptionist

General

Andoruu	アンドルー	Andrew
Atarashii	あたらしい	New, fresh
Awasete	あわせて	Altogether, the sum
Byooin	びょういん	Hospital
… chan	…ちゃん	Title for young people, particularly children — commonly used within families
Chigai	ちがい	Difference
Chigaimasu	ちがいます	I disagree (we differ in opinion)
Daigaku	だいがく	University
E	え	Picture, drawing, illustration
Erizabesu	エリザベス	Elizabeth
Futari	二人	Two people
Ginkoo	ぎんこう	Bank
Go	ご	Prefix added to certain words to indicate politeness
Hatake	はたけ	Field or farm (usually growing vegetables) — typically very small by Australian standards
Hataraiteimasu (hataraku)	はたらいています（はたらく）	I am/someone is working (to work)
Hitori	一人	One person
Hontooni	ほんとうに	Really, honestly
Hosutofamirii	ホスト ファミリー	Host family
… (to) iimasu	…（と）いいます	I/He/She/It is/am called
Imi	いみ	Meaning (throughout いっしょに, いみ is the heading under which are listed words that you might be expected to know using the particular kanji)
Imooto (san)	いもうと（さん）	Younger sister
Itoko	いとこ	Cousin
Juku	じゅく	Cram school
Kaisha	かいしゃ	Company (a business concern)
Kakijun	かきじゅん	Stroke order

Kanai	かない	Wife
Kao	かお	Face
Keeki	ケーキ	Cake
Kodomo (san)	こども（さん）	Child
Kono e ni	この　えに	In this photograph
Kotaemasu (kotaeru)	こたえます（こたえる）	I/someone answer(s) (to answer)
… kudasaimasenka	…くださいませんか	Won't you please …
Kun (yomi)	くん（よみ）	Japanese reading of a Chinese character
Kurasu	クラス	Class (at school)
Kutsuya	くつや	Shoe shop
Kyoodai	きょうだい	Brothers and sisters
Mada	まだ	Still, yet
Manga	まんが	Comics
Maria	マリア	Maria
Mashuu	マシュー	Matthew
Miruku	ミルク	Milk
… (to) mooshimasu	…（と）もうします	I am called …
Mugicha	むぎちゃ	Barley tea, a popular drink served cold in summer
Musuko (san)	むすこ（さん）	Son
Musume (san)	むすめ（さん）	Daughter
Nan, nani	何	What
Nandemo	何でも	Anything
Narimasu (naru)	なります（なる）	I/someone become(s) (to become)
Nihon	日本	Japan
… nin	…人	Counter for people
Nokori	のこり	Remainder, rest
Obaasan	おばあさん（そば）	Grandmother
Oba (san)	おば（さん）	Aunty
Oitokosan	おいとこさん	Your cousin
Ojiisan	おじいさん（そふ）	Grandfather
Oji (san)	おじ（さん）	Uncle
Okaasan	おかあさん（はは）	Mother
Okusan	おくさん	Wife
… (to) omoimasu	…（と）おもいます	I think …
On (yomi)	おん（よみ）	Chinese reading of a Chinese character
Oneesan	おねえさん（あね）	Older sister
Oniisan	おにいさん（あに）	Older brother
Oosutoraria	オーストラリア	Australia
Oshiemasu (oshieru)	おしえます（おしえる）	I/someone teach(es) (to teach)
Oshietekudasai (masenka)	おしえてください（ませんか）	(Won't you) please help (teach) me?
Otona	おとな	Adult
Otoosan	おとうさん（ちち）	Father
Otooto (san)	おとうと（さん）	Younger brother

Otto	おっと	My husband, my spouse
Ouchi	おうち	Your home (very polite)
PTAiin	PTAいいん	Member of Parent-Teacher Association
Rippa	りっぱ	Terrific
Ryooshin	りょうしん	Parents
Sandoitchi	サンドイッチ	Sandwich
Seifuku	せいふく	School uniform
Shinsetsu	しんせつ	Kind, considerate
Shitsumon	しつもん	Question
Shitsureishimasu	しつれいします	Excuse me
Shokugyoo	しょくぎょう	Occupation
Shujin	しゅじん	Husband
Sotsugyoogo	そつぎょうご	After graduation
… taidesu	… たいです	(I) want to …
Takusan (no)	たくさん（の）	Many
Tetsudattekudasai	てつだってください	Please help me! (I'm in danger!)
Tsugi	つぎ	Next
Tsuma	つま	My wife, my spouse
Tsutometeimasu (tsutomeru)	つとめています （つとめる）	I am/someone is employed (to be employed)
Yakkyoku, kusuriya	やっきょく、くすりや	Chemist (shop)
… yo	… よ	Used at the end of a sentence to indicate strong conviction or assertion
Zembude	ぜんぶで	In all, altogether

R

Kanji studied to the end of Unit 13:

Unit 13: 一 二 三 四 五 六 七 八 九 十 人 何
  1 2 3 4 5 6 7 8 9 10 11 12

A typical farm in Saitama Prefecture

Unit 14
Family and friends
家族と友達

Topics:
一 Colours and other descriptions
二 Personal characteristics
三 Exclamations

A

1. これは 父です。かいしゃの しゃちょうです。せは たかいですが すこし ふとっています。

これは いとこの グレゴリーです。だいがくせいです。ほけん たいいくを べんきょうしています。

2. グレゴリーさんは 目が 大きくて あおいですねえ。たいかくが いいですねえ。グレゴリーさんは きんぱつですね。

3. ええ。つぎのは いもうとの アナの しゃしんです。

4. アナさんは かわいいですねえ。

B | Colours

Once you know how to express colours in Japanese, your descriptions of people, things and places will become far more vivid.

Before analysing the nature of Japanese adjectives or describing words, study this colour chart and see what discoveries you can make about the Japanese equivalents for colours.

Description (left)	Image label	Colour	Image label	Description (right)
かのじょは きんぱつです。	きいろいたいよう	みどり／きいろ（い）	みどりの木	その人はみどりの目をしています。
その人のかみは オレンジ色です。	オレンジ（色）のみかん	オレンジ／ちゃいろ（い）	ちゃ色のくつ	その人はちゃ色のかみをしています。
その人は 赤げです。	赤いりんご	あか（い）／くろ（い）	黒いかばん	あにのかみは 黒いです。
むらさきの かみ ですか？	むらさきのぶどう	むらさき／しろ（い）	白いくも	おばあさんは 白がです。
おんなの人の目は あおいです。	あおいそら	あお（い）／ピンク（いろ）	ピンクいろのさくら	ピンクのドレスは きれいです。

An analysis of Japanese adjectives

1. In English, all words which describe nouns, pronouns or other adjectives are called adjectives. So "white", "black", "green", "blue" and "yellow" in *English* are adjectives.

2. In Japanese, not all describing words are true adjectives.

   - Some are actually nouns, for example みどり, which means "green". In this course, to help you recognise that these nouns have an adjectival or descriptive function but must be treated as nouns, such words will be called "adjectival nouns". You may also hear them referred to as quasi (or false) adjectives.

3. As you can see in the colour chart on the previous page, all adjectives have a noun base but

   - Some are more commonly used as adjectives with い added.

     For example: くろい、おかい、あおい、しろい

   - Some can only be used in the noun form.

     For example: むらさき、みどり

   - ちゃいろ（い）— brown — and きいろ（い）— yellow — are more commonly used in their noun forms.

   - Others can be used in their noun forms in compound words.

     For example: あおしんごう (green* traffic lights) and あかげ (red hair).

     *Although あおい means "blue" it is sometimes used for the colour green.

4. Adjectives in Japanese or English can be used either

   (a) before the word they are describing

     For example: あおい　め (blue eyes)

   or

   (b) at the end of a clause or sentence

     For example: かみは　くろいです。(His hair is black.)

5. To describe a noun with a true adjective, the procedure is simple.

Sentence Pattern 43a

True adjective + noun （です）
あかい　りんごです。　　It is a red apple.

(Have you noticed that true adjectives all end in あい、いい、うい、おい but *never* えい?)

To describe a noun using another noun or an adjectival noun, the procedure is simple but you have to *think first*. You need something between the two words to make sure they stick! The "glue" that is used between nouns and the noun form of the colours describing them is の.

Sentence Pattern 43b

むらさきの　ぶどうは　おいしいです。　　The purple grapes are delicious.

C₃

For most other adjectival nouns, for example,きれい (beautiful), the connector or "glue" used isな.

Sentence Pattern 43c

きれいな　おんなのこを　みました。　　I saw a beautiful girl.

D₁

Let's try to describe the following things using any colours or other adjectives you know that you think are appropriate.

Example:

しろい　ばら — White rose

1. ....かばん

2. ....いぬ

3. ....かみ

4. ....き

5. ....せいふく

Unit 14 **29**

6. .... りんご

5. .... みかん

6. .... くつ

7. .... かみ

8. .... くも

9. .... ぶどう

D₂ What does each of the following sentences mean in English?

1. まいにち　あかい　りんごを　たべます。
2. あおい　そらが　きれいです。
3. くろい　くつを　かいました。
4. あかい　りんごは　おいしいですね。
5. ちゃいろの　いぬは　わたしの　いぬです。
6. きいろい　ようふくは　いもうとさんの　ですか。
7. むらさきの　ジャカランダの　はなは　うつくしいです。
8. あそこに　みどりの　きが　あります。
9. くろい　ねこは　おおきい　さかなを　たべています。
10. わたしたちは　ピンクいろの　さくらを　みています。

E Find or draw pictures of at least fifteen things of which you know the names, and describe the thing in the picture. Use a variety of adjectival types so that you use な, の and い.

For example:

あかい　だるま

えいごでは、<ruby>何色<rt>なにいろ</rt></ruby>ですか

Can you work out what colours these are?

ねずみいろ　　そらいろ
ももいろ　　　くさいろ
くりいろ　　　みずいろ

F₂ ## スーパーマーケットで　**At the supermarket**

The fruit section of a Japanese supermarket is always alive with the bright colours of fresh, high-quality fruit and vegetables. In one long sentence, list all the fruit and vegetables mentioned below, describing each item with an adjective. Part of the sentence has been done for you.

あかい　いちご　と.........を　みました。

1. いちご
2. さくらんぼ
3. くり
4. りんご
5. すいか
6. かき

7. レモン
8. だいこん
9. バナナ
10. なし
11. にんじん
12. みかん

G₁ As with the other adjectives and nouns that you have learnt, you can always describe something simply by the following pattern:

Sentence Pattern 44

Q. あなたのうちの　ねこは　<ruby>何色<rt>なにいろ</rt></ruby>ですか。　　What colour is your cat?

A. <ruby>黒<rt>くろ</rt></ruby>です。　　It's black.

Q. ぶどうは　<ruby>何色<rt>なにいろ</rt></ruby>ですか。　　What colour are grapes?

A. むらさきです。　　They are purple.

Notice that in this pattern it is more common to give the answer in the noun form.

Answer these questions as you think appropriate:

1. りんごは　何色（なにいろ）ですか。
2. なしは　何色（なにいろ）ですか。
3. いぬは　何色（なにいろ）ですか。
4. かばんは　何色（なにいろ）ですか。
5. あなたの　せいふくは　何色（なにいろ）ですか。
6. すうがくの　ほんは　何色（なにいろ）ですか。
7. こくばんは　何色（なにいろ）ですか。
8. あなたの　がっこうの　くつは　何色（なにいろ）ですか。
9. あなたの　くるまは　何色（なにいろ）ですか。
10. きょうしつの　ドアは　何色（なにいろ）ですか。

H 書きしょう・漢字

13.　目　Eye

It's easy to see how the kanji for *eye* developed.

くん　め、ま　　おん　もく、ぼく　　いみ　目（め）

かきじゅん　｜ 冂 冂 月 目　　　　　　　　5かく

14.　口　Mouth

A person's *mouth* is diagrammatically represented in this kanji.

くん　くち　　おん　こう、く　　いみ　口（くち）、出口（でぐち） exit, 入口（いりぐち） entrance

かきじゅん　｜ 冂 口　　　　　　　　3かく

15. 日 Sun

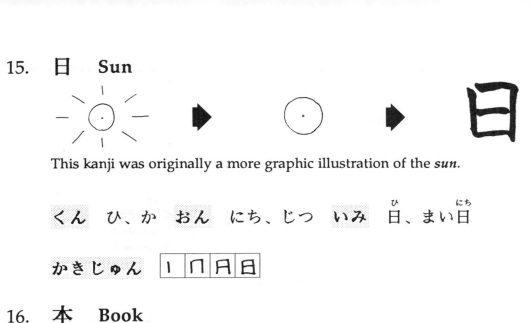

This kanji was originally a more graphic illustration of the *sun*.

くん ひ、か おん にち、じつ いみ 日、まい日

かきじゅん │ 冂 冃 日

4かく

16. 本 Book

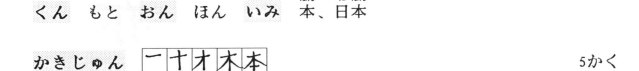

The kanji for *book* is represented by a tree — from which paper for books is made. The tree's roots also represent the origin or the beginning and so this kanji is used in the words for truth and honesty.

くん もと おん ほん いみ 本、日本

かきじゅん 一 十 才 木 本

5かく

17. 母 Mother

All that remains of the drawing of a *mother* feeding her baby is an outline of the baby and the mother's arms and breasts.

くん はは おん ぼ いみ 母 mother (This kanji is also used in the word お母さん.)

かきじゅん ㇈ 乄 乜 乜 母

5かく

18. 父 Father

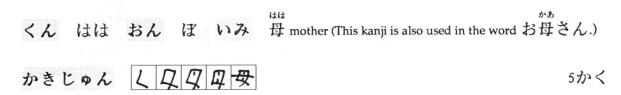

A *father* is represented by the remnants of the sketch of a wise man sitting cross-legged at the table.

くん　ちち　おん　ふ　いみ　父母 parents. (This kanji is also used in the word お父さん.)

かきじゅん　｜ノ　ハ　グ　父｜　4かく

19. 白　White

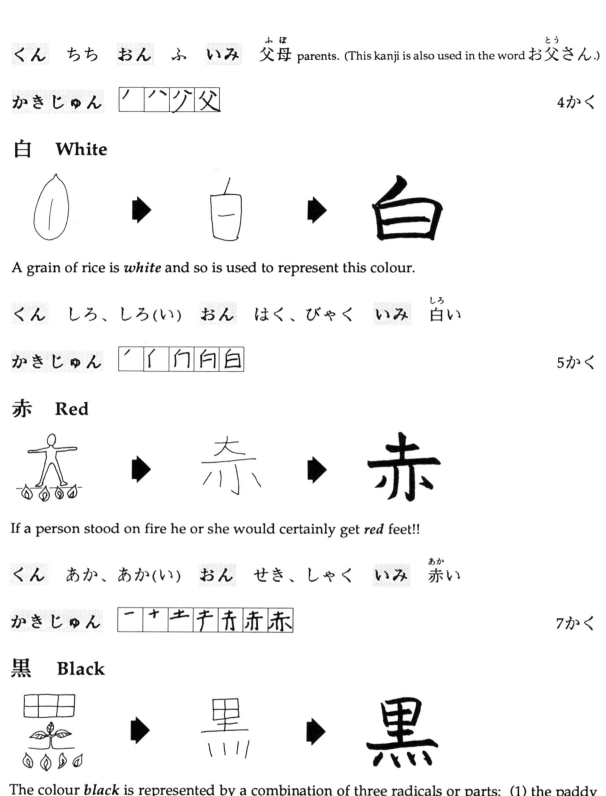

A grain of rice is *white* and so is used to represent this colour.

くん　しろ、しろ(い)　おん　はく、びゃく　いみ　白い

かきじゅん　｜′　′｜　′｜　白｜白｜　5かく

20. 赤　Red

If a person stood on fire he or she would certainly get *red* feet!!

くん　あか、あか(い)　おん　せき、しゃく　いみ　赤い

かきじゅん　｜一｜十｜土｜チ｜ホ｜赤｜赤｜　7かく

21. 黒　Black

The colour *black* is represented by a combination of three radicals or parts: (1) the paddy field, (2) the crops and earth, and (3) fire. The ground is blackened after fire has burnt out the crop.

くん　くろ、くろ(い)　おん　こく　いみ　黒

かきじゅん　｜｜｜冂｜冎｜日｜甲｜里｜里｜黒｜黒｜黒｜　11かく

22. 色 Colour

The character for "colour" shows a Peeping Tom looking down from the roof through the window — getting a full-*colour* view of everything.

くん いろ **おん** しょく、しき **いみ** 色(いろ)

かきじゅん ノ ク 勺 多 多 色

6かく

23. 大 Big

A person standing tall, stretching arms and legs, looks *big*.

くん おお（きい） **おん** だい、たい **いみ** 大(おお)きい、大好(だいす)き love
大学(だいがく) university

かきじゅん 一 ナ 大

3かく

24. 小 Little

A person standing with arms down and limp has *little* strength.

くん ちい（さい）、こ、お **おん** しょう **いみ** 小(ちい)さい
小学校(しょうがっこう) elementary school

かきじゅん 亅 小 小

3かく

In English there are often many ways of expressing an idea — especially when it comes to describing people. This is also the case in Japanese. The meanings may be exactly the same or they may be slightly different. By studying the next three patterns, you will see the variety of meanings that you can easily communicate.

Sentence Pattern 45

Q. ブラウンさんの　目は　何色ですか。　　What colour are Mr Brown's eyes?

A. ブラウンさんの　目は {あおい　です。　　Mr Brown's eyes are blue.
　　　　　　　　　　　　あお

This is a very common way of describing someone's features. The pattern …は …です is used more frequently in response to a question, and the は indicates that it is also a little emphatic and specific — that is, "as for Mr Brown's *eyes*, they are *blue*" (as opposed to his hair, which is brown).

Many Japanese say ひとみ, which means pupil, instead of 目 when talking about their eyes, and whether they use ひとみ or 目 the eye colouring is usually said to be くろ.

Can you work out what these sentences mean?

- たなかさんの　かみは　黒いです。
- アンドルーさんの　かみのけは　くり色です。

Sentence Pattern 46

いむらさんは　目が {黒です。　　Mr *Imura's* eyes are black (brown).
　　　　　　　　　　　黒いです。

This pattern is very similar in meaning to the previous one, but places greater emphasis on the *person* being spoken about (that is, Mr *Imura's* eyes are black, whereas Mr Kirwan's are blue).

Either the adjectival form or the noun form of くろ can be used.

This pattern has many uses, as you can see in the examples below. Can you work out what they mean?

- わたなべさんは　口が　大きいです。
- トムソンさんは　おかしが　すきです。
- マリアナちゃんは　目が　きれいですね。

The verb しています can be used in special descriptive expressions, as shown in the next pattern. The meaning of しています is not easy to explain, but as with many other phrases in Japanese, with a bit of practice you will find it both easy to use and useful!

Sentence Pattern 47

すずきさんは　黒い目を　しています。 Miss Suzuki has black eyes.

This pattern is usually used when one is simply describing someone (in a letter, for example). If you had been asked a question about the colour of her eyes, it would have been better to choose Sentence Pattern 45.

Can you work out the meanings of the following sentences which contain …を　しています? Numbers 1 and 2 are idiomatic (that is, they have a special meaning not based on a literal translation) so you may need to ask your teacher, but try to work them out first.

1. たなかさんは　あおいかおを　しています。

2. すずきさんは　赤いかおを　しています。

3. たなかさんは　黒いかみを　しています。

4. マイケルさんは　あおい目を　しています。

In certain other instances, set idioms are used to describe a person.

1. マリアさんは　きんぱつです。

2. スミスさんは　赤げです。

3. おばあさんは　白がです。

4. お父さんは　はげあたまです。

J₁ Using the information given, write a short paragraph about each of the following people.

1. アンドルー
   15さい
   ちゃ色のかみ
   みどりの　目

2. 日本人
   14さい
   黒いかみ
   黒い目

3. おばあさん
   73さい
   白が
   りょこうが　すき

J₂ In your exercise book, draw a picture of yourself and then describe yourself in as much detail as possible. Your teacher will tell you how much to write — you could just about write a book by now!

K ### 新しいことば

Can you work out what these expressions mean?

1. わたなべさんは　せが　たかいです。

2. わたなべさんの　おくさんは　せが
   ひくいです。

3. すずき　たろうさんは　すこし
　ふとっています。

4. ほんだ　みちこさんは　やせて
　います。

L Match each of the descriptions with the correct photograph by writing the correct description next to the katakana representing each picture from ア（あ）to オ（お）.

ア

イ

ウ

エ

オ

一　いもうとは　赤げです。やせています。かのじょは　みどりの目を　して
　います。

二　わたしは　白が　です。60さいです。わたしの　ひとみは　黒いです。

三 わたしは　ながい黒かみを　しています。黒い目を　しています。わたし
　は　やせています。せが　ひくいです。

四 わたしは　みじかい　ちゃ色のかみを　しています。せが　たかいです。
　目は　あおいです。

五 ぼくは　みじかい　黒いかみを　しています。やせています。

聞きましょう

M

You are listening to a Japanese radio programme in which a group of people introduce themselves. Draw a sketch of each of the people as you imagine them to be. Label your sketches, showing eye and hair colouring and anything else that you think is relevant.

N

Put each of these sentences around a different way, and write out the meaning of the new sentence as shown in the example.

Example:

　　ぼくは　くり色のかみを　しています。　***becomes***

　　ぼくの　かみは　くり色です。　　　My hair is (chestnut) brown.

1. アンドルーさんは　みどりの　目を　しています。
2. おにいさんは　オレンジ色の　かみを　しています。
3. いもうとさんは　ながいかみを　しています。
4. おじいさんは　白がです。
5. まりこさんの　かみは　黒いです。
6. いちろうさんのかみは　みどりです。
7. ジェニーさんは　赤げです。
8. あやのちゃんは　黒い目を　しています。
9. かれは　きんぱつです。
10. お母さんのかみは　みじかいです。

O₁

Separate statements such as "I have long hair. I have brown hair." sound just as boring in Japanese as they do in English. So let's try to join some short sentences together.

In Unit 12 we learnt how to make the て form of a verb. This may also be called the "connective" or "joining" form, and it can be used to mean " ... and ...".

Sentence Pattern 48a

ともだちは　ながいかみを　して
目_めが　みどりです。

My friend has long hair and her eyes are green.

Sentence Pattern 48b

わたしの　かみは　黒_{くろ}くて
目_めも　黒_{くろ}いです。

My hair is black and so are my eyes.

To make the "connective" form of a true adjective, the final い changes to くて.

For example:

おおきくて　big and ...　　みじかくて　short and ...　　あおくて　blue and ...

Sentence Pattern 48c

グレゴリーさんは　かみが
きんぱつで　せが　たかいです。

Gregory has blond hair and he is tall.

As you could guess, the 「で」 in this sentence is short for 「です」, so the connective of 「です」 when used after a noun or adjectival noun is 「で」.

O₂
Use the correct "connective" forms to join the two sentences in each set, making them one longer sentence as shown in the example. Write out the meaning of the sentences you have made.

For example:

みちこさんは　せが　ひくいです。　**+**　みちこさんの　かみは　黒いです。
Michiko is short.　　　　　　　　　Michiko's hair is black .

= みちこさんは　せが　ひくくて　かみは　黒いです。
Michiko is short and her hair is black.

1.　たろうさんは　むらさきの　かみを　しています。
　　たろうさんは　みじかいかみを　しています。

2. おじさんは　せが　たかいです。
   おじさんは　目が　あおいです。

3. その本は　やすいです。
   その本は　おもしろいです。

4. あきはばらへ　いきます。
   ワープロを　かいます。

5. この　きものは　きれいです。
   この　きものは　たかいです。

6. わたしは　せが　ひくいです。
   わたしは　ふとっています。

7. せんせいは　せが　たかいです。
   せんせいは　やせています。

8. がっこうへ　いきます。
   としょかんへ　いきます。

9. おかあさんは　本を　よみます。
   いもうとは　テレビを　みます。

10. せんせいは　日本人です。
    せが　ひくいです。

11. こうこうの　せんせいに　なります。
    ちりを　おしえたいです。

12. えいがは　みじかいです。
    えいがは　おもしろいです。

13. ともだちは　かみが　きんぱつです。
    ともどちは　かみが　ながいです。

14. これは　ともだちです。
    これは　あやのさん　といいます。

15. あしたは　どようびです。
    あしたは　やすみです。

16. わたしは　あおい目を　しています。
    わたしは　きんぱつです。

17. かいしゃいんに　なります。
    大きいかいしゃで　はたらきたいです。

18. 大きくて　赤いりんごを　かいます。
    りんごを　たべます。

19. びょうきです。
    ともだちは　かおが　あおいです。

20. おじさんは　目が　みどりです。
    おじさんは　かみが　みじかいです。

Put the sentences under each photograph into Japanese, using the appropriate connector.

1. My house is large and white

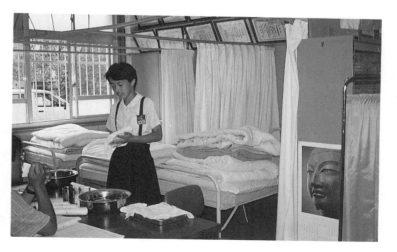

2. I want to become a doctor after I graduate and I want to work in a hospital.

This photograph shows a fairly typical sick bay or rest room (きゅうけいしつ) in a Japanese junior high school. One of the students is helping sterilise instruments while the teacher records "problem teeth" for the dentist during a routine dental check.

3. I have red hair and green eyes.
Students in this senior high school class are studying calligraphy.

4. I have black hair and brown eyes.
This boy is wearing the typical boys' school uniform.

5. Mount Fuji is beautiful and very high.

Unit 14 **43**

P Imagine that this is your family. Describe each family member to your Japanese host family. Try to make your description as interesting and as varied in form as possible.

Q Extension: **More maths!**

Test yourself on these.

ア 赤　2ほん。
　 白　1ぽん。
　 きいろ　　2ほん。
　 はなは　みんなで　なんぼん ｛あるでしょうか。
　　　　　　　　　　　　　　 ｛ですか。　　　　　＿＿＿＿＿＿＿ こたえ

イ 白と　あおの　おはじきが　ぜんぶで　6こ　あります。
　 白い　おはじきは　4こです。
　 あおい　あはじきは　なんこ ｛でしょうか！
　　　　　　　　　　　　　　 ｛ですか。

　 みんなで6こ  　　　　　　　　　　＿＿＿＿＿＿＿ こたえ

ウ ふうせんが　あります。
　 みどり　6つ、赤　8つ
　 ❶ みどりのふうせんが　4つ　とんでしまいました。
　　 みどりのふうせんは　いくつ　のこっていますか。
　　　　　　　　　　　　　　　　　　　　　＿＿＿＿＿＿＿ こたえ

　 ❷ 赤い　ふうせんも　4つ　とんでいってしまいました。
　　 赤い　ふうせんは　いくつ　のこっているでしょうか。
　　　　　　　　　　　　　　　　　　　　　＿＿＿＿＿＿＿ こたえ

エ 黒と 白の おはじきが あります。
どちらが いくつ おおいでしょうか!

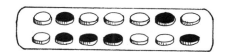

_____ こたえ

オ おとこのこが 22人、おんなのこも 22人 います。
いすは 36 あります。
いすは いくつ たりないでしょうか!

_____ こたえ

R Exclamations!

There'll be many instances during a stay in Japan when you'll want to make some kind of utterance (like "Wow!", "Oh!") where the English sounds would not be appropriate. Have a look at these expressions and see when you could use them in your role plays.

1. えっ?
What? Well? Eh? Are you sure?

2. ええ?
Eh? Huh? What? Really?

3. わあ、おどろいた!
Oh! I'm so surprised (at such a magnificent sight)!

4. じょうだんでしょう!
(_for females_) You're joking! You don't mean it!

5. じょうだんだろう!
(_for males_) You're joking! You don't mean it!

6. うん。
Yes. All right. Okay. (Said with a slight nod of the head)

7. あ、そうか。
I see.

8. （あれ）みて！
Look at that!

9. へえ。
What? (Really? Are you sure?)

10. びっくりした！
I'm surprised! You surprised me!

11. わあ！
Oh! Wow!

12. しっ！
Hush! Shh!

S₁ 書きましょう・カタカナ

By now you can probably read and recognise many katakana. In each unit from now on, you will learn how to write a number of katakana. Once you have mastered this second phonetic script you will be able to read many Japanese menus, signs and shop advertisements. It has even become quite "trendy" to use English words in katakana rather than use the correct Japanese word. (For example: ピンク is usually used instead of もﾓいろ.)

A complete katakana chart, showing the correct stroke order, is provided on page 323 for your reference.

ア a	ン n	ト to	ル ru	ナ na	ー ／
ア	ン	ト	ル	ナ	This symbol is used to lengthen any vowel. It is written horizontally when writing horizontally and vertically when writing vertically.
Stick out your tongue and say "*aaaa*"	Note: one tick will not make you pass the test	Spinning *top*	Kanga*roo*'s strong back legs and tail	Ban*ana*	

| フア | ヽン | Ｉト | ノル | ーナ | ー |

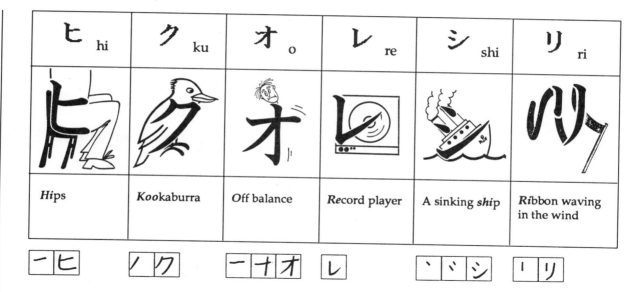

ヒ hi	ク ku	オ o	レ re	シ shi	リ ri
Hips	Kookaburra	Off balance	Record player	A sinking ship	Ribbon waving in the wind

一ヒ	ノク	一ナオレ	レ	` ゛シ	｜リ

S₂ ことばのれんしゅう　**Word practice**

Write out each of these words in your exercise book five times or until you can write them fluently without any need to check the katakana.

1. アンドルー (Andrew)
2. ドア (door)
3. グリル (grill)
4. ドン (Don)
5. アナ (Anna)
6. オーライ (All right)
7. アン (Anne)
8. ドナ (Donna)
9. グレゴリー (Gregory)

S₃ Copy out these words at least five times. Work out what each word is. (Some of them are first names.)

★ When trying to decipher katakana, you will often need to say the word over and over again, perhaps aloud, before you realise what the word is!

1. ピンク
2. レシート
3. ピン
4. アーン
5. クレア
6. オレンジ
7. グレー
8. オイル
9. アナ
10. ランドル
11. レール
12. グリーン
13. リー
14. オール
15. ルーク
16. リオン
17. アジア
18. ピーアールする
19. ドア
20. アリシア

S₄ What are the three words written in katakana? The illustrations should help you work out the katakana that you haven't yet learnt.

レストラン

パレード

カトゥン　キャンディ

S₅ Is this statement concerning you true or false?

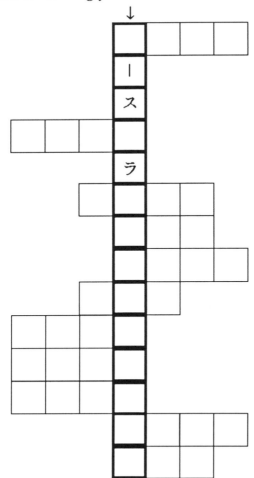

↓

1. Orange (katakana)

2. Katakana for す

3. Receipt (katakana)

4. Katakana for ら

5. Green (katakana)

6. Asia (katakana)

7. Carrot

8. Cheap

9. Balloons

10. By car

11. Short

12. Not bad, okay

13. Watermelon

T₁ Did you notice in the dialogue that there's a quick way of saying「これは　いとこです。グレゴリーと　いいます。」? It sounds odd in English, too, to say "This is my cousin. He is called Gregory." Why not try "This is my cousin Gregory"?

> *Sentence Pattern 49*
>
> これは　いとこの　グレゴリーです。　This is my cousin Gregory.

T₂ Whose photographs is Chie showing to her friends?

1. これは　いとこの　ゆうこです。
2. これは　いもうとの　まりこです。
3. これは　おとうとの　けんすけです。
4. これは　ともだちの　アンドルーです。
5. これは　いとこの　たろうです。

How would you explain to your Japanese friends that the photographs you show them are of the following people?

1. Your cousin Andrew.
2. Your friend Anne.
3. Your younger sister Donna.
4. Your uncle Don.
5. Your younger brother Greg.

U

(a) Write out the English equivalent of Seiji's letter so that you can tell your friends what he has said.

(b) Write a suitable reply to Seiji.

グレッグさんへ

お手紙と　ごかぞくの　しゃしん、ありがとうございました。グレッグさんの　グレートデンの　名前は　何ですか。ぼくの　いぬは　「ドーグ」と　言います。プードルです。ふつうは　ドーグに　えいごで　はなします。

「シットダウン」と「ステイ」と「ベッグ」と　言う　ことばを　よく　言います。ドーグは　白いです。でも　耳は　大きくて　茶色です。ドーグの　犬小屋（ドーグハウス）は　赤です。

まい日、ぼくと　母と　父は　ドーグを　さんぽに　つれていきます。かぞくの　うちは　とても　小さいですから　ドーグは　まい日の　さんぽを　たのしみに　しています。ときどき　さんぽの　あとで　こうえんで　ボールで　あそびます。

グレッグくんの　グレートデンは　どこで　はしり回りますか。いぬは　とても　いいペットですね。

では、　すぐ　へんじを　書いてください。

さようなら

平成三年五月十五日

せいじより

V You have taken these photographs while in Japan and you are sending them back to Australia. What would you write on the back of each photo describing who's who or what's what? Give as much detail as possible. Clues are given at the bottom of each photograph.

1. *You live in a "danchi" (apartment)*

2. *Your host mother and sister*

3. *Your host father, brother, sister and the dog*

4. *"Aunty" and baby (with a bottle of mugicha in front)*

5. *New Year's Day with "cousins"*

6. *Students in class having lunch*

調べましょう **Let's do some investigating**

しら

What do these two signs mean and where would you find them?

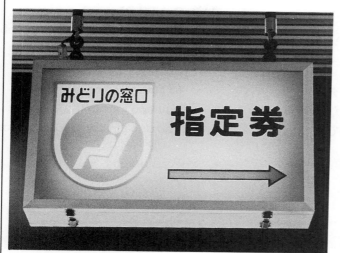

W₂ Have you heard this little rhyme before? What does it mean?

ばらは　赤い

すみれは　青い

さとうは　あまい

そして　あなたは　やさしい

X **New words and expressions** (words asterisked (*) are for recognition only)

A, sooka	あ、そうか	I see!
Akage	赤げ	Red hair
Akai	赤い	Red
Aoi	あおい	Blue
(Are) mite!	(あれ)みて！	Look at that!
Bara	ばら	Rose (flower)
Bikkurishita!	びっくりした！	I'm surprised! You surprised me!
Budoo	ぶどう	Grapes
Byooki	びょうき	Sick
Chairo (i)	ちゃいろ（い）	Brown
Daigakusei	だいがくせい	University student
Daikon	だいこん	Radish
Dochira*	どちら	Which one(s)?
Ee?	ええ？	Eh? Huh? What? Really?
Eh?	えっ？	What? Well? Eh? Are you sure?
Futotteiru	ふとっている	To be fat
Fuusen	ふうせん	Balloon
Hage (atama)	はげ（あたま）	Bald-headed

Unit 14 **51**

Hana	はな	Flower
Hashirimawaru	はしり回る	To run about (around)
Hee?	へえ？	What? Really? Are you sure?
Hikui	ひくい	Low
Hitomi	ひとみ	Pupil (of the eye)
Hon	ほん（ぽん、ぼん）	Counter for long cylindrical objects
Ichigo	いちご	Strawberry
Iro	色	Colour
Jakaranda	ジャカランダ	Jacaranda
Joodandaroo?	じょうだんだろう？	You don't mean it? (*for males*)
Joodandeshoo?	じょうだんでしょう？	You don't mean it? You're joking! (*for females*)
Kaki	かき	Persimmon
Kami	かみ	Paper
Kami (noke)	かみ（のけ）	Hair
Kanojo	かの女	She
Kawaii	かわいい	Cute
Ki	木	Plants, trees
Kiiro(i)	き色（い）	Yellow
Kimpatsu	きんぱつ	Blond hair
Kookoo	こうこう	High school
Kuchi	口	Mouth
Kumo	くも	Cloud
Kuri	くり	Chestnut
Kuroi	黒い	Black
Kurokami	黒かみ	Black hair
Kusa	くさ	Grass
Kyuukeishitsu	きゅうけいしつ	Sick bay, rest room
Me	目	Eye
Midori (no)	みどり（の）	Green
Mijikai	みじかい	Short
Momo	もも	Peach
Murasaki (no)	むらさき（の）	Purple
Nagai	ながい	Long
Nashi	なし	Japanese pear
Nezumi	ねずみ	Mouse
Ninjin	にんじん	Carrot
Nokotteiru*	のこっている	To remain behind
Ohajiki*	おはじき	Marbles
Omou	おもう	To think
Ooi	おおい	Many, numerous
Orenji(iro) (no)	オレンジ（色）（の）	Orange (coloured)
Pinku(iro) (no)	ピンク（色）（の）	Pink
Remon	レモン	Lemon
Sakana	さかな	Fish
Sakurambo	さくらんぼ	Cherry (fruit)

Sampo	さんぽ	A stroll, a walk
Se	せ	Back
Sh	しっ	Hush! Shh!
Shiraberu	調べる	To investigate, to look into
Shiraga	白が（しらが）	White (grey) haired
Shiroi	白い	White
Sora	そら	Sky
Suika	すいか	Watermelon
Sukoshi	すこし	A little
Sumire	すみれ	Violet (flower)
Suupaa (maaketto)	スーパー（マーケット）	Supermarket
Taikaku	たいかく	Physique, build
Taikaku ga ii	たいかくが　いい	Have an excellent physique
Takai	たかい	Tall, high
Tanoshii	たのしい	Enjoyable
Tanoshimini shite imasu	たのしみに　しています	Looking forward to …
Tarinai*	たりない	Be short of, insufficient
Tondeshimau*	とんでしまう	To fly away
Totemo	とても	Very
Un	うん	Yes, all right. Okay
Utsukushii	うつくしい	Beautiful
Waa odoroita!	わあ　おどろいた！	Oh! I'm surprised (*at such a magnificent sight*)!
Waa!	わあ！	Oh!
Waapuro	ワープロ	Word processor
Yaseteiru	やせている	To be thin

Kanji studied to the end of Unit 14:

Unit 13:	一	二	三	四	五	六	七	八	九	十	人	何
	1	2	3	4	5	6	7	8	9	10	11	12
Unit 14:	目	口	日	本	母	父	白	赤	黒	色	大	小
	13	14	15	16	17	18	19	20	21	22	23	24

Katakana studied to the end of Unit 14:

Unit 14:	ア	ン	ト	ル	ナ	ー	ヒ	ク	オ	レ	シ	リ
	1	2	3	4	5	6	7	8	9	10	11	12

Unit 15
Special times
とくべつ　じかん
特別な時間

A

1. おたん生日は　いつですか。

2. 三月の　三日です。

3. ほんとうですか。日本では　三月三日に　ひなまつりを
いわいます。その日は　小さい　女の　子は　パーティーを
します。たくさんの　女の　子は　きれいな　きものを
きます。春は　日本では　うつくしい　きせつです。さくら
の花が　さきます。

4. ええ、それに　天気が　いいです。よく
えんそくに　いきます。

5. 春を　たのしみに　しています。

How much of the dialogue could you guess? By now, given a few clues from your teacher, you'll find that you can start "guessing" what many words and expressions could mean. This is no different from what will happen in real life, where you will be required to use your common sense, and your ability to deduce from the context, when you hear or see a word that you haven't yet learnt.

B₁ ## Flowers and seasons

When planning a trip to Japan it is important to consider the season and the associated weather. Each of the four seasons is very different — each being characterised by its own flowers and festivals.

Summer sunflowers

Autumn leaves have fallen

Winter snowfall

Kimono-clad women on Adults' Day, January 15

Hinamatsuri in March

School culture festivals in September/October

Athletics carnivals in October

(a) Using a Japanese–English dictionary or the glossary at the end of this book, find out the names in English of each of the flowers illustrated in the diagram below. Also find out something about the events or festivals illustrated.

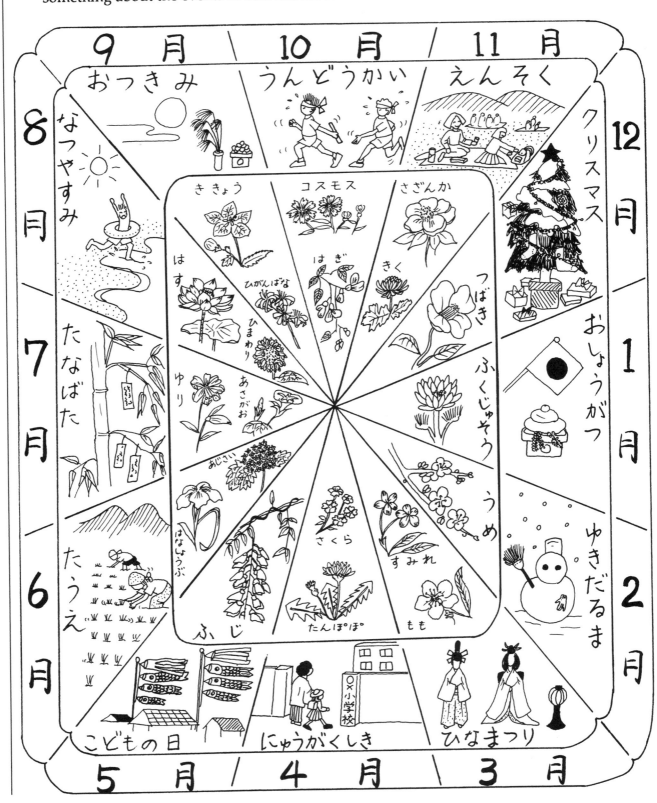

(b) By consulting gardening books or by asking a keen gardening friend, find out the colour of each flower and, on the copy of the diagram that your teacher will give you, colour them in appropriately.

(c) Write a short description of each of the twenty flowers, using one or other of the following patterns:

- ひまわりは　き色です。

- これは　き色の　ひまわりす。

- き色の　ひまわりを　みました。

If you cannot find out the colour of a particular flower, write 「わかりません」 or its less formal equivalent 「わからない」, and then complete this activity with your teacher's help.

C 書きましょう・漢字

25. 月　Moon

Clouds are floating past the *moon*.

| くん | つき | おん | げつ、がつ | いみ | 月、こん月、一月 |

| かきじゅん | ノ 几 月 月 |

4かく

26. 花　Flower

Here a person is seen cutting *flowers*.

| くん | はな | おん | か | いみ | 花、花火 fireworks |

| かきじゅん | 一 十 サ ヴ ヴ 花 花 |

7かく

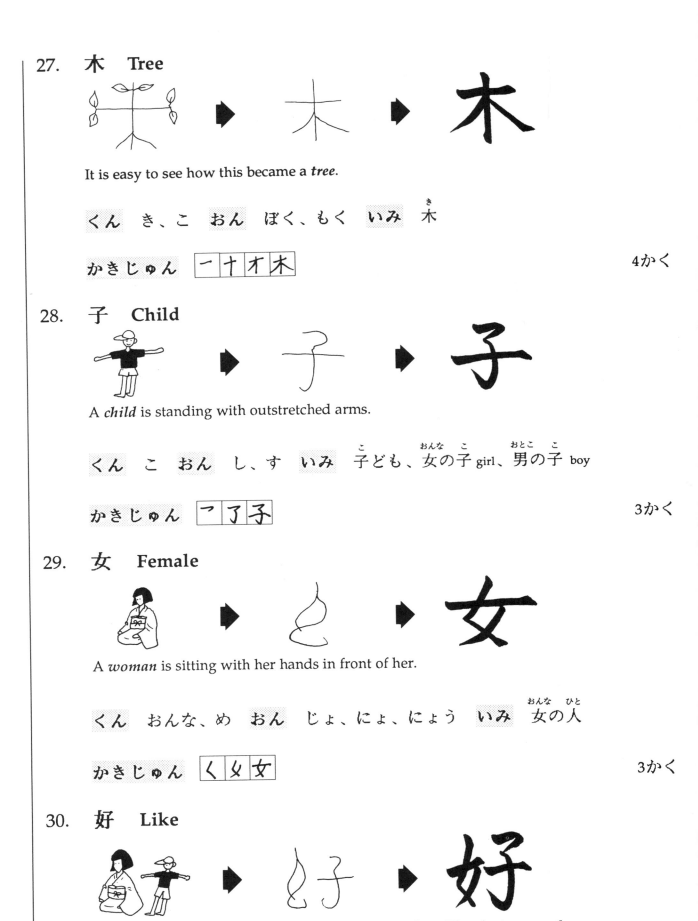

27. 木 Tree

It is easy to see how this became a *tree*.

くん き、こ　おん ぼく、もく　いみ 木（き）

かきじゅん ─ 十 オ 木

4かく

28. 子 Child

A *child* is standing with outstretched arms.

くん こ　おん し、す　いみ 子ども、女の子（おんな こ）girl、男の子（おとこ こ）boy

かきじゅん 了 了 子

3かく

29. 女 Female

A *woman* is sitting with her hands in front of her.

くん おんな、め　おん じょ、にょ、にょう　いみ 女の人（おんな ひと）

かきじゅん く 女 女

3かく

30. 好 Like

Love is strong between a woman and her child. They *like* playing together.

くん　す（き）、この（む）　おん　こう　いみ　好き _す like

かきじゅん　| し | 女 | 女 | 女 | 好 | 好 |　　　　　　　　6かく

31. 言　Say

When people speak, they use both their heart and their mouth.

くん　い（う）、こと　おん　げん、ごん　いみ　言_いう、言_{こと}ば words

かきじゅん　| ` | ﾗ | 二 | 三 | ﾗ | 言 | 言 |　　　　　　　7かく

★ Remember, write out each kanji as often as is necessary for you to be able to write and read it fluently!

D

(a)　Rewrite the following dialogue, inserting the missing words from the list at the foot.

(b)　In what month would this dialogue most likely take place?

アンドルー：　ああ！□の　にわは　きれいですね。

まりこ：　　ええ、そうですね！

アンドルー：　むらさきの□は　何と言いますか。

まりこ：　　これは　□です。

アンドルー：　ああ！□の　びょうどういんの
　　　　　　　まえに　ふじが　ありますね。
　　　　　　　(in front of)

まりこ：　　ええ、そうです。

アンドルー：　□たんぽぽは　きれいですね。

まりこ：　　ええ、わたしは　さくらの□が
　　　　　　　だい□です。あしたは　いっしょに
　　　　　　　花みに　いきましょうか。

The Byodoin, Kyoto

| 好き、き色の、ふじ、きょうと、花、あなたのうち、花 |

Japanese appreciate your knowing something about their daily life and culture. They will also be impressed if you show an interest in and knowledge of their flowers, plants and trees. You could show your appreciation of the beauty of their garden by commenting in this way:

き色の　ひまわりは　とても　うつくしいですね。

日本で　ひまわりを　たくさん　みます。

いつ　さきますか。

or　この花は　何と　言いますか。
(This flower)

or　その花は　コスモスですか。
ko su mo su
(That flower)

Cosmos

or　あの木は　さくらの木ですか。
(That tree over there)

Using the scene illustrated above as a base, write a dialogue between yourself and a member of your host family as you are shown around their garden. Try to *make* conversation and initiate discussion.

Use the adjectives that you learnt in the previous unit as often as possible, and be careful of which "glue" you use — の or な or い.

Indicating which flowers

In the previous exercise, you saw how it was possible to say "*This* flower" 「この花」, "*That* flower" 「その花」 and "*That* tree *over* there" 「あの木」.

The three words この、その and あの are very useful in indicating exactly which things you are talking about. They are demonstrative adjectives and it's easy to work out what kind of "glue" you'd use, isn't it. The の is already there. Study the examples given in Sentence Pattern 50 to see how they are used.

Sentence Pattern 50

Q. どの 花が 好きですか。 — Which flowers do you like?

A. この 花が 好きです。 — I like this flower.

でも その ピンク色の 花も — However, that pink flower is beautiful too, isn't it.
きれいですね。

あの 木は 何と 言いますか。 — What is that tree over there called?

F₂ Whether この、その or あの is used depends on the distance between the object and the speaker. Remember that the same principle applied for これ、それ and あれ (Unit 6, Sentence Pattern 17).

What does each of the following sentences mean?

1. この ぶどうは むらさきで そのぶどうは 白いです。
2. あの みせは ゆうめいな デパートです。「そごう」と 言います。
3. この 人は 父です。いい しゃしんじゃないです。
4. あの やまは ふじさんですね。
5. その レストランで たべましょうか。
6. この 大きいあじさいは きれいですね。
7. その 木の 花は 何色ですか。
8. その 花火は あぶないです。
9. あの ひ行きは ジャルの ひ行きです。
   ジャルの シンボルは 白いつるです。
10. この 子どもは テレビを みています。

花火

F₃ Study the photographs on page 62 and write eight sentences using この、その or あの as would be appropriate if you were showing your photo album to a Japanese friend. Be as creative as possible.

Eating chawan mushi, inari zushi and other dishes

A person "sleeping" on a train

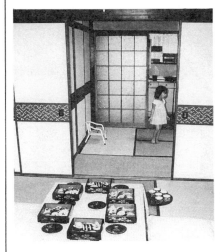

*Mariko absorbed in a TV programme.
There is sushi on the table.*

*Students bowing to their principal. "Father" works in
the building behind the school*

G 書きましょう・漢字

32. 夏　**Summer**

During the *summer* festival masks are worn. It is extremely hot under the masks, and even
when the mask is taken off the person is still left feeling hot — because it is *summer*.

くん　なつ　おん　か、げ　いみ　夏、夏休み summer holiday

かきじゅん　一　ア　ア　万　万　百　百　頁　頁　夏　　　10かく

33. 火　Fire

The crossed logs are burning brightly in the *fire*.

くん　ひ、ほ　おん　か　いみ　火よう日

かきじゅん　｜ヽ　ヽ｜　ソ　火

4かく

34. 秋　Autumn

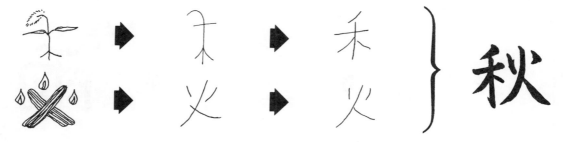

Autumn is harvest time, so あき is represented partly by a rice plant ready for harvesting and partly by a fire, used to burn the left-over plants.

くん　あき　おん　しゅう　いみ　秋

かきじゅん　ノ　ニ　千　チ　禾　禾　秒　秋

9かく

35. 春　Spring

Spring is represented by the growth of many plants and by the warm sun.

くん　はる　おん　しゅん　いみ　春

かきじゅん　一　二　三　声　夫　表　春　春

9かく

36. 冬　Winter

The waterfall stops flowing in *winter*; it freezes up completely except for a trickle!

くん　ふゆ　おん　とう　いみ　<ruby>冬<rt>ふゆ</rt></ruby>

かきじゅん　ノ　ク　夂　冬　冬　　　　　　5かく

37. 雨　Rain

It is easy to see the clouds and *rain* falling in あめ .

くん　あめ　おん　う　いみ　<ruby>雨<rt>あめ</rt></ruby>

かきじゅん　一　厂　冂　雨　雨　雨　雨　雨　　　　8かく

38. 雲　Cloud

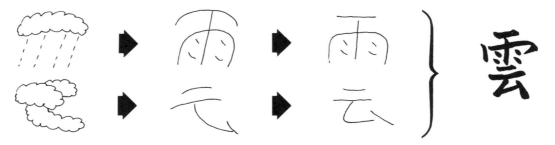

The kanji for *cloud* consists of two radicals or parts. The first part is the same as for "rain", as explained in the previous description. The second part comes from a drawing of a cloud.

くん　くも　おん　うん　いみ　<ruby>雲<rt>くも</rt></ruby>

かきじゅん　一　厂　冖　雨　雨　雨　雨　雫　雫　雫　雲　雲　　　12かく

39. 天　Heaven

Above a person's head is an expansive roof. This represents the idea of the *heaven*s or sky above us all.

くん　あめ、あま　　おん　てん　　いみ　天気 weather

かきじゅん　｜一　二　チ　天｜　　　　　　　　　　　　4かく

40. 気　Spirit, energy

In winter, when we breathe out, we can see "steam". Steam (or heat) is added to rice to cook it. When we eat, we get *energy*.

The character for rice started from a sketch of many grains of rice.

くん　　　おん　き、け　　いみ　元気 energy、びょう気 sick

かきじゅん　｜ノ　ヒ　ヒ　气　気　気｜　　　　　　6かく

41. 年　Year

Traditionally, the Japanese *year* revolved around the rice crop and its harvest, so it is appropriate that "year" be represented by a person carrying the harvested crop on his or her back.

くん　とし　おん　ねん　いみ　一年 one year、まい年 every year、今年 this year

かきじゅん　｜ノ　ヒ　ヒ　ヒ　ヒ　年｜　　　　　　　6かく

てんき
天気　Weather

Talking about the weather is a typical and common way of beginning a conversation. Look at some of the ways we could comment on the weather.

天気は　どうですか。

1. あついです。

It is hot!

2. むしあついですね。

It is humid, isn't it.

3. 雨が　ふります。

It will rain.

4. あたたかいです。

It is warm.

5. いい天気ですね。

It's good weather, isn't it.

6. はれです。

It is fine.

7. すずしいですね！

It's cool, isn't it.

8. くもりです。

It's cloudy.

9. さむいです。
It is cold.

10. とても　さむいです。
It is very cold.

11. いやな　天気ですね。
It's awful weather, isn't it.

12. かぜが　あります。
It will be windy.

13. ゆきが　ふります。
It will snow.

14. はれます。
It will be fine.

H₂ Look at the example on page 68 of how the weather forecast is presented in Japanese newspapers. Using the kanji listed below to help you read the weather report, and using the map on page 321 with the names of the cities in Japanese, work out what the weather will be like in six of the cities.

Kanji and useful expressions:

1. 北 North
2. 南 South
3. 東 East
4. 西 West
5. 曇り Cloudy
6. 晴れたり曇ったり Alternately clear and cloudy
7. 時々 Sometimes/with occasional

8. 朝 Morning
9. 午後 Afternoon
10. 夜 Night
11. 雪 Snow
12. 晴れ Fine
13. 曇一時雪 Cloudy with brief snow
14. 雨 Rain

15. にわか雨	Sudden showers	18. 曇後晴れ	Cloudy; fine later
16. 曇所により雨	Cloudy with scattered showers	19. 風	Wind
17. 後	After	20. 午前	Morning

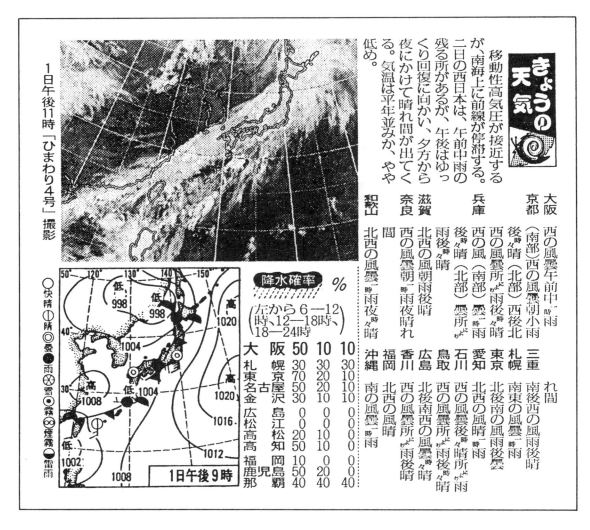

聞きましょう — 天気は どうですか

H3

Listen to the weather forecasts and write in your exercise book the closest English equivalent of the forecast — A, B or C.

(If C is your answer, write down what the weather forecast is.)

1. A. Windy and then snow   B. Windy, then rain   C. Other

2. A. Cloudy, then rain   B. Fine but rain in the evening   C. Other

3. A. Rain in the morning but humid in the afternoon   B. Rain in the morning but will fine up in the afternoon   C. Other

4. A. Typhoon, but will become fine   B. Rain all day because of a typhoon   C. Other

5. A. Cloudy and snow   B. Cloudy, then rain   C. Other

6. A. Strong winds and cold   B. Heavy rain and cold   C. Other

7. A. Alternating fine and cloudy   B. Cloudy with some rain   C. Other

8. A. Possible rain   B. Cloudy and some rain   C. Other

9. A. Fine, becoming cloudy and cold   B. Cool, cloudy after a clear morning   C. Other

10. A. Hot but fine   B. Snow   C. Other

きせつと月   The seasons and months

★ If you have difficulty in remembering vocabulary, why not make up some word-associations? For example:

In *fu*yu (winter) it is *fu*reezing.

In *ha*ru (spring) the birds are *hu*mming.

In *na*tsu (summer) the heat and humidity can be *na*sty.

In *a*ki (autumn) the rains can be *yu*kky!

Before long you'll find that you don't need to rely on the mnemonics.

I2 The following sentence patterns demonstrate how to use the seasons in sentences, and the particles that are used in each case.

Sentence Pattern 51a

<ruby>春<rt>はる</rt></ruby>が　きました。

Spring has come.

(Particle が is usually used instead of は when talking about a natural phenomenon, except when you wish to emphasise it — in that case you would use は, as in Sentence Pattern 51b.)

Sentence Pattern 51b

<ruby>冬<rt>ふゆ</rt></ruby>は　とても　さむいです。

Winter is very cold.

Sentence Pattern 51c

すぐ　<ruby>冬<rt>ふゆ</rt></ruby>に　なります。

It will become winter soon.

Sentence Pattern 51d

<ruby>冬<rt>ふゆ</rt></ruby>は　さむさが　きびしいですね。

The cold is bitter in winter, isn't it.

Notice that the pattern ... は ... が in 51d is the same as in Sentence Pattern 46. In this sentence 「冬」 is the topic, so は is used, even though in English it is translated as "in".

Sentence Pattern 51e

<ruby>冬<rt>ふゆ</rt></ruby>に　せんだいへ　いきます。

I go to Sendai in winter.

I3 Use the hints given to answer the following questions:

1. らい<ruby>月<rt>げつ</rt></ruby>は　<ruby>何<rt>なん</rt></ruby>の　きせつですか。(It will be spring.)

2. せん月は　何の　きせつでしたか。(It was winter.)

3. こん月は　何の　きせつですか。(Winter)

4. オーストラリアで　クリスマスは　何の　きせつですか。(Summer)

5. 日本では　つゆのきせつは　何ですか。(Summer)

調べましょう

Answer the following questions in Japanese. (The は after the で further emphasises "Japan" or "Australia" as the topic of the sentence.)

1. 日本では　春は　何月^{なんがつ}ですか。

1. 日本では　春は　何月ですか。

2. 日本では　夏は　何月ですか。

3. オーストラリアでは　夏は　何月ですか。

4. 日本では　秋は　何月ですか。

5. 日本では　冬は　何月ですか。

6. オーストラリアでは　夏やすみは　何月ですか。

7. 日本では　いつ　スキーに　いきますか。

8. オーストラリアでは　冬やすみは　何月ですか。

J₁

When specifying the month in which something occurs, use particle に to indicate "in". However, if the month is the topic of the sentence, it should be followed by the topic indicator は.

Sentence Pattern 52a

Q. 何月に　さくらの　花が　さきますか。　　When do the cherry blossoms come out?

A. 四月に　さきます。　　They bloom in April.

Sentence Pattern 52b

日本では　12月は　さむいです。　　December is cold in Japan.

J₂

Answer each of the following questions according to the clues given. (Note which particles are used depending on the meaning being conveyed. に is used when designating a *specific* point of time.)

1. さくらの　花は　何月に　さきますか。(April)

2. ひなまつりは　何月ですか。(March)

3. こどもの日は　何月ですか。(May)

4. 何月に　にゅうがくしますか。(April)

5. 何月に　日本へ　いきましたか。(November)

6. オーストラリアでは　夏やすみは　何月に　はじまりますか。(December)

7. 何月に　花みに　いきますか。(April)

8. 日本では　何月に　ゆきが　ふりますか。(January)

9. オーストラリアでは　お父さんの　日は　何月ですか。(September)

10. せつぶんは　何月ですか。(February)

11. ふつう　イースターは　何月ですか。(March)

12. おぼんは　何月ですか。(July)

J₃ Use the hints given to answer the following questions:

1. 日本では　いつ　たいふうが　たくさん　きますか。(August/September)

2. 日本では　がっこうは　一月に　はじまりますか。(No, it starts in April.)

3. オーストラリアでは　六月は　夏やすみ　ですか。(No. In Australia the summer holidays are in December and January.)

4. 日本では　九月は　むしあついですか。(Yes, it's humid in September.)

5. いつ　日本へ　いきたいですか。(In September)

K Your Japanese friend sends you some photographs he or she has taken at various times of the year and he or she tells you a few things about each season.

(a)　At the end of each story, rate your comprehension by using the scale below.

(b)　Then go back over and over again until you understand everything perfectly.

(c)　Write a summary in English of the description of each season.

Comprehension scale:

I only understood a few words	➡	I got the general idea	➡	I understood everything (I think)

1. 日本では　十二月と　一月と　二月は　冬です。
冬は　とても　さむいです。　かぜが　つよく*
ふきます。よく　ゆきが　ふります。ゆきだるま
を　つくります。冬には　日本アルプスで
スキーを　します。お母さんと　おねえさんは
十二月に　おしょう月の　りょうりを　つくり
ます。おもちも　つくります。ときどき
ともだちは　クリスマス　パーティーを
します。
　　　　　* Strong

Enjoying osechiryoori on New Year's Day

2.

A group of children on a school picnic

日本では　三月と　四月と　五月は　春です。
天気が　いいです。三月三日は[1]　ひなまつりで
女の子の日です。さくらの花が　さきますから
ピクニックに　いきます。春は　花が　いつも
きれいです。き色の　たんぽぽが　好きです。
来年　四月に　にゅうがくして　こうこう
せいに　なります。たのしみに　しています。
五月五日は[2]　子どもの日で　男の子の日です。

[1]三日（みっか）= the third
[2]五日（いつか）= the fifth

3.　オーストラリアでは　十二月と　一月と　二月は
　　夏です。でも　日本では　六月、七月と　八月は
　　夏です。六月に　つゆ*の雨が　ふりますから
　　ときどき　てるてるぼうずを　つくります。
　　七月に　たなばたまつりが　あります。花火を
　　します。夏休みを　たのしみに　しています。
　　夏は　むしあついです。わたしは　かぞくと
　　うみへ　いきます。七月は　とても　あついです。

Teruteruboozu

* The つゆ is Japan's rainy season, which lasts usually from mid June to mid July. This season is characterised by
much rain and often the weather is very humid (むしあつい).

4.

Taiikusai

日本では　九月と　十月と　十一月は　秋です。
ときどき　九月に　たいふうが　きます。雨が
ふります。十月に　お月みを　します。お月みだんご
を　たべます。十一月に　がっこうの　たいいくさい
が　あります。秋は　きくが　さきます。きくは
大きくて　きれいです。十一月は　だんだん
さむくなります*。

* Gradually gets colder

L

Describe the weather in each month of the Japanese calendar and illustrate or find pictures of this
kind of weather.

For example:

　　日本で　一月は　とても　さむいです。
　　一月に　雪（ゆき）が　ふります。

Note the use of 「で」 to denote the place of action!

M₁ | なんにち
何日ですか　Days of the month

Now things really are becoming specific! Once you've mastered this section, you can start making plans for special events, for birthdays, and for other things that will happen in the future; or you can talk specifically about what you did on specific days.

注意 The words for the *first* (1st) and *twentieth* (20th) of any month are quite irregular, so pay special attention to them. Look carefully at the *fourth*, *fourteenth* and *twenty-fourth*, too.

何日　　なんにち　　What day?	
1st　一日(ついたち)	17th　十七日(じゅうしちにち)
2nd　二日(ふつか)	18th　十八日(じゅうはちにち)
3rd　三日(みっか)	19th　十九日(じゅうくにち)
4th　四日(よっか)	20th　二十日(はつか)
5th　五日(いつか)	21st　二十一日(にじゅういちにち)
6th　六日(むいか)	22nd　二十二日(にじゅうににち)
7th　七日(なのか)	23rd　二十三日(にじゅうさんにち)
8th　八日(ようか)	24th　二十四日(にじゅうよっか)
9th　九日(ここのか)	25th　二十五日(にじゅうごにち)
10th　十日(とおか)	26th　二十六日(にじゅうろくにち)
11th　十一日(じゅういちにち)	27th　二十七日(にじゅうしちにち)
12th　十二日(じゅうににち)	28th　二十八日(にじゅうはちにち)
13th　十三日(じゅうさんにち)	29th　二十九日(にじゅうくにち)
14th　十四日(じゅうよっか)	30th　三十日(さんじゅうにち)
15th　十五日(じゅうごにち)	31st　三十一日(さんじゅういちにち)
16th　十六日(じゅうろくにち)	

M₂ Like other specific forms of time, the days of the month require particle に when specifying a certain day. Study the sentence patterns below to see how you can use dates.

Sentence Pattern 53

(a) Q.　ダンスは　何日ですか。　　　　On what date is the dance?
　　　　Da n su　なんにち

　　A.　五日です。　　　　　　　　　It's (on) the fifth.
　　　　いつか

(b) Q.　何日に　えんそくに　いきますか。　On what date will we go on the excursion?
　　　　なんにち

　　A.　24日に　いきます。　　　　　　We'll go on the twenty-fourth.

(c) Q.　16日は　がっこうの　　　　　Is the school dance on the sixteenth?
　　　　ダンスパーティーですか。
　　　　da n su paa tii

　　A.　いいえ、17日です。　　　　　No, it's the seventeenth.

Sentence Pattern 54

Q. おたんじょう日は　いつですか。　　　　When is your birthday?

A. （わたしの　たんじょう日は）　4月7日です。　(My birthday is) It's on April the 7th.

or

A. 4月の　7日です。*　　　　　　　It's on the 7th of April.

注意 * Never use particle に before です。

N What do you know about each of these people and what they are doing?

1.  たんじょう日は　五月の　二十三日です。ことし
十五さいに　なります。二十三日は　月よう日です。
それで　二十二日に　小さいパーティーを　します。

2.  わたしは　ぎんこうで　はたらいています。六月の
七日から　六月十七日まで　やすみます。

3.  マリアさんは　九月の　九日に　「なりたくうこう」
に　つきます。お父さんと　わたしは　マリアさんに
七じはんに　あいます。

4.  子どもの日は　五月の　五日です。いつも　やすみ
です。ことし　おばあさんと　おじいさんと
いっしょに　きょうとへ　いきます。

5. 七月の　二十三日に　よるの　八じはんに
とうきょうを　でます。あさの　六じはんに
ブリスベンに　つきます。

Answer these questions as indicated and then try to find out how each of the events is celebrated in Japan.

1.　てんのうの　おたんじょう日は　いつですか。
(23 December)

Emperor

2.　クリスマスの日は　いつですか。
(25 December)

3.　けいろうの日は　いつですか。
(15 September)

4.　たいいくの日は　いつですか。
(10 October)

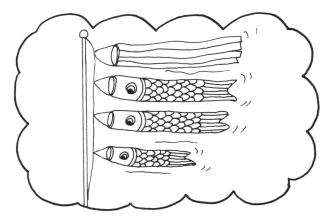

5.　たなばたまつりは　いつですか。
(7 July) (or 7 August in some districts)

6.　子どもの日は　いつですか。
(5 May)

7. おおみそかは　いつですか。
(31 December)

8. せつぶんは　いつですか。
(3 February) (3rd or 4th, depending on the beginning of spring according to the lunar calendar)

9. ひなまつりは　いつですか。
(3 March)

10. おぼんは　いつですか。(15 July)
(or 15 August, depending on the region)

P # 聞きましょう

Your teacher will read out ten dates. Circle each of these dates on a copy of this calendar which your teacher will give you.

一月						
日	月	火	水	木	金	土
	1	2	3	4	5	6
7	8	9	10	11	12	13
14	15	16	17	18	19	20
21	22	23	24	25	26	27
28	29	30	31			

二月						
日	月	火	水	木	金	土
					1	2	3
4	5	6	7	8	9	10
11	12	13	14	15	16	17
18	19	20	21	22	23	24
25	26	27	28	29		

三月						
日	月	火	水	木	金	土
					1	2
3	4	5	6	7	8	9
10	11	12	13	14	15	16
17	18	19	20	21	22	23
24	25	26	27	28	29	30
31						

四月						
日	月	火	水	木	金	土
	1	2	3	4	5	6
7	8	9	10	11	12	13
14	15	16	17	18	19	20
21	22	23	24	25	26	27
28	29	30				

五月						
日	月	火	水	木	金	土
			1	2	3	4
5	6	7	8	9	10	11
12	13	14	15	16	17	18
19	20	21	22	23	24	25
26	27	28	29	30	31	

六月						
日	月	火	水	木	金	土
						1
2	3	4	5	6	7	8
9	10	11	12	13	14	15
16	17	18	19	20	21	22
23	24	25	26	27	28	29
30						

七月						
日	月	火	水	木	金	土
	1	2	3	4	5	6
7	8	9	10	11	12	13
14	15	16	17	18	19	20
21	22	23	24	25	26	27
28	29	30	31			

八月						
日	月	火	水	木	金	土
					1	2	3
4	5	6	7	8	9	10
11	12	13	14	15	16	17
18	19	20	21	22	23	24
25	26	27	28	29	30	31

九月						
日	月	火	水	木	金	土
1	2	3	4	5	6	7
8	9	10	11	12	13	14
15	16	17	18	19	20	21
22	23	24	25	26	27	28
29	30					

十月						
日	月	火	水	木	金	土
		1	2	3	4	5
6	7	8	9	10	11	12
13	14	15	16	17	18	19
20	21	22	23	24	25	26
27	28	29	30	31		

十一月						
日	月	火	水	木	金	土
					1	2
3	4	5	6	7	8	9
10	11	12	13	14	15	16
17	18	19	20	21	22	23
24	25	26	27	28	29	30

十二月						
日	月	火	水	木	金	土
1	2	3	4	5	6	7
8	9	10	11	12	13	14
15	16	17	18	19	20	21
22	23	24	25	26	27	28
29	30	31				

Q Answer each of the following questions according to the clues given.

1. まりこさんの　おたんじょう日は　何月　何日ですか。(13 May)
2. いつ　あさくさへ　いきたいですか。(Thursday of next week)
3. ふねは　いつ　つきますか。(24 July)
4. いつ　ぎんざへ　いきたいですか。(15th of this month)
5. あきはばらへ　いつ　いきましたか。(7th of last month)
6. いつ　レストランへ　たべに　いきますか。(30 November)
7. いつ　がっこうは　はじまりますか。(4 April)
8. いつ　夏やすみは　はじまりますか。(20 July)
9. いつ　はこねへ　たけしくんと　いきますか。(16 December)
10. うんどうかいは　いつですか。(29 September)

R Draw pictures of ten friends or members of your family, or find pictures of ten people whose birthdays you know. Next to each picture, write down when that person's birthday is.

S₁ ## いつ　うまれましたか　When were you born?

Although the Japanese traditionally counted years by historical periods as shown in the chart on the next page, today they also use the Western method. As you can see, each year in the Japanese calendar is timed according to how long the current emperor has been on the throne. So, when talking about the year 1991, Japanese could say either 1991 or へいせい　さんねん meaning the third year of the reign of Akihito, in the era "Enlightened Peace".

Japanese take their babies to the local shrine when they are about one month old to express thanks and pray for the child's good health—this is called omiyamairi

Western Calendar		Japanese Calendar		
1868	せんはっぴゃくろくじゅうはちねん 千八百六十八年	がんねん めいじ元年	Meiji Era	1st year
1912	千九百十二年	たいしょう元年	Taisho Era	1st year
1926	千九百二十六年	しょうわ元年	Showa Era	1st year
1945	千九百四十五年	しょうわ二十年		20th year
1976	せんきゅうひゃくななじゅうろくねん 千九百七十六年	しょうわ五十一年		51st year
1977	千九百七十七年	しょうわ五十二年		52nd year
1978	千九百七十八年	しょうわ五十三年		53rd year
1979	千九百七十九年	しょうわ五十四年		54th year
1980	千九百八十年	しょうわ五十五年		55th year
1981	千九百八十一年	しょうわ五十六年		56th year
1982	千九百八十二年	しょうわ五十七年		57th year
1983	千九百八十三年	しょうわ五十八年		58th year
1984	千九百八十四年	しょうわ五十九年		59th year
1985	千九百八十五年	しょうわ六十年		60th year
1986	千九百八十六年	しょうわ六十一年		61st year
1987	千九百八十七年	しょうわ六十二年		62nd year
1988	千九百八十八年	しょうわ六十三年		63rd year
1989	千九百八十九年	へいせい元年	Heisei Era	1st year
1990	千九百九十年	へいせい二年		2nd year
1991	千九百九十一年	へいせい三年		3rd year
1992	千九百九十二年	へいせい四年		4th year

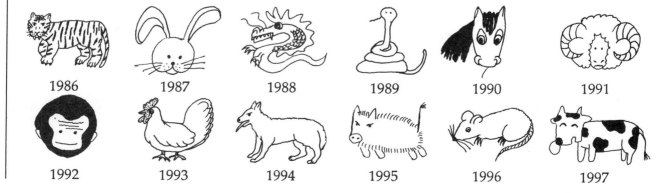

1986	1987	1988	1989	1990	1991
1992	1993	1994	1995	1996	1997

Sentence Pattern 55

(a) **Q.** 何年に　うまれましたか。   In what year were you born?

     A. 1977年に　うまれました。   I was born in 1977.

     （1977 = せんきゅうひゃくななじゅうなな）

(b) **Q.** いつ　うまれましたか。   When were you born?

     A. 1977年　6月　15日に　うまれました。   I was born on 15 June 1977.

Find out the year, month and day of the birth of at least ten of your relatives and friends.

Record them as follows:

　　おばあさんは　1930年　5月　3日に　うまれました。

　　（1930 = せんきゅうひゃくさんじゅうねん）

After reading this dialogue, answer the questions which follow.

えみこ：	もしもし
としゆき：	マリア^{Ma}さん　ですか。

えみこ：　いいえ、ちがいます。マリア^{Ma}さんは　います。ちょっと
　　　　　まってください。

　　　　　　………

マリア：　もしもし、マリア^{Ma}です。

としゆき：　ああ、マリア^{Ma}さん　こちらは　としゆきです。

　　　　　わたしの　たんじょう日は

　　　　　こん月の　二日で　パーティーを　します。マリアさんを

　　　　　しょうたいしたいの[*]ですが …

マリア：　ああ、どうも　ありがとう。   *Note: の in this context makes the sentence politer.

もちろん　いきたいです。

こん月の　二日ですね。

としゆき：　　ええ。

マリア：　　何じに　はじまりますか。

としゆき：　　六じに　はじまります。どうですか。

マリア：　　いいです。何年に　うまれましたか。

としゆき：　　1977年です。

マリア：　　あ、15さいに　なりますか。

としゆき：　　ええ、そうです。

マリア：　　では　ありがとう。またね。

としゆき：　　ええ、バイバイ。

1. Can you guess who Emiko might be?
2. Why does Toshiyuki ring Maria? (Give full details.)
3. What do you know about Toshiyuki's birthday and age?

Can you now act out this or a similar dialogue? Try to be creative in your scripting and use as many different sentence patterns and idioms as you can think of.

U₁ 書きましょう・カタカナ

Let's now add a few more katakana to our repertoire!

ハ ha	イ i	マ ma	テ te	ス su	ラ ra	ツ tsu
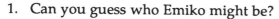						
Hard as nails	Indian chief	*Ma's* sore back	Temple	*Su*perman	*Rugby Rat* with his *ru*gby ball	Rugby Rat has a cold: "Aah-*tsu*."
ノ ハ	ノ イ	フ マ	ニ テ	フ ス	ラ	ィ ッ

ことばのれんしゅう

Copy out these words at least five times and work out the meaning of each.

1.	レストラン	11.	ライオン	22.	バット
2.	バイバイ	12.	テーラー	23.	シルクハット
3.	マリア	13.	パリ	24.	トマト
4.	ステレオ	14.	パーラー	25.	ズームレンズ
5.	スパイ	15.	パパ	26.	ハイツ
6.	ママ	16.	バイパス	27.	ベビー
7.	スペリング	17.	トイレ	28.	シリーズ
8.	スペイン	18.	バス	29.	スペード
9.	スペア	19.	マスク	30.	オーストラリア
10.	スーパー	20.	スト (less commonly written as ストライキ)		
	(マーケット)	21.	ドイツ		

U₃

What's the movie? Can you work out the actor's name?

V ワンダーワード **Wonderword**

With a pencil, circle the hiragana which link up to make words. They can be read horizontally, vertically or diagonally. All the words have been used in the いっしょに course to date. Seven of the eight hiragana needed for the "wonderword" will be left uncircled. The third hiragana is already provided for you. Write down the uncircled hiragana in the order that they are presented from top to bottom to find the "wonderword".

せ	つ	は	れ	ま	す	ん	て	も	か	じ	ち	せ
お	く	こ	ど	も	の	ひ	も	ん	お	ゅ	ゃ	い
ふ	る	き	き	さ	た	ん	ぽ	ぽ	の	く	い	ぶ
ろ	く	つ	ぎ	く	く	ゅ	え	き	く	う	ろ	つ
た	た	い	ふ	う	も	ら	い	い	つ	ま	ね	う
な	お	も	ち	ち	り	し	ご	う	う	れ	ず	ひ
ば	ゃ	す	い	が	り	ょ	う	り	い	ま	み	く
た	て	ず	つ	あ	つ	う	ん	ょ	ぬ	す	み	れ
き	る	し	つ	た	に	じ	ど	う	し	ゃ	か	し
う	て	い	い	た	ご	ゅ	う	り	あ	き	が	さ
つ	る	り	う	か	が	く	か	い	た	つ	く	ね
く	ぼ	ん	い	い	な	い	い	ち	く	ら	き	ふ
し	う	ご	な	つ	ほ	ん	と	う	さ	い	る	た
い	ず	じ	ゅ	う	い	ち	が	つ	ん	み	っ	つ

Wonderword:

W **New words and expressions**

Abunai	あぶない	Dangerous
Ajisai	あじさい	Hydrangea (flower)
Aki	秋	Autumn
Ame	雨	Rain
Ano	あの	That (over there) (*adjective*)
Asa	あさ	(in the) Morning
Asagao	あさがお	Morning glory (flower)
Atatakai	あたたかい	Warm

Atsui	あつい	Hot
Chigaimasu	ちがいます	I/We disagree. No (it isn't)
Chuugakusei	ちゅうがくせい	Junior high school student
Daisukidesu	大好きです	(I) love/like … very much
Dandan	だんだん	Gradually
Dansu	ダンス	Dance
Dansupaatii	ダンスパーティー	School dance, dance party
Dono	どの	Which (one) ?
Fuji	ふじ	Wisteria
Fuku (fukimasu, fuite)	ふく（ふきます、ふいて）	To blow
Fukujusoo	ふくじゅそう	Adonis, a pheasant's eye (flower)
Furu (furimasu, futte)	ふる（ふります、ふって）	To rain, to snow
Futsuka	二日	The second (day of the month)
Fuyu	冬	Winter
Gogatsu	五月	May
Hachigatsu	八月	August
Hagi	はぎ	Bush clover
Hanabi	花火	Fireworks
Hanabi o suru	花火を　する	To let off fireworks
Hanashoobu	はなしょうぶ	Iris (flower)
Hare desu	はれです	It is fine
Haremasu	はれます	It will be fine
Hareteimasu	はれています	It is fine
Haru	春	Spring
Hasu	はす	Lotus
Hatsuka	二十日	Twentieth (day of the month)
Himawari	ひまわり	Sunflower
Hinamatsuri	ひなまつり	Doll Festival
Hiraku (hirakimasu, hiraite)	ひらく（ひらきます、ひらいて）	To hold (an event)
Hontoo	ほんとう	True, truth
Hyaku	百	One hundred
Ichigatsu	一月	January
Iisutaa	イースター	Easter (not celebrated in Japan)
Itsuka	五日	Fifth (day of the month)
Iu	言う	To say
Iwau (iwaimasu, iwatte)	いわう(いわいます、いわって)	To celebrate
Iya (na)	いや（な）	Awful
Jaru	ジャル	Japan Air Lines (JAL)
Juugatsu	十月	October
Juuichigatsu	十一月	November
Juunigatsu	十二月	December
Kaze	かぜ	Wind
Kedo	けど	But, however
Keiroonohi	けいろうの日	Day of Respect for the Aged
Kibishii	きびしい	Severe, bitter

Kiku	きく	Chrysanthemum
Kikyoo	ききょう	Chinese bell flower
Kiru (kimasu, kite)	きる（きます、きて）	To wear
Kisetsu	きせつ	Season
Kokonoka	九日	Ninth (day of the month)
Kongetsu	こん月	This month
Kono	この	This (*adjective*)
Kookoosei	こうこうせい（こうとう がっこうのせいと）	Senior high school student
Kosumosu	コスモス	Cosmos (flower)
Kugatsu	九月	September
Kumori	くもり	Cloudy
Kurisumasu	クリスマス	Christmas
Matsuri	まつり	Festival
Midorinohi	みどりの日	Green Day (29 April)
Mikka	三日	Third (day of the month)
Muika	六日	Sixth (day of the month)
Mushiatsui	むしあつい	Humid
Nangatsu	何月	What month?
Nannichi	何日	What day?
Nanoka	七日	Seventh (day of the month)
Narita kuukoo	なりた　くうこう	Narita airport
Natsu	夏	Summer
Nen	年	Year
Nigatsu	二月	February
Nihonarupusu	日本アルプス	Japan Alps
Nochi	後	Future, after
Nyuugakusuru	にゅうがくする	To start school
Obon	おぼん	Festival of Ancestral Souls
Omochi	おもち	Rice cakes
Onnanoko	女の子	Girl
Oomisoka	おおみそか	New Year's Eve
Osechiryoori	おせちりょうり	Special New Year's Day food arranged in layered lacquered dishes
Oshoogatsu	おしょう月	New Year
Otsukimi	お月み	Moon viewing on the night of the full moon in mid-autumn
Paatii o suru	パーティーを　する	To have a party
Pikunikku	ピクニック	Picnic
Raigetsu	らい月	Next month
Rokugatsu	六月	June
Ryoori	りょうり	Cooking
Saku (sakimasu, saite)	さく（さきます、さいて）	To bloom
Sakura	さくら	Cherry
Sakuranohana	さくらの花	Cherry blossoms

Sakuranohana	さくらの花	Cherry blossoms
Samui	さむい	Cold (when referring to weather)
Samusa	さむさ	Coldness
Sangatsu	三月	March
Sazanka	さざんか	Sasanqua (camellia)
Sen	せん（千）	One thousand
Sengetsu	せん月	Last month
Setsubun	せつぶん	Bean Throwing Festival
Shichigatsu	七月	July
Shigatsu	四月	April
Shootaisuru	しょうたいする	To invite
Sono	その	That (*adjective*)
Sonohi	その日	On this day
Sorede	それで	Therefore
Soreni	それに	Besides this, moreover
Suzushii	すずしい	Cool
Taifuu	たいふう	Typhoon
Taiikunohi	たいいくの日	Sports Day
Taiikusai	たいいくさい	Athletics carnival
Tampopo	たんぽぽ	Dandelion
Tanabata	たなばた	Star Festival
Tanjoobi	たんじょう日	Birthday
Taue	たうえ	Rice planting
Tenki	天気	Weather
Tennoo	てんのう	Emperor
Teruteruboozu	てるてるぼうず	A doll made of white tissue paper
Tooka	十日	Tenth (day of the month)
Tsubaki	つばき	Camellia
Tsuitachi	一日	First (day of the month)
Tsukimidango	つきみだんご	Rice cakes made for Otsukimi
Tsukuru	つくる	To make
Tsuru	つる	Crane (bird)
Tsuyoi	つよい	Strong (*adjective*)
Tsuyoku	つよく	Strong (*adverb*)
Tsuyu	つゆ	Rainy season
Umareru	うまれる	To be born
Ume	うめ	Plum
Undookai	うんどうかい	Sports festival —primary school
Wakaranai	わからない	I don't understand/know
Yokka	四日	Fourth (day of the month)
Yooka	八日	Eighth (day of the month)
Yoru	よる	(in the) Evening
Yuki	ゆき	Snow (*noun*)
Yukidaruma	ゆきだるま	Snowman
Yuri	ゆり	Lily

Kanji studied to the end of Unit 15:

Unit 13:	一	二	三	四	五	六	七	八	九	十	人	何
	1	2	3	4	5	6	7	8	9	10	11	12
Unit 14:	目	口	日	本	母	父	白	赤	黒	色	大	小
	13	14	15	16	17	18	19	20	21	22	23	24
Unit 15:	月	花	木	子	女	好	言	夏	火	秋	春	冬
	25	26	27	28	29	30	31	32	33	34	35	36
	雨	雲	天	気	年							
	37	38	39	40	41							

Katakana studied to the end of Unit 15:

Unit 14:	ア	ン	ト	ル	ナ	ー	ヒ	ク	オ	レ	シ	リ
	1	2	3	4	5	6	7	8	9	10	11	12
Unit 15:	ハ	イ	マ	テ	ス	ラ	ッ					
	13	14	15	16	17	18	19					

As the school athletics carnival is not too far away, these students are in sports uniform ready for practice.
Here they are on assembly bowing to the principal

Unit 16

Student life
がくせい せいかつ
学生 生活

Topics:

一　Comparisons and descriptions
二　Abilities
三　Schools and speeches
四　School rules

A　しょうかいする。

みなさん、今日は。　マリア　アレンと　もうします。わたしは「しんりょうだい中学校」に
これたことを　とても　うれしく　おもいます。　日本の　かぞく生かつや　学校について[1]
しりたい {です。
　　　　 {と　おもいます。[2]
みなさんに　オーストラリアの　いろいろな　ことを　おしえたいです。
日本語は　むずかしい {です。
　　　　　　　　　　　 {と　おもいます。
まだ　わたしは　日本語が　下手だから　おしえてください。がんばります。

---

[1]について ... concerning ...　　　[2]と　おもいます　I think

(The second alternative in each sentence is more formal or polite and should be learned as an extension sentence only.)

Enjoying a stay of any length in a Japanese school means that you will have to:

- Give many speeches.
- Get used to four or five-storeyed buildings.
- Observe everything going on around you and learn from your experiences.
- Ask lots of questions.
- Give lots of explanations.
- Learn some "protocol" or customs.
- Learn some more Japanese.

So let's get started!

You will be asked many times over to talk about life as a student in Australia as compared with Japan.

So why not say:

オーストラリアの　学生生<ruby>かつと<rt>がくせいせい</rt></ruby>
日本の　学生生<ruby>かつの<rt>がくせいせい</rt></ruby>　ちがいは
or { たくさん　あります。
あまり　ありません。

There are many/not many differences between student life in Japan and in Australia.

たとえば … (for instance …)

1.
オーストラリアで

- きゅうしょくは　ありません。
- じゅくは　ありません。
- ぶんかさいは　ありません。

- 六さいで　こどもは　にゅう
  <ruby>学<rt>がく</rt></ruby>します。
- いつも　くつを　はきます。
- スリッパを　はきません。

In Australia …
- We don't have school lunch.
- We don't have cram schools.
- We don't have culture festivals.
- Six-year-olds start school.

- We always wear shoes.
- We don't wear slippers.

2.
わたしの　学校で

- しょどうを　しません。
- いけばなを　ならいません。

- コンピューターを
  つかいます。

At my school …
- We don't do calligraphy.
- We don't learn flower arranging.
- We use the computer.

3.

日本で

- 生とは　土よう日
  にも　学校へ　いきます。
- グランドは　ふつう
  小さいですが
  オーストラリアでは
  グランドは　大きいです。

In Japan …

- Pupils go to school on Saturday too.

- The playgrounds are usually small but in Australia they are large.

But …

日本の　学校でも　オーストラリアの　学校でも
生とは　せいふくを　きます。

In both Australia and Japan, students wear uniforms.

B₂ 調べましょう

After carrying out research into the Japanese education system and schooling in Japan, see if you can make 3–5 other comparisons of Australian and Japanese schools.

C₁

In using combined particles or signposts (じょし), as in the sentences in Box 3 above, the literal meanings of each separate じょし do not change much.

> ### Sentence Pattern 56
>
> 日本では　生とは　土よう日にも
> 学校へ　いきます。
>
> In Japan the students go to school *on* Saturday *too*.

The は after 日本で emphasises "Japan" as the topic of the sentence ("As for in Japan"). The に and も still retain their original meanings, so together they mean "on … also".

… And if you think students wouldn't want to go to school on Saturdays, read this sign in a classroom window!

C₂ What does each of the following sentences mean?

1. 日本の　デパートは　日よう日にも　あいています。
2. ときどき　日本で　学生は　日よう日にも　学校に　いきます。
3. 三じにも　ともだちに　あいます。
4. 九じに　かいものに　いきました。二じにも　かいものに　いきました。
5. 五月にも　日本へ　いきましたね。
6. まりこさんに　あいました。たけしさんにも　あいましたか。
7. ねんがじょうを　おばあさんと　おじいさんにも　おくりました。
8. 小さいノートに　かきました。大きいノートにも　かきました。

C₃ も can be added to で in the same way that it can be to に.

> ### Sentence Pattern 57
>
> オーストラリアでも　生とは　　　　In Australia, too, students wear school uniform.
> せいふくを　きます。

Australian and Japanese students in a school tea room

C₄ Try putting these into Japanese:

1. In Japan, too, students do homework.
2. In Japan, too, school finishes at 3.00 p.m.
3. In Australia, too, students take books to school.
4. In Japan, too, students learn English.
5. In Australia, too, after lessons, students talk with their teachers.

The じょし or particle 「も」 has many uses, as you can see from the above. It is simple to use, but it can make your Japanese sound so much better. Try using the following patterns:

Sentence Pattern 58a

Q. 本を　もってきましたか。　　Did you bring the books?

A. ええ、本も　ざっしも　　　Yes, I brought both the books and the magazines.
　　もってきました。

Sentence Pattern 58b

Q. 本を　よみましたか。　　　Have you read the books?

A. 本も　ざっしも　よんでいません。　I have read neither books nor magazines.

Explanation

Because you are still in the state of not having read the books or magazines, the present tense is used in the answer in Sentence Pattern 58b.

D₂

Use the clues given to answer each of the following questions:

1. しゅくだいは　何を　しましたか。 (Both maths and science)
2. だれが　パーティーに　いきましたか。 (Both Kensuke and Ayano)
3. としあきさんは　パーティーに　いきましたか。 (No, neither Toshiaki nor Taroo)
4. 日本では　こうとう学校に　たべものを　もっていきますか。(Yes, both food and drink)
5. 四日は　やすみですか。 (Yes, both the 4th and the 5th)
6. フランス語を　ならいますか。 (No, neither French nor German)

E₁

書きましょう・カタカナ

コ ko	ユ yu	タ ta	ノ no	キ ki	ニ ni	カ ka
コ	ユ	タ	ノ	キ	ニ	カ
Play "connect the dots"	U-boat	Tarpaulin used to keep the firewood dry	The nozzle on the hose	Kindling	Ichi, ni	A cup of tea
フ コ	フ ユ	′ ク タ ノ	ノ	ー ニ キ	ー ニ	フ カ

フ fu	ケ ke	チ chi	エ e	ロ ro	ミ mi
					HITOTSU FUTATSU MITTSU
The *food* Rugby Rat is trying to sniff	*Ken* is a boy's name	*Cheer* leader	The *extra* periscope on the U-boat	"*Rock* around the clock"	*Mittsu*
フ	ノ ト ケ	ノ ニ チ	一 イ エ	l ロ ロ	` ミ ミ

E₂ Try working out how to write the following words in katakana. When you have finished, check the glossary at the back of the book to see how close you were.

1. Computer
2. Cards
3. Sydney
4. Dance
5. Rugby
6. Chicken
7. Ski
8. Leigh
9. Cake
10. Piano
11. Taxi
12. Escalator
13. Tennis
14. Kangaroo
15. Colour television

E₃ What items of food and drink are available at this restaurant? Write out the English equivalent of each item and the approximate price you would pay for it in Australia.

★ You will not have learnt every katakana. Work out what they could be by reading the katakana that you do know.

せいようりょうり
西洋料理

コーンスープ	¥300	コーンサラダ	¥500
ハンバーガー	¥350	フライドポテト	¥250
サンドイッチ		グリーンサラダ	¥500
• ハムサンド	¥380	トマトサラダ	¥500
• トマトサンド	¥400	アスパラガスサラダ	¥500
パイナップルジュース	¥300	コーヒー	¥300
オレンジジュース	¥300	カフェオーレ	¥350
		ビール	¥350

Expressing abilities

> *Sentence Pattern 59*
>
> Q. アンドルーさんは　ギター（gi taa）が　できますか。　　Can you play the guitar, Andrew?
>
> A. いいえ、できません。　　No, I can't.
>
> A. はい、できます。　　Yes, I can.

Try using this pattern with the activities illustrated below. Write out the questions as shown in Sentence Pattern 59, but include each of the hobbies/skills illustrated below. Answer "yes" or "no" — whichever is true for you — and leave a blank line after each answer for a later exercise.

> ★ You will be using many new words in this exercise. Where you are presented with so many new words, start by learning off by heart the words that apply more particularly to you or that are easiest to remember.
>
> For example:　スキー
>
> Then gradually try to learn the others.

1. ダンス

2. テニス

3. ゴルフ

4. やきゅう

5. ラグビー

6. ピアノ

7. ギター

8. スケート

9. スキー   10. すいえい   11. りょうり

12. 日本語

13. オートバイのうんてん   14. チェス   15. トランプ   16. うた

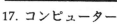

17. コンピューター   18. コンピューター
ゲーム   19. コンピューター
プログラミング   20. くるまの　うんてん

F₂

The following pattern shows you how to be specific in your replies to the question "Can you do … ?"

Sentence Pattern 60

Q. マリアさんは　ピアノが　できますか。   Maria, can you play the piano?

A. はい、すこし　できます。   Yes, I can play a little.

or

A. あまり　できません。   I can't play very well.

or

A. いいえ、ぜんぜん　できません。   No, I can't play it at all.

Go back to F1 and, for each activity illustrated, answer the question 「 ... が できますか」 by using one of the responses in Sentence Pattern 60. Write your answers in the spaces that you left.

Go back to F1 and

F3

Try answering these questions according to the clues:

1. たけしくんは　ギターが　できますか。Yes, a little.
2. うめこさんは　ピアノが　できますか。Yes, she can.
3. せんせいは　オートバイのうんてんが　できますか。Not very well.
4. こうちょうせんせいは　スキーが　できますか。No, she can't.
5. たなかさんの　お母さんは　りょうりが　できますか。Yes, of course.
6. りこちゃんは　すうがくが　できますか。No, not at all.
7. アンドルーさんは　日本語が　できますか。Yes, a little.
8. リーサさんは　すいえいが　できますか。Yes, she can.
9. トムさんは　やきゅうが　できますか。No, not at all.
10. としあきさんは　ラグビーが　できますか。Not very well.

F4

Let's be honest!!

There will be many times at school in Japan where you will need to clarify just how well you understand something or how well you can do something. Look at some further examples of how you could clarify things:

(a) これが　わかりますか。 — Do you understand this?
いいえ、ぜんぜん　わかりません。 — No, I don't understand it at all.

(b) テリーさんは　日本語が　できますか。 — Can Terry speak Japanese?
いいえ、テリーさんは　ぜんぜん　日本語が　できません。 — No, he can't speak it at all.

(c) よく　えいがに　いきますか。 — Do you go to the movies often?
いいえ、あまり　えいがに　いきません。 — No, I seldom go to the movies.
(I don't go to the movies very often.)

(d) さしみが　好きですか。 — Do you like sashimi?
いいえ、あまり　好きじゃないです。 — No, I don't like it very much.

(e) マリアさんは　りょうりが　できますか。 — Maria, can you cook?
わたしは　りょうりが　かなり　できます。 — I can cook fairly well.

(f) コーヒーショップで　ぜんぜん　のみません。 — I never drink at a coffee shop.

F₅ Answer these questions honestly, using any sentence patterns that you think are appropriate:

1. 日本語が　できますか。
2. コンピューターが　できますか。
3. ギターが　できますか。
4. スキーが　できますか。
5. 「ご」が　できますか。
6. かていかが　好きですか。
7. くるまのうんてんが　できますか。
8. かがくが　好きですか。
9. ダンスが　できますか。
10. しょどうが　できますか。

F₆ Put the following sentences into Japanese:

1. I never forget my homework.
2. I'm not very good at calligraphy.
3. I'm not good at computer programming.
4. I'm fairly good at Japanese
5. I'm fairly good at cooking.
6. I'm fairly good at skiing.
7. I can't sing at all.
8. I'm not very good at golf.
9. I'm fairly good at swimming.
10. I'm not very good at chess at all.
11. I'm fairly good at cards.

Singing in a karaoke bar

G₁ 書きましょう・漢字

42. 上　**Above**

The plant is growing *above* the ground and the flower is at the *top* of the stem.

くん うえ、あ（げる）、のぼ(る)、かみ　**おん** じょう、しょう

いみ 上 on top of,　上手 skilful

かきじゅん | ｜ | ト | 上 |

3かく

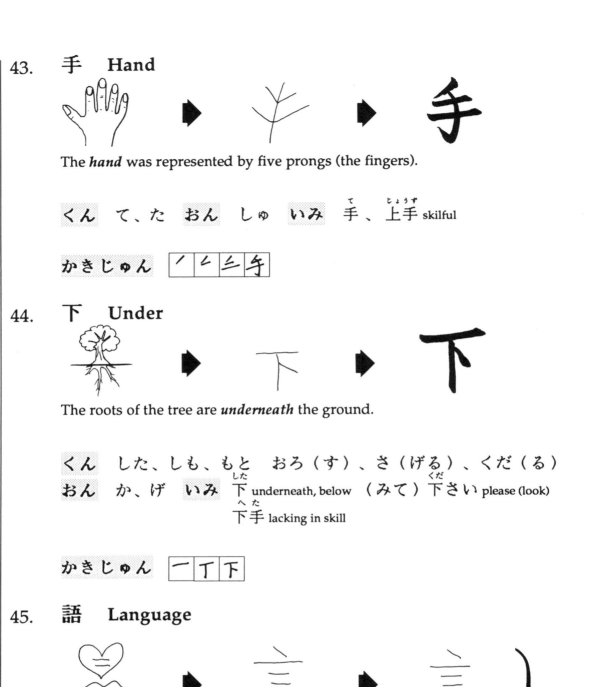

43.　手　Hand

The *hand* was represented by five prongs (the fingers).

| くん | て、た | おん | しゅ | いみ | 手、上手 skilful |

かきじゅん　｜ ノ ｜ ´ ｜ ‐ ｜ 手 ｜

4かく

44.　下　Under

The roots of the tree are *underneath* the ground.

くん	した、しも、もと	おろ（す）、さ（げる）、くだ（る）
おん	か、げ	いみ　下 underneath, below　（みて）下さい please (look)
		下手 lacking in skill

かきじゅん　｜ 一 ｜ 丁 ｜ 下 ｜

3かく

45.　語　Language

When people speak, they use both their heart and their mouth.

A cross is drawn to represent friendship (crossing of ideas), and friendships are developed through talking (with the mouth). Friendships, therefore, rely on *language.*

| くん | かた（る） | おん | ご | いみ | 日本語 Japanese language |
| | | | | | ドイツ語 German language |

46.　中　Middle, inside

Both the top and the bottom part of a top are in the exact *centre* of the toy. In fact, it's often the one piece of wood going right through the top.

くん　なか　おん　ちゅう　いみ　中、中 during

かきじゅん 　｜　口　口　中　4かく

47.　学　Learning

Learning takes place in a building which has tiles on the roof and children inside.

くん　まな（ぶ）おん　がく　いみ　学生 student, 学ぶ to learn, 学校 school

かきじゅん 　｀　＂　ヅ　ヅ　ツ　学　学　学　8かく

48.　校　School

A child is sitting cross-legged at a low table, studying. Learning can take place anywhere — even under a tree.

くん　　おん　こう　いみ　学校 school

かきじゅん 　一　十　オ　オ　木　朾　栌　栌　栌　校　10かく

49.　外　Outside

Once the moon comes up, children don't go *outside*. The radical on the right shows a fortune teller's divining rod. Fortune tellers only used to work at night outside under the moonlight. So together these radicals mean *outside*.

くん　そと、ほか、はず(す)　おん　がい、げ　いみ　外,外人 foreigner
（そと）（がいじん）

かきじゅん　｜ノ｜ク｜タ｜夕｜外｜　　　　　　　5かく

50.　男　Male

This picture represents the subdivisions within a paddy field.

This radical always represents strength. It combines with 田 to illustrate that the *men* use their strength and energy to cultivate the rice fields.

くん　おとこ　おん　だん、なん　いみ　男
（おとこ）

かきじゅん　｜丶｜丨冂｜冂丌｜甲｜田｜甼｜男｜　　　　7かく

51.　生　Life, birth

When a flower is at the peak of its growth, it is ready to start a new cycle of *life*. (The seeds drop and give *birth* to a new plant.)

くん　い（きる）、う（まれる）、き、なま　おん　せい、しょう
いみ　生まれる to be born, 生かつ life, 生と pupil, 学生 student
（う）　　　　　　（せい）　　（せい）　　（がくせい）

かきじゅん ｜ノ｜ﾉｰ｜ﾉｰ｜牛｜生 5かく

52. 今 Now, this

The top radical of three lines is always symbolic of a meeting or gathering — represented by three people. The lower radical looks like a question mark, perhaps for the question "when is the meeting being held?" Together the two radicals represent the idea of "*now*" or "*this*".

くん いま おん こん、きん いみ 今、今日は、今日、今月、今年

かきじゅん ｜ノ｜ハ｜ﾑ｜今 4かく

53. 階 Storey, floor

The first radical is a terraced mountain side, indicating a series of levels. The second part of this kanji is みんな (everybody). "Everybody" is represented by two people and me (the nose). Everybody in society has a particular rank or level. This kanji is used to represent the words "*rank*", "*grade*" or "*floor*" of a building.

くん おん かい いみ 二階 2 floors, 2 storeyed, 階だん steps

かきじゅん ｜ ﾞ｜ ﾜ｜阝｜阝'｜阝ヒ｜阝ヒ'｜阝ﾋﾋ｜阝ﾋﾋ｜阝ﾋﾋ｜階｜階｜階 12かく

G₂ Write the following words in the most appropriate form — using kanji wherever possible:

1. This year	8. Hanako	15. Fireworks	22. Girl
2. Boy	9. Man	16. Woman	23. Student
3. Hello	10. Pupil	17. Foreigner	24. University
4. French language	11. Sunday	18. Summer	25. Monday
5. Winter	12. Skilful	19. Japan	26. Poor, weak
6. Japanese person	13. Japanese language	20. Moon	27. German language
7. Rain	14. School	21. Snow	28. Japanese language school

Did you need to look up any of the kanji in G2? If you did, go back to where they were originally taught and write them out several more times until you can remember them better .

G3 Write these telephone numbers in kanji:

1. 612 4577	4. 351 5285	7. 968 7543	10. 741 9863
2. 436 4294	5. 576 2989	8. 209 5376	11. 490 5728
3. 274 0012	6. 384 2167	9. 842 5432	12. 705 8765

Zero (0) in a telephone number is read as ゼロ（ぜろ） and the "space" between the first three numbers and the next four is indicated by の. So 351 0653 would be read as さんごいちの ゼロろくごさん.

G4 What is the difference between these two tickets to get into the Kobe City Suma Aquarium?

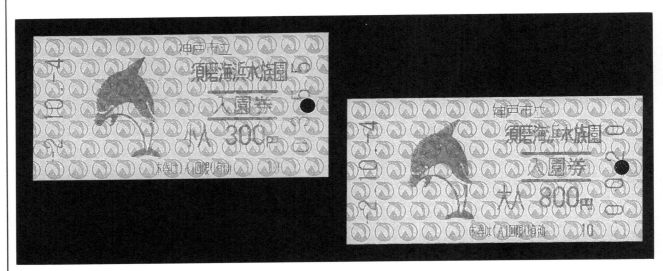

H1

How good *are* you?

As a general rule, Japanese do not comment on people's skills and abilities in a social context if they are being polite. In other words, you don't say to the art teacher at your Japanese school that he is a skilful artist. Instead, you would comment on the quality of the painting.

For example:

きれい　です ね。 Isn't it beautiful!　**or**　すてき　です ね。 Isn't it superb!

However, when talking amongst friends at school, commenting on how well someone can do something is quite permissible. It is also the custom to comment on how poorly you do something yourself. (In fact, Japanese often begin important speeches with an apology for the speech being so bad and ill-prepared!)

Sentence Pattern 61

Q. アンドルーさんは　ギターが　上手<ruby>じょうず</ruby>ですか。　　Are you good at the guitar, Andrew?

A. いいえ、下手<ruby>へた</ruby>です。　　No, I am not. (I'm bad at it.)

In this pattern, は once again marks the topic and が denotes the subject.

H₂

You are now able to describe how good or weak *you* are at certain things.

For example, in answering the question あなたは　日本語が　上手　ですか, you could give one of a variety of possible answers:

えX、すこし　できます。　　　　or　いいえ、下手です。

えX、できます。　　　　　　　　or　えX、もちろん。

Using the above patterns, answer the following questions:

1. あなたは　にんてんどうの　ゲーム^{mu}が　上手ですか。
2. あなたは　うたが　上手ですか。
3. あなたは　えい語<ruby>ご</ruby>が　上手ですか。
4. お母さんは　日本語が　できますか。
5. お父さんは　テニスが　できますか。
6. あなたは　やきゅうが　上手ですか。
7. あなたは　コンピューターが　できますか。
8. ピアノ^{no}が　できますか。

9. しょどうが　上手ですか。　　　10. あなたは　りょうりが　できますか。

In many respects a Japanese school will **look** different from an Australian school. One obvious difference will be the number of floors in a Japanese school compared with most Australian schools.

A typical Japanese school

500 pairs of shoes removed in orderly fashion

Even Year 1 students must serve kyuushoku

A typical name tag worn on a school uniform

Calligraphy class in a junior high school

Everyone helps clean the school

The counter for "floors" is used in a sentence in the same way that other counters (for example, ひとつ、ふたつ) are used.

Sentence Pattern 62a

Q. あなたの　学校は　何階だて　ですか。　　How many floors/storeys is your school?

A. （わたしたちの）　学校は　四階だて　です。　　Our school has four floors.

Sentence Pattern 62b

わたしたちの　学校は　四階だての

たてもの　です。　　Our school is a four-storey building.

J₂

Counting floors

何階 How many floors? (which floor?)

いっかい	1階
にかい	2階
さんがい	3階
よんかい	4階
ごかい	5階
ろっかい	6階
ななかい	7階
はちかい	8階
きゅうかい	9階
じゅっかい	10階
じゅういっかい	11階
じゅうにかい	12階
じゅうさんかい	13階
じゅうよんかい	14階
じゅうごかい	15階
じゅうろっかい	16階
じゅうななかい	17階
じゅうはちかい	18階
じゅうきゅうかい	19階
にじゅっかい	20階

Also　ちか　いっかい　　1st basement

　　　ちか　にかい　　2nd basement

A multi-storeyed building in Shinjuku

J₃ Using the clues given, answer each of the following questions as shown in J1.

1. あなたの　うちは　何階だてですか。(2)
2. あなたの　学校は　何階だてですか。(1)
3. ぎんこうは　何階だてですか。(6)
4. デパートは　何階だてですか。(10)
5. まちの　としょかんは　何階だてですか。(4)
6. はくぶつかんは　何階だてですか。(11)
7. マリアさんの　オーストラリアの　学校は　何階だてですか。(1)
8. たけしさんの　学校は　何階だてですか。(5)
9. にほんばしの　まるぜんは　何階だてですか。(8)
10. この　学校の　ちずを　みてください。
    • 学校は　何階だてですか。
    • 生とホールは　何階だてですか。

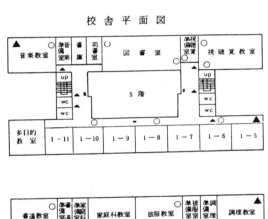

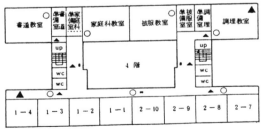

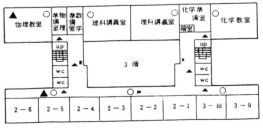

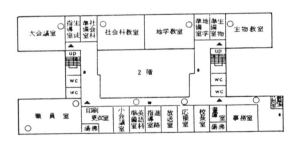

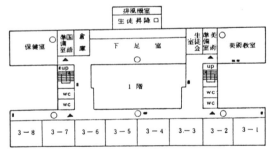

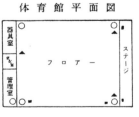

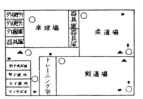

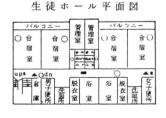

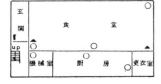

Answer these questions as they relate to you:

1. あなたの　学校は　何階だてですか。
2. あなたの　うちは　何階だてですか。
3. まちの　としょかんは　何階だてですか。
4. ちかくの　デパートは　何階だてですか。
5. おばあさんと　おじいさんの　うちは　何階だてですか。

森の劇場
テアトル・ド・ボア

銀座のお地蔵さん
銀座出世地蔵尊

グリーンセンター
園芸用品

店内ご案内
STORE GUIDE

R		
8	宝石のフロア 催物会場	宝石・貴金属 時計・カメラ（フィルム・DPE）
7	音とインテリア 食器フロア	和、洋家具・直輸入家具・カーテン・敷物 和、洋陶器・ガラス器・花瓶・金属食器 テーブルウェア・漆器・七宝・テレビ・ラジオ ステレオ・レコード・ピアノ・暖、冷房器具・書籍
6	お子さまと ビジネス用品フロア	女児服・男児服・幼児服・新生児用品 マタニティーウェア・おもちゃ・人形・文房具 女子学生服・ユニホーム・ビジネス用品（万年筆 電卓・タイプライター）・ゲーム用品（囲碁・将棋・麻雀）
5	きもののフロア	特選きもの・趣味のきもの・帯・和装コート 男のきもの・和装小もの・風呂敷・和装バッグ 草履・ショール・和装肌着・ふとん・毛布 シーツ・タオル
4	メンズフロア	スーツ・コート・ジャケット・スラックス・オーダー メード・イージーオーダー・紳士服地・男子学生服 オーダーワイシャツ・ワイシャツ・セーター・ニット シャツ・くつ下・ナイトウェア・肌着・帽子・紳士靴
3	レディスフロア	プレタポルテ（ドレス・コート）・ドレス・スーツ コート・セーター・ブラウス・スカート・パンタロン ジャケット・毛皮・レザーウェア・婦人服地 ストッキング
2	ティーンズと ヤングレディのフロア	ヤングレディスウェア（ドレス・スーツ・コート セーター・ブラウス・スカート・ジーンズ）・スカーフ ハンカチーフ・ナイティ・肌着・帽子 婦人靴
1	輸入特選と ファッショングッズ フロア	ティファニー・ロエベ・バレンシアガ・ファブリス ダンヒル・バルトロメイ・ハンドバッグ・ネクタイ 傘・紳士、婦人アクセサリー・化粧品・石けん カバン・スーツケース・ライター・喫煙具・タバコ
B1	食料品のフロア	輸入、国産洋酒・日本酒・和、洋菓子 フルーツ・佃煮・珍味・銘茶・海苔・缶詰 瓶詰・調味品
B2	豊かな暮らしを提案する ギンザ・デリカテッセンと 生活用品フロア	精肉・鮮魚・冷凍食品・野菜・お惣菜・漬物・寿司・弁当 冷蔵庫・電子レンジ・ミキサー・洗濯機 トースター・調理器具・システムキッチン 薬品・健康食品・化粧用具・理容器具 バス、トイレ用品・エプロン・肌着・ストッキング
B3	スポーツ ファッションプラザ 食堂街	ゴルフ、テニス用品・野球用品・スキー用品 スイムスーツ・トレーニングウェア・ジーンズ コットンパンツ・スポーツウェア・カップ トロフィー・釣用品

エスカレーター

Answer the following questions as they relate to this typical store guide:

1. 何階に　ドレスが　ありますか。
2. 何階で　テレビを　かいますか。
3. 何階で　トースターを　かいましたか。
4. きものうりばは　何階ですか。
5. レディスフロアは　何階ですか。

K You would probably have observed that the number of students per class is much greater in Japan. In fact, there are between 43 and 47 students per class! The total population per school is about the same as ours; that is, large senior high schools will have about 1500 students.

With these facts in mind, answer the following questions as they relate to you:

1. おなたの　日本語の　クラスに　生とが　何人　いますか。
2. あなたの　学校に　生とが　何人　いますか。
3. あなたの　すうがくの　クラスに　生とが　何人　いますか。
4. あなたの　えい語の　クラスに　生とが　三十人　いますか。
5. あなたの　学校に　せん生が　何人　いますか。

L ## Giving speeches

A stay (no matter how long or short) in a Japanese school will inevitably mean that you have to give speeches. There are numerous expressions and sentences that you might need to use. To begin with, master a few like the ones below; then, as time goes by, with your teacher's help you could add to them.

In a speech of *introduction*:

1. わたしは (name of school) に　これたことを　とても　うれしく　おもいます。
   I am very happy to be able to come to (name of school) school.

2. 日本の　かぞく生かつや　学校について　しりたいと　おもいます。
   I would like to learn about school and family life.

3. オーストラリアの　いろいろな　ことを　おしえたいです。
   I would like to teach you many things about Australia.

4. がんばります。
   I will try very hard.

5. おしえてください (ませんか)。

   (Won't you) please teach (help) me?

In a *thank-you* or *farewell* speech:

6. わたしの　日本語を　たすけてくださって　どうも　ありがとう　ございました。
   Thank you very much for helping me with my Japanese.

7. たいへん　すばらしい　じかんを　すごすことができ、どうも　ありがとう
   ございました。
   I had a really wonderful time. Thank you very much.

8. みなさんの　ごしんせつを　けっして　わすれません。
   I will never forget your (everyone's) kindness.

Sentence Pattern 63a

たくさんの　生_{せい}とは　日本語_{にほんご}を
べんきょうしています。　　　　Many students are studying Japanese.

Sentence Pattern 63b

生_{せい}とは　ここに　たくさん　います。　　There are many students here.

Sentence Pattern 63c

いろいろな　ことを　ならいました。　　I learnt many (various) things.

Explanation

When たくさん (many) is used in its more common function as a counter, it is positioned after the thing it "counts". When it is used like an adjectival noun it is linked to the noun it is describing with の. Although いろいろ means "various", it can also mean "many". Either の or な can be used to link it with the noun it is describing.

What does each of the following sentences mean?

1. いろいろな　ことを　学_{まな}びました。どうも　ありがとう　ごさいました。
2. あなたに　オーストラリアの　いろいろな　ことを　おしえたいです。
3. おもしろい　たてものを　たくさん　みました。
4. 人に　たくさん　あいたいです。
5. わたしの　クラスに　生とは　たくさん　います。
6. ぎんざに　たかいみせが　たくさん　あります。
7. わたしの　学校には　外人の　生とが　たくさん　います。
8. オーストラリア人は　たくさん　います。
9. アメリカ人も　たくさん　います。
10. 日よう日に　たくさんの　人は　ぎんざへ　かいものに　いきます。

It was explained briefly in Unit 14, Part C, that there are "true adjectives" (ending in ai, ii, ui, oi) and there are other describing words which we call "adjectival nouns". When we describe a word with a true adjective, the link is simple!

おもしろい　たてもの　　　　　　… an interesting building

ふるい　うち　　　　　　　　　… an old house

The final い is like "self-adhesive" glue that joins the two words. But adjectival nouns require "special glue". Remember that when we linked colour we used の, as in ちゃいろの くつ (brown shoes). When using most other adjectival nouns, the "glue" to make sure that they can be attached to the noun is な (see Unit 14, Part C3). The next three exercises provide an opportunity to revise the use of the adjectival nouns.

Remember:

(a) Connecting *true adjectives* with nouns (revision):

たかい みせは たくさん あります。　　There are many expensive shops.

(b) Connecting *adjectival nouns* with nouns:

きれいな みせは たくさん あります。　　There are many beautiful shops.

N₂ Put these two phrases into sentences and add an extra sentence about the person or place in the photograph.

1. しんせつな せんせい
   (A kind teacher)
   This teacher is saying 「がんばって。」
   to a visiting student.

2. ゆうめいな ところ
   (A famous place)
   Shops in Asakusa with the
   Kaminarimon in background

N₃ Try putting these sentences into Japanese:

1. The complicated story is interesting.
2. I live in a quiet place.
3. My lazy younger brother never does his homework.
4. We went to a noisy party last week.
5. Many busy people work here.
6. I want to drink cold water.*

7. The Ginza is a famous place in Tokyo.
8. My teacher is a kind person.
9. The polite student studies English every day at cram school.
10. It was a horrible movie.
11. The old museum is a three-storeyed building.
12. He is a lazy person.

* The word for "cold" when referring to objects is つめたい.

N4 Read the two dialogues which follow. What do they mean?

Make up three dialogues of your own in which you use an adjectival noun.

With a partner, act out one of your dialogues.

A

マリア:	ただいま！
ホスト:	おかえりなさい。
	学校は　どうでしたか。
マリア:	日本語の　せん生は　しんせつな　女の人　です。よく　せつめいします。だから、わたしは　よく　わかります。

B

お父さん:	たけしちゃん、今日　アンドルーさんの　お母さんに　手がみを　かきましたか。
たけし:	いいえ、かきませんでした。テレビを　みて　いました。
お父さん:	ああ、たけしちゃんは　なまけもの　ですね。
たけし:	お父さん、すぐ　かきます。

O 学校のきそく　School rules

Many of the rules in Japanese schools are probably much the same as the rules at your school. In talking about these with your friends, the following pattern will be useful.

Sentence Pattern 64

はいっては　いけません。　You must not enter.

Explanation

By adding は　いけません to the て form of a verb, you are indicating prohibition — something that should not be done.

Do these rules apply in your school or in any areas of your school?

1.
じゅぎょうのあいだ たべては いけません。

2.
はなしては、いけません。

3.
たばこをすっては いけません。

4.
せいとは、このスリッパを はいては いけません。おきゃくさまのスリッパです。
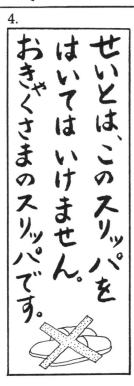

5.
さけを のんでは いけません。

6.
はしっては いけない。

Lockers for guests' slippers —in the school foyer

Note: ない is less polite than ません.
おきゃくさま = Guest

P 調べましょう

Using a Japanese–English dictionary, see if you can work out the gist of these signs.

1.
よく考(かんが)える子(こ)。
げんきで よく、がんばる子。
おおきな心(こころ)のやさしい子。

2.

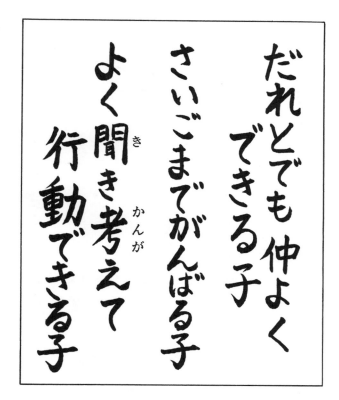

だれとでも　仲よく
できる子
さいごまでがんばる子
よく聞き考えて
行動できる子

These meanings may help you:

- だれとでも仲よく = Get on well with others
- さいご = End
- 行動 = Act (in a way)

3. And what is this sign in a Year 3 class trying to tell the children?

はい ‥‥‥‥‥ です。

‥‥‥‥‥ と思います。

大きな声ではっきりと

Q1

For those who like a challenge ...

Your penpal, Aiko, has written the following reply to your letter. Typically, you will not understand *everything* she or any penpal writes to you, but see how much you can understand without any help. When you have tried to work out the meanings of as many words as possible, your teacher will give you a vocabulary list to help you. But do try to work out the unfamiliar words first!

Your task: Using Aiko's letter as a basis, write a summary of school life in a Japanese junior high school.

マリアナさんへ

お手がみ、ありがとうございました。お元気ですか。学校の
生かつについて　かきます。

一がっきは　4月　から　7月、

二がっきは　9月　から　12月、

三がっきは　1月　から　3月　です。

10月には　たいいくさいが　あります。ぜんいんが　何かの
スポーツに　さんか　しなければなりません。たいいくさいの
日には、みんなで　たいそう、きょうそう、フォークダンス
などを　して　たのしみます。

11月には　ぶんかさいが　あります。すいそうがくぶの
えんそうや　えんげきぶの　げきを　みて　たのしみます。

かもくは　9つ　あります。こく語、しゃかい、すうがく、
りか、えい語、びじゅつ、おんがく、たいいく、ぎじゅつ
（男）、かていか（女）です。あさは　生とと　おなじ
じかんに　学校へきて、よるは　おそく　かえります。ひるご
はんは　みんな　おべんとうを　もってきて　きょうしつで
たべます。きゅうしょくの学校も　あります。パンを　かって
たべる人も　います。まいしゅう　月よう日に　ちょうれいが
あって、ぜんこうせいとが　グランドに　あつまります。
こうちょうせんせいの　おはなしが　あります。

じゅくは　ほとんどの　せいとが　いっています。学校には
ぶんかと　スポーツの　クラブが　たくさん　あります。

わたしたちかぞくは　みんな　元気です。お父さんは　今
べんきょうを　しています。とても　むずかしい　べんきょう
だ　そうです。わたしは　6月　12日から　14日まで　しゅう学
りょ行に行きます。きゅうしゅうです。とても　たのしみ
です。マリアナさんも　がんばってください。
みなさんに　よろしく。　　さようなら
　　　　　　あいこ

Q₂ Write a letter back to Aiko, telling her about life and routine at your school.

- Tell her about your school festivals, sports carnivals and so on.
- Explain when school starts and finishes, and when you have holidays.
- Describe your school to her—how many floors it has, whether it is new (あたらしい) or not, and so on.
- Describe some of your teachers.
- Tell her about some of your subjects and which ones you are good or bad at.

R Listen carefully as the radio announcer talks to Masayoshi about school rules at his junior high school.

(a) Make a list of the rules that he gives.

(b) What is 「オアシス」?

S しりとりあそびを　しましょう

Can you work out the rules to this popular Japanese game?

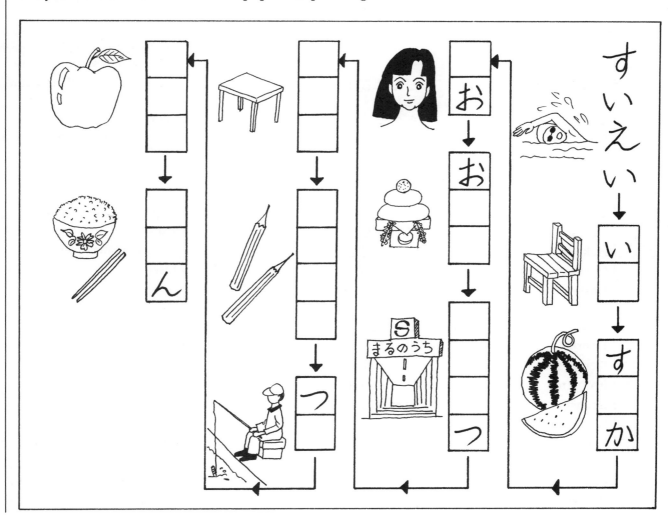

New words and expressions

... (no) Aida (ni)	... （の）あいだ（に）	During
Aisatsu	あいさつ	Greetings
Aku (aiteimasu)	あく（あいています）	To be opened, open
Amari ... masen	あまり ... ません	Not very (much)
Arumono	あるもの	Some
Bunkasai	ぶんかさい	Culture festival
Chesu	チェス	Chess
Chikaikkai	ちか一階	First basement
Chikaku (no)	ちかく（の）	Nearby, local
Chikanikai	ちか二階	Second basement
Choorei	ちょうれい	Morning assembly
... date	... だて	... building
Dekiru (dekimasu)	できる（できます）	To be able to do, can do
Depaato	デパート	Department store
Doresu	ドレス	Dress
Fukuzatsu (na)	ふくざつ（な）	Complicated
Furui	ふるい	Old (not used for people)
Gaijin, gaikokujin	外人、外国人	Foreigner
Gakusei	学生	Student (usually reserved for university students and perhaps senior high school students)
Gambaru (gambarimasu)	がんばる（がんばります）	To persevere (I will persevere, stick at it)
Gitaa	ギター	Guitar
Go	ご	Japanese board game using black and white stones
Gorufu	ゴルフ	Golf
Goshinsetsu (na)	ごしんせつ（な）	Your kindness
Gurando	グランド	Playground, school oval
Hakkiri	はっきり	Clearly
Haku (hakimasu, haite)	はく（はきます、はいて）	To wear on one's feet
Hakubutsukan	はくぶつかん	Museum
Hashiru (hashirimasu, hashitte)	はしる（はしります、はしって）	To run
Heta (na)	下手（な）	Lacking in skill
Hooru	ホール	Hall
Ikemasen	いけません	Must not do
Iroiro (na)	いろいろ（な）	Various, all kinds of, many
Isogashii	いそがしい	Busy
Jikan	じかん	Time
Joozu (na)	上手（な）	Skilful
Kafeoore	カフェオーレ	Cafe au lait (milk coffee)
Kai	階	Counter for floors or storeys
Kanari	かなり	Fairly, okay

Kesshite … masen	けっして … ません	Never
Kisoku	きそく	Rules
Koe	こえ	Voice
Kokoro	こころ	Heart
Kompyuutaa	コンピューター	Computer
Kompyuutaa geemu	コンピューター　ゲーム	Computer game
Kompyuutaa puroguramingu	コンピューター　プログラミング	Computer programming
Koretakoto	これたこと	The fact that I could come
Koto	こと	Things
Kyampu	キャンプ	Camp
Manabu (manabimasu)	まなぶ（まなびます）	To learn
Maruzen	まるぜん	The name of a large bookstore which stocks many books written in English
Mottekuru (mottekimasu)	もってくる（もってきます）	To bring
Namakemono (no)	なまけもの（の）	Lazy (person)
Nankai (nangai)	何階	How many floors? Which floor?
Nengajoo	ねんがじょう	New Year's greeting card
Nintendoo	にんてんどう	Popular Japanese computer game
Nomu (nomimasu, nonde)	のむ（のみます、のんで）	To drink
Nooto	ノート	Notebook
Okuru (okurimasu, okutte)	おくる（おくります、おくって）	To send
Ootobai	オートバイ	Motor bike
Ootobai no unten	オートバイの　うんてん	Driving a motor bike
Oshieru (oshiemasu)	おしえる（おしえます）	To teach
Piano	ピアノ	Piano
Ragubii	ラグビー	Rugby
Rakugaki	らくがき	Scribble
Redisufuroa	レディスフロア	Ladies' floor
Sankasuru	さんかする	To participate (in)
Seikatsu	生かつ	Life
Setsumeisuru (setsumeishimasu)	せつめいする（せつめいします）	To explain
Shookaisuru	しょうかいする	To introduce oneself
Subarashii	すばらしい	Wonderful
Sugosukoto ga dekiru	すごすことが　できる	To be able to spend one's time
Suiei	すいえい	Swimming
Sukeeto	スケート	Skate (ice skate)
Sukii	スキー	Ski
Sukunai	すくない	Not many, not much, few, little
Suteki (na)	すてき（な）	Superb, excellent, great, wonderful
Taisetsu (na)	大せつ（な）	Important
Tanoshimi desu	たのしみです	(I am) looking forward to … [(Because) it will be enjoyable.]
Tanoshimu	たのしむ	To take pleasure in, enjoy
Tasuketekudasai	たすけて　ください	Please help me (I'm in danger!)

Tatemono	たてもの	Building
Teinei (na)	ていねい（な）	Polite
Tenisu	テニス	Tennis
… te wa ikemasen	… ては　いけません	You must not …
Tokoro	ところ	Place
Toosutaa	トースター	Toaster
Torampu	トランプ	Playing cards
… (ni) Tsuite	…（に）　ついて	Concerning
Tsukau (tsukaimasu, tsukatte)	つかう（つかいます、つかって）	To use
Tsumetai	つめたい	Cold (used for things that are cold to touch)
Undoo	うんどう	Training, exercise, athletics
Unten (suru)	うんてん（する）	(To) drive, operate
Ureshii	うれしい	Happy
Uriba	うりば	Counter (with cash register)
Uru (utte, urimasu)	うる（うって、うります）	To sell
Urusai	うるさい	Noisy, annoying
Uta	うた	Song
Wasureru (wasurete, wasuremasu)	わすれる　（わすれて、わすれます）	To forget
Yasashii	やさしい	Gentle, kind-hearted
Yasumi	やすみ	Holiday
Yonkaidate no tatemono	四階だての　たてもの	Four-storeyed building
Zenzen … masen	ぜんぜん … ません	Not at all
Zero	ゼロ	Zero

U₁

Kanji studied to the end of Unit 16:

Unit 13:	一	二	三	四	五	六	七	八	九	十	人	何
	1	2	3	4	5	6	7	8	9	10	11	12
Unit 14:	目	口	日	本	母	父	白	赤	黒	色	大	小
	13	14	15	16	17	18	19	20	21	22	23	24
Unit 15:	月	花	木	子	女	好	言	夏	火	秋	春	冬
	25	26	27	28	29	30	31	32	33	34	35	36
	雨	雲	天	気	年							
	37	38	39	40	41							
Unit 16:	上	手	下	語	中	学	校	外	男	生	今	階
	42	43	44	45	46	47	48	49	50	51	52	53

Unit 14: ア ン ト ル ナ ー ヒ ク オ レ シ リ
           1   2   3   4   5   6   7   8   9   10   11   12

Unit 15: ハ イ マ テ ス ラ ッ
           13   14   15   16   17   18   19

Unit 16: コ ユ タ ノ キ ニ カ フ ケ チ エ ロ ミ
           20   21   22   23   24   25   26   27   28   29   30   31   32

A floor guide in Seiden Department Store

A floor guide in an electrical shop in Akihabara

Unit 17

Favourite things
いちばん　す　　　　もの
一番好きな物

A

一

ちゃのゆの　しずけさが　大好きです。

二

しょどうを　するのは　むずかしいと
思います。

ええ、わたしも　そうだと
思います。

三

この　おびは　わたしの　一ばん　好きな
おびだと　思います。

わたしも　それが　好きです。

四

一ばん　好きな　しゅみは
テレビを　見ることです。

B1 Being able to express your likes, dislikes and opinions can be a great way to break the ice with your host family. Let's go over what you should already be able to say.

Revision:

Q.	かぶきが　好きですか。	Do you like kabuki?
A.	ええ、大好きです。	Yes, I *love* it.
or	いいえ、好きじゃないです。	No, I don't like it.
or	いいえ、きらいです。	No, I dislike it. (This is perhaps too strong in polite speech.)
or	まあまあ　です。	It's not bad.

or why not try this one:

かぶきを　見たことが
ありませんから　わかりません。

I don't know because I've never seen kabuki.

> ★習い方
> * When talking about your likes and dislikes, always use the joshi が with the thing that you like or don't like.
> * The words 好き (like) and 大好き (like very much) may be replaced by their opposites きらい (dislike) and 大きらい (really dislike).

B2 Before answering the following questions, find out as much as you can about each of the high-lighted leisure pursuits or forms of theatre or entertainment. Then answer each of the questions to the best of your understanding of the particular thing referred to.

1. ぶんらくが　好きですか。
2. のうが　好きですか。
3. お父さんは　カラオケが　好きですか。
4. かぶきが　好きですか。
5. きょうげんが　好きですか。
6. しょどうが　好きですか。
7. もくはんがが　好きですか。
8. ぼんさいが　好きですか。
9. おりがみが　好きですか。
10. やきものが　好きですか。

A kabuki actor (print by Yuriko Nakayama)

C1 Japanese usually do not give opinions in black-and-white terms; they generally include an element of doubt or respect for another's opinion by adding "... I think". Look at Sentence Pattern 65 to see how this is done.

Sentence Pattern 65

Q. かぶきを　どう　思いますか。   What do you think of kabuki?

A. かぶきは　つまらないと　思います。   I think that kabuki is boring.

A. かぶきは　ふくざつだと　思います。   I think that kabuki is complicated.

True adjective   + と　思います。

Adjectival noun
Noun   } + だ + と　思います。

C2 Answer these questions according to the clues given and as shown in the example.

Example:

てんぷらを　どう　思いますか。　　(Delicious)

てんぷらは　おいしいと　思います。

1. まんじゅうを　どう　思いますか。(Sweet)
2. のうを　どう　思いますか。　(Boring)
3. ぶんらくを　どう　思いますか。　(Interesting)
4. 日本語を　どう　思いますか。　　(Difficult)
5. かがくを　どう　思いますか。　　(Difficult)
6. ごを　どう　思いますか。　　(Complicated)
7. カラオケを　とう　思いますか。　(Interesting)
8. パチンコを　どう　思いますか。　(Enjoyable)
9. コンピューターを　どう　思いますか。　(Complicated)
10. 日本の　じゅぎょうを　どう　思いますか。　(Boring)

Manjuu store

C3 Put these sentences into Japanese:

1. I think that Japan is beautiful.
2. I think that Tokyo is very noisy.
3. I think that it is a camellia.
4. I think that today is very hot.
5. I think that my school is fantastic.

A busy street in the Ginza, Tokyo

6. I think that Japanese language is interesting.

7. I think that school excursions are fun.

8. I think he is a senior high school student.

9. I think that hydrangeas are blue.

10. I think that dandelions are yellow.

Hydrangea

D 書きましょう・漢字

54. 思 Think

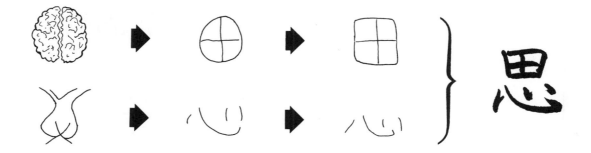

Thinking involves using the brain and the heart.

くん　おも(う)　おん　し　いみ　思う

かきじゅん　｜ 冂 冊 用 田 甲 思 思 思　　　9かく

55. 見 See

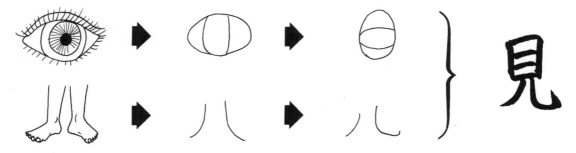

"Looking around" and *seeing* everything involves both the eyes and the legs.

くん　み(る)　おん　けん　いみ　見る

かきじゅん　｜ 冂 冂 目 目 貝 見　　　7かく

56. 聞 Listen

"To *listen*" is represented by shooji screens and an eavesdropper's ear pressed against them. The person is *listening* to conversation on the other side of the screen doors.

くん　き（く）　おん　ぶん、もん　いみ　聞く、しん聞 newspaper

かきじゅん　｜ ｢ ｢ ｢ ｢ 門 門 門 門 門 門 聞 聞 聞　　14かく

57. 行 Go

The kanji for "go" represents a crossroad where people can *go* in any of four directions. This kanji also illustrates the Confucian belief that you should always take time to stop and check life's progress before going on.

くん　い（く）、おこな（う）　おん　こう、ぎょう、あん
いみ　りょ行 travel, 行く

かきじゅん　ノ ク イ 彳 仁 行　　6かく

58. 話 Speak

When we *speak* we use the heart and mouth and, as shown in the second radical, the tongue.

くん　はな（す）、はなし　あん　わ　いみ　話 talk, 電話 telephone

かきじゅん　丶 一 ニ 三 言 言 言 言 訴 許 許 話 話　　13かく

59. 電 **Electricity**

Streaks of lightning and rain form part of an *electrical* storm. (Originally the character simply meant "lightning", but as it was discovered that lightning is a form of electricity the same character came to be used for both words.)

くん　　　　おん　でん　いみ　電話 telephone, 電車 electric train

かきじゅん 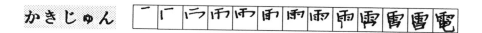　　　13かく

60. 買 **Buy**

The first business in Japan is said to have been a fortune-telling business, with tortoise shell used as the currency in which one paid to have one's fortune told. Nets were used to catch many tortoises. The word *buy*, then, is represented by the net (the top part of the kanji) and the tortoise shell.

くん　か（う）　おん　ばい　いみ　買う、買いもの shopping

かきじゅん 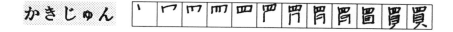　　　12かく

61. 売 **Sell**

When the kanji for "buy" is written underneath a sketch of some plants shooting up out of or leaving the ground, this final character means to *sell*. In other words, *selling* involves something leaving (your hands) to go to someone who buys it. This kanji has been simplified in recent times from 賣 so that it is now written as 売.

くん　う（る）　おん　ばい　いみ　売る

かきじゅん 一 十 士 去 声 声 売　　　7かく

62. 読　Read

The character for "read" is a combination of the kanji for "sell" (売) and "say" (言). It represents the idea that reading involves saying and it is through *reading* advertisements that things get sold.

くん　よ(む)　おん　どく、とく、とう　いみ　読む

かきじゅん　`　`　亠　亠　宣　言　言　計　計　試　試　誌　読　読　　14かく

63. 入　Enter

The river is shown *entering* the sea.

くん　い(る)、い(れる)、はい(る)　おん　にゅう　いみ　入口 entrance、入る to enter,
入学 enter school、入学しけん school entrance exam

かきじゅん　ノ　入　　2かく

64. 食　Eat

Meals are taken as family units or groups. This is shown abstractly by the top three lines. (A group consists of at least three people.) As rice was eaten at every meal this character for *eat* also shows rice being cooked over a fire. It is also possible that the first part 𠆢 comes from the idea of eating under a roof.

くん　く(う)、た(べる)　おん　しょく、じき　いみ　食べる

かきじゅん　ノ　人　𠆢　今　今　今　食　食　食　　9かく

E₁ | I like doing ...

Until now you've only been able to tell someone what you like, or what you think of something. Now let's try explaining what we like *doing* or what we think about *doing* certain things.

The basic patterns for both structures are the same:

noun or **noun phrase** $\begin{cases} が　好きです。\\ は　おもしろいと　思います。\end{cases}$

For example:

ふるい　えいがが　好きです。	I like old movies.
ふるい　えいがを　見ることが　好きです。	I like watching old movies.
ふるい　えいがは　おもしろいと　思います。	I think old movies are interesting.
ふるい　えいがを　見るのは　おもしろいと　思います。	I think watching old movies is interesting.

If talking about something that is *not* a noun, *make* it into a "noun".
For example, you know how to say:

> I like old movies ふるい　えいが が　好きです。　　　("Movies" is a noun.)

but when saying "I like *watching old movies* " "watching old movies" has to be a "noun" so that the same pattern can be used.

- We do this by adding こと or の to the "dictionary" form of the verb (in this case, 見る).

- The dictionary form is simply the way the verb is written in a dictionary (and it always ends in an う sound).

- How do you find the dictionary form?

  Look up the English word in a dictionary that gives the reading in hiragana — so that you know how to say it.

  For instance, you want to know the dictionary form of "see", so you look up "see" in your dictionary and you find the following entry:

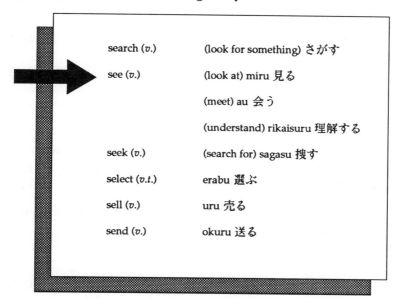

search (*v.*)	(look for something) さがす
see (*v.*)	(look at) miru 見る
	(meet) au 会う
	(understand) rikaisuru 理解する
seek (*v.*)	(search for) sagasu 捜す
select (*v.t.*)	erabu 選ぶ
sell (*v.*)	uru 売る
send (*v.*)	okuru 送る

Alternatively, you know that みます or みる means "see", so go to the appropriate entry in a Japanese–English dictionary:

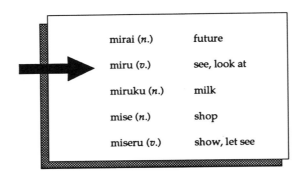

mirai (*n.*)	future
miru (*v.*)	see, look at
miruku (*n.*)	milk
mise (*n.*)	shop
miseru (*v.*)	show, let see

Or consult the verb-form summary on pages 324–26 of this book and look up "see".

Once you've followed these steps often enough, you won't have to go anywhere to retrieve the verb form but your own brain!

Sentence Pattern 66

(a) Q. 何を　するのが　好きですか。   What do you like doing?

  A.

- テレビを　見るのが　好きです。   I like watching television.
- ともだちと　話すのが　好きです。   I like talking with friends.
- えいがへ　行くことは　好きじゃないです。   I don't like going to the movies

(b) Q. …を　どう　思いますか。   What do you think of …?

  A.

- かんじを　ならうのは　むずかしいと
  思います。   I think learning kanji is difficult.
- はらじゅくへ　行くことは　たのしいと
  思います。   I think going to Harajuku is fun.

Explanation

こと and の in these phrases are called "noun nominalisers". That is, they make verbs into "nouns" or noun phrases. They are generally interchangeable, except in some set phrases that you will learn much later on. You may think of them as meaning something like "…ing".

When saying that you ***don't*** like doing something, for example, "I don't like going to the movies", particle は is used instead of が.

E₂   Using one of the techniques described above, work out the dictionary forms of the following verbs.

Write the English meaning next to each dictionary form. Can you see any patterns or rules that you could use in working out dictionary forms? The separate boxes form a clue.

1
a. みます
b. おきます (to get up)
c. おしえます
d. あけます
e. でます
f. みせます
g. ねます
h. たべます

2
a. かいます
b. ならいます
c. あらいます
d. あいます

4
a. あそびます
b. よみます
c. やすみます
d. すみます
e. のみます

3
a. べんきょうします
b. します
c. れんしゅうします
d. そうじします
e. スケートします
f. せんたくします

5
a. ききます
b. つきます
c. いきます
d. かきます

6
a. はいります
b. かえります
c. はじまります
d. はしります
e. まちます

7
およぎます

9
はなします

8
きます (come)

★ Don't panic if you can't remember all these forms. However, the more you practise, the quicker they will come to you. When learning these words, always say them aloud to give your brain that extra chance of remembering.

E₃

You really *do* have an inquisitive friend. Try answering these questions.

For example:

テレビを　見るのが　好きですか。
はい、テレビを　見るのが　好きです。
or いいえ、テレビを　見るのは　好きじゃないです。
or いいえ、テレビを　見るのは　あまり　好きじゃないです。

1. 日本りょうりを　食べることが　好きですか。
2. レコードを　聞くことが　好きですか。
3. コンピューターを　つかうことが　好きですか。
4. 日本語を　ならうことが　好きですか。

5. りょ行するのが　好きですか。

6. はしを　つかうことが　好きですか。

7. ふとんで　ねるのが　好きですか。

8. 学校へ　行くのが　好きですか。

9. うまに　のるのが　好きですか。

10. まんがを　読むのが　好きですか。

Reading まんが

E4 Use the clues given to answer these questions in full sentences. Make sure that you check the meaning of anything you don't understand.

1. ピアノを　ひくのが　好きですか。　　　　　　　　　(Yes)

2. しゅくだいを　することが　好きですか。　　　　　　(Not very much)

3. うまに　のることを　どう　思ますか。　　　　　　　(It's fun)

4. 日本語を　ならうのを　どう　思いますか。　　　　　(It's interesting)

5. ぎんざへ　買いものに　行くのを　どう　思いますか。(It's expensive)

6. りょ行するのを　どう　思いますか。　　　　　　　　(It's fun)

7. じゅくへ　行くのが　好きですか。　　　　　　　　　(No, not at all)

8. すう学が　好きですか。　　　　　　　　　　　　　　(Yes, I do)

9. とうきょうを　どう　思いますか。　　　　　　　　　(It's noisy)

10. すしが　好きですか。　　　　　　　　　　　　　　　(It's okay)

E5 Put these sentences into Japanese:

1. I like going to school.

2. I love studying Japanese.

3. I love going to the movies.

4. Going to Harajuku on Sunday is fun.

5. Working in a hospital is satisfying.

6. I don't like riding horses.

7. I don't like going by train very much.

8. Travelling by plane is terrific.

9. Reading magazines is enjoyable.

10. I think using a computer is difficult.

A happy student

F Fill in the spaces with appropriate questions, answers, words or phrases. Can you work out the meaning of the last sentence?

おばあさん： わたしたちは　マリアさんの　とうちゃくを

　　　　　　 たのしみに .... 。

あとで...

けんすけ： マリアさん　うまに　のる ....。

マリア： はい、..。

　　　　 でも　よく　うまに　のりません。

おじいさん： マリアさん　オーストラリア人は　つりに　行くことが　好き

　　　　　　 ですね。

マリア： はい、..。

　　　　 おじいさん ....　つりに　行く ....。

おじいさん： ....　大好きです。

あやの： なし ....。

マリア： はい、...。

おかあさん： わたしたちは ....　に　ねます。

　　　　　　 よろしい　ですか。

マリア： ....。

おとうさん： しん聞を ....　のが　好きですか。

マリア： はい、...............　わたしの　日本語は ....です。

おとうさん： じゃ...　えい語で　かいてある　しん聞を　買います。

G Can you work out an occupation that the people on the following page could be engaged in? Do you know how to say these occupations in Japanese? Use a dictionary if necessary.

Answer according to this example:

わたしは　四十さいです。生とに　おしえるのが　好きです。生との

りょうしんと　話すのは　おもしろいと　思います。

Answer: This person could be a teacher (せんせい).

1. 本を　読むことが　大好きです。としょかんで　はたらい
ているのは　おもしろいと　思います。生とに　話すのが
好きです。

2. わたしの　しごとが　好きです。きものを　売るのは
たのしいと　思います。デパートに　つとめています。
デパートの　五階で　はたらいています。

3. 学校で　せいぶつが　好きでした。大学で　べんきょう
していました。今　びょういんで　はたらいています。
ここで　はたらいているのが　大好きです。たくさんの
人に　あいます。

4. じむしつに　つとめるのが　きらいです。どうぶつが
好きです。きょねん　じむしつで　はたらいていました。
たいへん　でした。きらい　でした。でも、今　大きい
どうぶつえんに　つとめています。とても　たのしいと
思います。

5. 学校が　きらいです。つまらないと　思います。よく
じゅぎょうを　やすみたい　ですが　もちろん　それを
しません。よく　ねます。そつぎょうご、ぜんぜん
わかりません。

H₁ 書きましょう・カタカナ

セ se	ネ ne	ウ u	ヘ he	サ sa	ホ ho
A sharp *set* of *sec*ateurs	You can *nev*er catch a pixie	*Oo*ps! The crab is escaping through the hole in the crab pot	*He*ad to the top of the mountain	Toss the "*sara*-da"	It is so *ho*t
⏋セ	⟍ ⟍ ⟍	⟍ ⟍ ウ	ヘ	一 十 サ	一 ナ オ ホ

Katakana — revision

What can be purchased from these two restaurants?

How good are you at working out all these foreign words? On the handout that your teacher gives you, label each item of clothing by writing its name next to it in katakana. Select the words from the list below.

スーツケース	スカート	ネクタイ	バッグ	スーツ
ジーンズ	ベルト	オーバー	ドレス	シャツ
レインコート	ハンドバッグ	ワンピース	スラックス	ブラウス
ワイシャツ	セーター			

Shopping — and being specific

Whether we are shopping by ourselves or with others, we constantly compare items in order to decide which one to buy.

When shopping, we need to be specific about the thing we are talking about.

Sentence Pattern 67

Q. この　スカーフ　ですか。　　Is it this scarf? (Is this the scarf that you want to look at?)

A. いいえ、その　あおいの　です。　No, that blue one.

Explanation

In this pattern, the の before です is a pronoun meaning "one".

Read the following dialogue. You should have little trouble working out what it means. With a partner, prepare a similar type of dialogue in which you point out something that you want to buy.

てんいん：　　　いらっしゃいませ。

マリア：　　　セーターを　見せてください。

てんいん：　　　はい、この　セーター　ですか。

マリア：　　　いいえ、その　あおいの　です。

てんいん：　　　この　あおいの　ですか。

マリア：　　　はい、どうも。

　　　　　　　...うん...　ちょっと　小さいですね。

てんいん：　　　ええ、すこし。

　　　　　　　この　セーターは　どうですか。

マリア：　　　その　セーターも　きれいですね。

てんいん：　　　ええ、きれいです。

マリア：　　　(looks in mirror) うん...　いいですね。

　　　　　　　いくらですか。

てんいん：　　　3000円　です。

マリア：　　　じゃ、この　あおいセーターを　ください。

J₁　What does each of the following sentences mean in English?

1. その　男の子は　そのみどりの　シャツは　好きじゃないです。
2. その　女の子は　ウインドーショッピングを　することが　好きです。
3. この　ドレスを　あらっても　いいですか。
4. この　本は　あなたの　ですか。
5. だれが　あの　ゆきだるまを　つくりましたか。
6. この　みどりのが　好きです。
7. ちゃ色のは　たろうくんの　だと　思います。
8. その　赤いのは　ちょっと　大きいです。
9. むらさきの　花は　とても　うつくしいと　思います。
10. 黒いのが　きらいです。

Express these sentences in Japanese as best you can:

1. I thought that that movie was very complicated. I didn't understand it.

2. I think that that red one is a little expensive.

3. My aunt is employed at this company.

4. I did not come to this park yesterday.

5. I read that one last week.

6. I think these shoes are mine!

7. May I eat this nashi?

8. Is this green scarf Maria's?

9. The blue one is not mine.

10. The little one is cute, isn't it.

だれの くつですか
(A typical entry to an apartment)

K₁

Getting down to specifics ...

Sentence Pattern 68

Q. どの ドレスが 一ばん 好きですか。   Which one/what one do you like best?

A. あおい ドレスが 一ばん きれい ですが たかいです。   The blue dress is the prettiest but it is expensive.

ピンク色の ドレスが 一ばん やすいです。   The pink dress is the cheapest.

だから 赤いのを 買いたいと 思います。   Therefore, I think I'll buy the red one.

Explanation

When expressing one's preference for something where there are three or more things to choose from, use the pattern shown in the above question and the first and second sentences of the responses. By putting いちばん before an adjective, you are expressing it in the "superlative" degree, that is:

一ばん きれい   (the pretti*est*)

一ばん たかい   (the *most* expensive)

一ばん 好き（な）is often used as an adjective to mean "my favourite".

が is used when you are required to make a selection of one item only.

K₂

Answer each of the following questions according to the clues given, and then answer each question again as it relates to you:

1. どの　スポーツが　一ばん　好きですか。 (Baseball)

2. どの　ズボンが　一ばん　たかいですか。 (The black ones)

3. どの　食べものが　一ばん　好きですか。(Sushi)

4. 一ばん　好きな　のみものは　何ですか。(Tea)

5. 一ばん　好きな　シャツは　何ですか。 (The blue one)

6. 一ばん　好きな　かもくは　何ですか。 (Japanese)

7. 一ばん　きらいな　かもくは　何ですか。 (History)

8. どの　本が　一ばん　おもしろいと　思いますか。 (This book)

9. 一ばん　好きな　テレビの　プログラムは　何と　言いますか。("47 Roonin")

10. みつこしは　一ばん　いいデパートですか。 (I don't know but I think it is the oldest.)

 K₃ Try putting these sentences into Japanese:

1. Which (pop) group is your favourite? My favourite (pop) group is … (*Name it*)

2. I think that this shop's fruit is the cheapest and the best.

3. Hidemi's favourite teacher is the English teacher.

4. My favourite teacher is the maths teacher.

5. I like going to the pool.

6. My favourite season is spring.

7. My favourite hobby is reading.

8. My favourite town is Takayama.

9. This book is my favourite.

10. This is the tallest building in Japan.

This photograph was taken from the 54th floor of the Shinjuku Centre building. This means that the tall building in the foreground must not be very tall at all!

 L Write complete sentences in which the people illustrated are matched with the activities on page 138.

1. ダビンチ

2. ディズニー

3. セルズ

4. ジェーン　トービル

5. レノン

6. ジェシ　ジェームス

7. アブラハム　リンカン

8. プリンセス　ダイアナ

9. グレック　ノーマン

Activities:

a. えを　かくのが　上手でした。

b. ゴルフが　上手です。

c. スケートが　できます。

d. アメリカ人　でした。

e. おもしろい　話を　たくさん　書きました。

f. たかい　ようふくが　たくさん　あります。

g. テニスを　するのが　大好きです。

h. うまに　のりました。

i. うたが　できました。

M

Beat the clock

Your teacher will give you a copy of this exercise so there's no need to write in your text.

Complete each line with the dictionary form of the verb. Try to finish this exercise in just 60 seconds. If you don't complete it in time, relearn your verb endings and try again.

1. き☐ to listen
2. か☐ to write
3. す☐ to do
4. よ☐ to read
5. そうじす☐ to clean
6. やす☐ to have a rest
7. わか☐ to understand
8. ひ☐ to play (the piano)
9. つか☐ to use
10. み☐ to see

11. あら☐ to wash
12. おしえ☐ to teach
13. の☐ to drink
14. たべ☐ to eat
15. あそ☐ to play
16. い☐ to go
17. さ☐ to bloom
18. つく☐ to make
19. か☐ to buy
20. つ☐ to arrive

書きましょう

Listen to the dialogue read by your teacher and then answer these questions:

- Why does Andrew like karate?

- What does Tomoko say about her hobby?

- Does Tomoko go to concerts often or not? Explain.

- What does the word おんがくか mean?

- What is Tomoko talking about when she says あたらしいですね？

O 調べましょう

1. シェークスピアは　何を　するのが　好きでしたか。
2. ミケランジェロは　何を　することが　好きでしたか。
3. ショパンは　何を　するのが　好きでしたか。
4. ピタゴラスは　何を　するのが　好きでしたか。

P

You have just received a letter from your friend けんすけ.

(a) Rewrite his letter in English.

(b) Write an informative letter back to him. Mention when our rainy season is, where you go for school excursions and what your interests are.

(c) Knowing what ちかてつ means, can you work what てつどうけんきゅう means? (See No. 23 in Kensuke's list of clubs.)

デイビッドさん、　お元気ですか。

オーストラリアでは　冬ですね。さむさは　きびしいですか。日本は　つゆに　入りました。これからは　雨の　おおい　シーズンに　なります。こめを　つくる人には　ひつような　シーズンですが　サラリーマンには　いやな　シーズンです。

あねの　まき子は　あしたから　しゅう学りょ行に　行きます。かの女は　とても　たのしみに　しています。にっこうへ　行きます。まき子は　「とうしょうぐう」と「ちゅうぜんじ　こ」を　見に　行きます。きょ年　冬にぼくは　にっこうへ　行きました。しゃしんを　2まい　どうふうします。

今年、学校で　チェスの　クラブに　入りました。あまり　上手じゃな

いですが この ゲームを するのは おもしろいと 思います。まい日、じゅ
ぎょうの あとで チェスを します。あなたの ハイ
スクールに クラブが ありますか。

ぼくの 中学校には 23の クラブが あります。

クラブ:

1. バスケット
2. テニス
3. ソフトボール
4. 書どう
5. しゃしん
6. ちり
7. えい語
8. ワンダーフォーゲル ^(ハイキング)

9. バレーボール
10. サッカー
11. やきゅう
12. さどう
13. ギター
14. かていか
15. オーケストラ

16. バドミントン
17. まんが けんきゅう
18. いけばな
19. アメリカけんきゅう
20. チェス
21. うんどう
22. ハード ランニング
23. てつどうけんきゅう

まき子さんは 三年生の オーケストラ クラブに 入っています。
かの女は バイオリンを ひくことが 大好きで 上手です。

ところで、今日から あたらしい 電話 ばんごうに なりました。
あたらしいのは 451–5892です。

では、へんじを まっています。おげんきで。さようなら

6月29日

けんすけ

デイビッドさんへ

Toshogu Shrine, Nikko

A school excursion group at the Toshogu Shrine

Q Situational dialogue — ringing home from Japan

On arriving in Japan, most students will want to ring their parents to let them know that they've arrived safely. But at the same time you don't want to be a nuisance to your host family. The following dialogue allows you to call home with the minimum amount of bother to your Japanese hosts.

Step 1

Ask if you may ring your parents, reverse charges:

コレクト　コールで　りょうしんに　電話を　かけても　いいですか。

or

Say that you'd like to call your parents, or ask if you may use the phone:

I'd like to ring my parents but … りょうしんに　電話したいんですが…

Is it okay if I use the telephone? 電話を　つかっても ｛よろしいですか。
　　　　　　　　　　　　　　　　　　　いいですか。

Step 2

Wait for a reply such as … はい、どうぞ。

Then …

Dial the international operator on 0051.

Step 3

He or she will say something like …

What number do you want? 何ばんに　おかけに　なりますか。

or

Please give me the number that you want to call. あいての　電話ばんごうを　言って下さい。

Don't forget your area code.

So …

"Australia 07 765 932, please" is:

オーストラリアの　ゼロななの　ななろくごの　きゅうさんに　ばん　おねがいします。

He or she will ask you politely to wait a moment. しょうしょう　おまちください。

Step 4

The operator may tell you to go ahead please … どうぞ　お話（はな）しください。

or he or she may say that the line is busy. お話（はな）し中（ちゅう）です。

If the line is busy, you may be asked if you'd like to wait. おまちに　なりますか。

You could be asked if you'd mind calling again (later). また、かけなおして　くださいますか。

Don't forget to thank your hosts for the use of the phone (and tell them that your parents are now relieved to hear that everything is fine).

りょうしんは　あんしんしました。どうも　ありがとうございました。

R | **New words and expressions**

Akeru	あける	To open
Amai	あまい	Sweet, sugary
Anshinsuru	あんしんする	To be relieved, free from worry
Bonsai	ぼんさい	Miniature potted tree or plant
Bunraku	ぶんらく	Classical puppet theatre
Burausu	ブラウス	Blouse
Chanoyu	ちゃのゆ	Tea ceremony
Chuuzenjiko	ちゅうぜんじこ	Lake Chuzenji
Da	だ	Plain form of です
Denwa bangoo	電話ばんごう	Telephone number
Denwa o kakeru	電話を　かける	To ring, to make a telephone call
Doofuusuru	どうふうする	To enclose (in a letter)
Doo omoimasuka	どう思いますか	What do you think about it?
Hairu	入る	To enter
Hashi	はし	Chopsticks
Hiku	ひく	To play (the piano, guitar, violin)
Hitsuyoo (na)	ひつよう（な）	Necessary
Ichiban	一ばん	Number one
Jimushitsu	じむしつ	Office
Jugyoo	じゅぎょう	Lesson, class
Kabuki	かぶき	Highly stylised traditional Japanese theatre with singing and dancing, performed exclusively by male actors
Kagaku	かがく	Science
Kakeru	かける	To telephone, ring
Kamoku	かもく	(School) Subject
Karaoke	カラオケ	Form of nightclub entertainment where customers pay to sing popular songs to pre-recorded accompaniment
Kenkyuusuru	けんきゅうする	To research
Keredomo	けれども	However
Kiku	聞く	To listen
Kirai (na)	きらい（な）	Dislike, unlikeable
Korekara	これから	From now on
Korekuto kooru	コレクト　コール	Collect call, reverse charges
Koto	こと	Fact, used as a noun nominaliser

Kyoogen	きょうげん	Traditional drama reflecting everyday and social conditions in olden times
Mai	まい	Counter for flat objects, e.g. photographs, pages, tickets
Manzoku (na)	まんぞく（な）	Contented, satisfied, satisfying
Matsu	まつ	To wait
Miru	見る	To see
Mokuhanga	もくはんが	Woodblock print
Mono	もの	Thing
Nanban	何ばん	What number?
Narau	ならう	To learn
Neru	ねる	To sleep
Nihonryoori	日本りょうり	Japanese cooking
No	の	One (thing), used as a noun nominaliser
Noo	のう	Traditional theatre with highly stylised acting, wooden masks and elaborate costumes
Ohanashichuu	お話し中	Busy (on the telephone)
Omachi kudasai	おまちください	Please wait
Omou	思う	To think
Origami	おりがみ	Paper folding
Pachinko	パチンコ	Japanese pinball
Puroguramu	プログラム	Programme, e.g. television programme
Rekoodo	レコード	Record
Ryokoosuru	りょ行する	To travel
Sadoo	さどう	(The study of) Tea ceremony
Sarariiman	サラリーマン	Salary man (white-collar worker)
Seetaa	セーター	Sweater
Shatsu	シャツ	Singlet or casual shirt with no buttons, T-shirt
Shigoto	しごと	Job, work
Shiizun	シーズン	Season
Shimbun	しん聞	Newspaper
Shizukesa	しずけさ	Silence, tranquillity, serenity
Shooshoo	しょうしょう	A little, a bit, a moment
Shumi	しゅみ	Hobby, interest
Shuugakuryokoo	しゅう学りょ行	School excursion
Soodato omoimasu	そうだと思います	I think that is so
Soojisuru	そうじする	To clean, sweep (a house)
Sukaafu	スカーフ	Scarf
Suki (na)	好き（な）	Like
Sumu	すむ	To live
Suru (shimasu)	する（します）	To do
Taberu	食べる	To eat

Taihen deshita	たいへん　でした	It was awful
Tokorode	ところで	By the way, well then
Toochaku	とうちゃく	Arrival
Tsumaranai	つまらない	Boring
Uindooshoppingu ni iku	ウインドーショッピングに行く	To go window shopping
Uindooshoppingu o suru	ウインドーショッピングをする	To window shop
Uma ni noru	うまにのる	To ride a horse
Uru	売る	To sell
Waishatsu	ワイシャツ	Men's shirt (with a collar and buttons)
Yakimono	やきもの	Pottery, earthenware
Yomu	読む	To read
Yoroshii	よろしい	Okay
Zubon	ズボン	Trousers, pants

S₁ Kanji studied to the end of Unit 17:

Unit 13:	一	二	三	四	五	六	七	八	九	十	人	何
	1	2	3	4	5	6	7	8	9	10	11	12
Unit 14:	目	口	日	本	母	父	白	赤	黒	色	大	小
	13	14	15	16	17	18	19	20	21	22	23	24
Unit 15:	月	花	木	子	女	好	言	夏	火	秋	春	冬
	25	26	27	28	29	30	31	32	33	34	35	36
	雨	雲	天	気	年							
	37	38	39	40	41							
Unit 16:	上	手	下	語	中	学	校	外	男	生	今	階
	42	43	44	45	46	47	48	49	50	51	52	53
Unit 17:	思	見	聞	行	話	電	買	売	読	入	食	
	54	55	56	57	58	59	60	61	62	63	64	

S₂ Katakana studied to the end of Unit 17:

Unit 14:	ア	ン	ト	ル	ナ	ー	ヒ	ク	オ	レ	シ	リ
	1	2	3	4	5	6	7	8	9	10	11	12
Unit 15:	ハ	イ	マ	テ	ス	ラ	ツ					
	13	14	15	16	17	18	19					

Unit 16:	コ	ユ	タ	ノ	キ	ニ	カ	フ	ケ	チ	エ	ロ	ミ
	20	21	22	23	24	25	26	27	28	29	30	31	32
Unit 17:	セ	ネ	ウ	ヘ	サ	ホ							
	33	34	35	36	37	38							

Reading is a popular pastime — even in the bookshops

From reading the blackboard, can you work out what club this senior high school student is probably in?

Unit 18

At the zoo
どうぶつえん
動物園で

Topics:

一　Animals and their sounds
二　Adjectives
三　Signs and messages
四　At the photographers

動物園で

やぎ、うし、ぶた、あひる、うま、クジャク、うさぎ、にわとり、ろば

しろくま　くま

出口

便所

ぞう、かば

さい

カンガルー　コアラ

さる　チンパンジー

ライオン

きりん

チータ

とら

とり

しか　フラミンゴ

らくだ　いんこ

入口　わに　へび

パンダ　ペンギン

ヤ ya	モ mo	ソ so	ヌ nu	メ me	ヨ yo	ム mu
Yarn pulled through by a crochet hook	A **mo**th attracted to the light	**So**mbrero	An American's "**noo**" dagger	Two roads have **met**	**Ya**chts berthed at the marina	**Mo**ve over!
⼀ヤ	一 ニ モ	丶 ソ	フ ヌ	ノ メ	フ ヨ ヨ	ノ ム ム

C₂ Can you work out what the following birds and animals are? Write out the katakana first and then the English equivalent. When you have corrected your work, decide which stamp would be most appropriate for the standard you reached and rewrite it into your book.

1. プードル
2. フラミンゴ
3. サイ
4. ライオン
5. チータ
6. コアラ
7. カンガルー
8. チンパンジー
9. パンダ
10. ペンギン
11. セントバーナード
12. カメレオン
13. ポニー
14. アフリカライオン
15. ペルシャねこ
16. ペリカン
17. ビーバー
18. ゴリラ
19. グレイハウンド
20. コリー
21. グレートデン
22. シェパード
23. シャムねこ
24. コッカースパニエル
25. スピッツ

Chameleon

How do you rate?

22 – 25

18 – 21

12 – 17  *or*
perhaps

You tried! *Try harder!*

0 – 12

You need to do a lot more work! *More effort needed!*

C₃ What do these two shops sell?

D₁ When visiting a zoo or any other tourist attraction with your host family, you will need to know how to comment on the animals and birds so that they know you are enjoying and appreciating your visit. You have already learnt some exclamations in Unit 14 and you already know much about adjectives.

The following two exercises will help you bring together what you know so far.

Put each of the following sentences into English. (The sentence pattern used is also given so that it is easy for you to refer back if you've forgotten something.)

1. きれいな　コアラは　ねています。 (43c)

2. くさい　らくだは　いやだと　思います。 (43a, 65)

3. カンガルーを　見ているのは　とても　おもしろいですね。 (66)

4. この　動物園に　めずらしい　動物が　たくさん　いますね。 (32b, 63b)

5. さるは　にぎやかで　おもしろい　ですね。 (48c)

6. この　動物園は　ひろくて　きれい　です。 (48b)

7. すてき　ですね！

8. かわいい　ですね！

9. ぞうの　ながいはなは　べんりですね。 (43a)

10. その　みどりのとりは　何と言いますか。 (43b)

A sleepy koala

D₂ Try expressing these questions or statements in Japanese:

1. The huge hippopotamus is very ugly, don't you think?

2. Are there any platypuses in this zoo? No, there aren't any.

3. The koala is sleepy. It's over there.

4. Is the green snake dangerous?

5. Monkeys are always lively, aren't they.

6. What is that brown animal called?

7. Where is the koala?

8. The macaw is a beautiful bird, isn't it.

9. Are chimpanzees really clever?

10. The smelly pigs are disgusting, aren't they.

11. I think pigs are smelly and disgusting.

12. The long green snake is over there.

E₁ ## More about adjectives

By now you have mastered quite a few ways of using adjectives.

We can say	It *is* …(clean) (*adjectival noun*)
	It *is* …(dirty) (*adjective*)
But how do we say	It *is not* …(clean) (*adjectival noun*)
	It *is not* …(dirty) (*adjective*)
or	It *was* clean
	It *was* dirty
or	It *was not* clean
	It *was not* dirty

The next six sentence patterns will show you how.

NEGATIVES: It is *not* …

Sentence Pattern 69

True adjectives

おおきい	です。	It is big.
おおきく	ないです。	It is *not* big.

Sentence Pattern 70

Adjectival nouns

にぎやか　です。　　It is noisy.

にぎやか

or ⎰ じゃ　ないです。　It is *not* noisy.
⎱ じゃ　ありません。
⎱ では　ありません。

Explanation

As you can see, true adjectives are treated in Japanese just like verbs and so the ending has to be adjusted, depending on the meaning being conveyed. In Sentence Pattern 42, you learnt how to say "I don't want to work …":

はたらきたくないです。

Expressing a true adjective in the negative is exactly the same. Just change the い to く and add ない（です）.

For example:
It is not big. 大きくない(です)。
It is not small. ちいさくない(です)。
It is not red. あかくない(です)。

In this pattern, 「です」at the end makes the sentence a little more polite. For this reason, it is better to use it. Once you get to know your new Japanese friends better, you may feel that it is appropriate to leave it off.

Explanation

Because adjectival nouns are used like nouns, this pattern is exactly the same as Sentence Pattern 19:

すし　じゃないです。

It is useful to know all the endings shown in Sentence Pattern 70.

じゃない（です）is less formal than じゃありますん and では　ありません is even more polite and less colloquial than the other two.

A simple way of remembering the *negative* form is that both the Japanese and the English words contain the *N* sound: *N*ot and se*N* or *N*ai.

Put each of the following adjectives into the negative form. Put the adjectival nouns in *all* forms: じゃないです, じゃありません and では　ありません.

1. おおきい	9. ひくい	17. にぎやか	
2. あぶない	10. いそがしい	18. いや	
3. みにくい	11. きたない	19. きれい	
4. くさい	12. ちいさい	20. げんき	
5. おそい	13. うつくしい	21. りこう	
6. はやい	14. うるさい	22. べんり	
7. ねむい	15. おもしろい	23. へん	
8. かわいい	16. ふべん	24. ゆうめい	

Flamingos at Oji Zoo, Kobe

E₄ Join each phrase from column A with a suitable clause from column B. Rewrite the completed sentence and write its English meaning next to it.

A

1. びょう気の
2. みどりの
3. オーストラリアでは
4. この黒い
5. パンダは
6. あぶない
7. 元気な
8. みにくくて
9. 大きい
10. ちゃ色の
11. きれいな
12. 白い
13. この　ペンギンは
14. 小さいねずみは
15. この　小さいわには

B

a. あまり　大きくないですね。
b. 元気じゃありません。
c. ぶたは　くさくないです。
d. コアラは　食べていません。
e. チータは　はやく　はしります。
f. 馬は　はやく　はしりません。
g. こわいです。
h. にわとりは　あまり　りこうじゃないです。
i. かばは　とても　みにくいです。
j. へびは　あぶなくないです。
k. あまり　あぶなくないです。
l. うるさいやぎは　女の人の　手がみを　食べました。
m. さるは　いつも　うるさいです。
n. カンガルーは　めずらしくないです。
o. ゴリラは　なまけものです。

E₅ **Surely you don't agree!**

Respond to each of the following questions in the negative and then add what you think is a more suitable description, as shown in the example. Write out the English meaning as well.

Example:

パンダは　きたないですか。 (Clean)

いいえ　パンダは　きたなくないです。

きれいだと思います。　　(No, the panda is not dirty. I think it is clean.)

1. その　くまは　みにくいですか。　(Cute)
2. わには　かわいいですか。　(Dangerous)
3. ぶたは　きれいですか。　(Dirty)
4. らくだは　くさいですか。　(Clean)
5. かばは　びょうきですか。　(Sleepy)
6. さるは　ねむいですか。　(Lively)
7. とりは　うるさいですか。　(Busy)
8. ぞうのはなは　みにくいですか。　(Convenient)
9. チンパンジーは　うるさいと　思いますか。　(Clever)
10. その　へびは　ねむいと　思いますか。　(No. Be careful)

*A hungry hippopotamus
at the Beppu Zoo*

E₆　Look at how a Japanese would reassure another that a snake is not dangerous:

その　へびは　あぶないですか。

- その　へびは　あぶなくないです。
- かまないから　だいじょうぶです。
  It's okay because they won't bite.
- ここは　あんぜんです。
  We're safe here.
- あんしん　してください。
  Don't worry. (Please feel safe.)
- だいじょうぶです。
  You're okay.
- しんぱいしないでください。
  Please don't worry.

E₇　By using the negative form of adjectives with expressions such as ぜんぜん and あまり your descriptions can be made much more specific and graphic.

For example:

(a) うちの　ねこは　きたなくないです。　　My cat is not dirty.

(b) うちの　ねこは　あまり　きたなくないです。　　My cat is not very dirty.

(c) うちの　ねこは　ぜんぜん　きたなくないです。　　My cat is not dirty at all.

In at least two sentences per picture, describe each of the animals or people illustrated below. You should use あまり or ぜんぜん at least once in each description.

1.
2.
3.
4.
5.
6.
7.
8.
9.

F 調べましょう

What is the meaning of this sign near the entrance to the Nikko National Park? Can you find out the origins of the proverb 「見ざる・言わざる・聞かざる」?

65. 動 Move

The first radical represents a pile of boxes. To *move* the boxes you'd need plenty of strength, symbolised by the arm muscle.

くん うご(く) **おん** どう **いみ** 動物 animal

かきじゅん 丿 仁 仨 佮 伯 白 車 車 重 動 動

11かく

66. 物 Thing

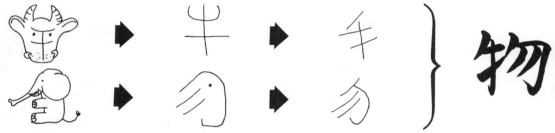

An elephant and an ox could move all *things*. This now very abstract character means "thing" or "article".

くん もの **おん** ぶつ、もつ **いみ** 動物 animal, 生物 biology

かきじゅん 丿 仁 仨 牛 牪 牞 物 物

8かく

67. 園 Park

A *park* has a definite boundary or a fence around it. It has trees and plants, and children (represented by the open, happy mouth); there is usually a lake or pond there too. The water is a modified version of みず.

くん　その　おん　えん　いみ　動物園 zoo, こう園 park

かきじゅん  13かく

68.　馬　Horse

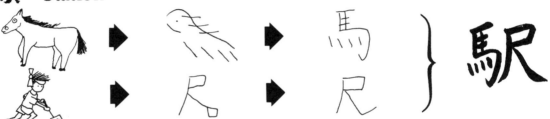

The character for *horse* has been progressively abbreviated to its present form.

くん　うま、ま　おん　ば　いみ　馬

かきじゅん　一　厂　厂　厍　馬　馬　馬　馬　馬　馬 10かく

69.　駅　Station

A *station* was traditionally a meeting place that was reached by horse. Men had to work with shovels to build these stations.

くん　　おん　えき　いみ　駅

かきじゅん　一　厂　厂　厍　馬　馬　馬　馬　馬　馬　馬　馬　駅　駅 14かく

70.　時　Time

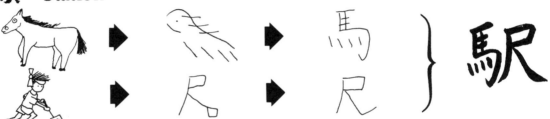

A hand with a dot measures how far the pulse can be taken from the wrist. It symbolises "measure" — of either distance or justice. When it is placed under "earth" it means "temple" because that is where the laws of the land were made. When the character for temple, 寺, is placed next to the character for the sun, 日, it means *time* or *hour* because in days gone by the temples measured time and kept the calendar.

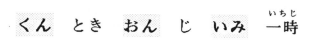 くん とき おん じ いみ 一時

かきじゅん 〔1 ｜ 冂 冂 日 日ˉ 日ⁿ 旷 昨 時 時〕 10かく

71. 青 Blue, green

As the days and nights pass, the plants grow more *green* leaves.

くん あお、あお(い) おん せい、しょう いみ 青い blue

かきじゅん 〔一 十 キ 主 丰 青 青 青〕 8かく

72. 土 Earth

Plants grow up from the ground or *earth*.

くん つち おん ど、と いみ 土よう日 Saturday

かきじゅん 〔一 十 土〕 3かく

73. 水 Water

The *water* is flowing down the river.

くん みず おん すい いみ 水、水よう日 Wednesday

かきじゅん 〔丿 才 水 水〕 4かく

74. 金　**Gold**

To find *gold* you pitch a tent and start digging; the gold is not on the surface and not in the top layer of soil, but where the arrow is pointing — in the next layer below.

くん　かね、かな　おん　きん、こん　いみ　金、お金 money, 金よう日 Friday

かきじゅん　｜ ｜八 ｜仝 ｜仝 ｜仝 ｜仝 ｜金 ｜金　8かく

75. 美　**Beauty**

Beauty is a rural scene of the shepherd (a strong man) tending his flock. Both the shepherd and the sheep are represented in this kanji.

くん　うつく(しい)　おん　び　いみ　美しい beautiful

かきじゅん　｜'｜'｜'｜'｜'｜'｜'｜'｜'｜'｜'｜'｜'｜'｜羊 ｜美　9かく

G₂　Write out the following words or phrases, using kanji wherever possible:

1. Little girl	7. Zoo	13. 7 o'clock	19. Beautiful park
2. Man	8. Park	14. Animals	20. Black horse
3. Tuesday	9. White snow	15. Big animals	21. Big station
4. Skilful	10. Favourite book	16. To think	22. To sell
5. To see	11. (I) say	17. Friday	23. Train
6. Food	12. (I) heard	18. Saturday	24. Junior high school

H　Read this dialogue between Andrew and Emiko as they wander through part of the zoo. Then answer in English the questions that follow.

アンドルー：　その　動物は　日本語で　何と　言いますか。

えみこ：　その　大きいのですか。

アンドルー：　ええ。

えみこ：　それは　かばと　言います。みにくいですね。

アンドルー：　　　ええ、そうですね。食べ物のくずを　食べますか。

えみこ：　　　　そうだと思います。
　　　　　　　　この　へんに　ぶたが　すんでいます。

アンドルー：　　びっくりしました。ふつうは　ぶたのいるところ*は　くさいです。
　　　　　　　　でも　この　へんは　くさくないです。きれいです。
　　　　　　　　ああ、えみこさん、あそこの　せが　たかいとりは　何と　言い
　　　　　　　　ますか。

えみこ：　　　　あそこの　ピンク色の　とりは　フラミンゴと　言います。きれいです
　　　　　　　　ね。おおいですね。

アンドルー：　　一わ、二わ、三わ、四わ、五わ、六わ、七わ、八わ、九わ、十わ、
　　　　　　　　十一わ　います。

えみこ：　　　　アンドルーさん、もう　二時です。何か　食べに　行きましょうか。

アンドルー：　　ええ、それは　よいかんがえですね。

*ぶたのいるところ The place where there are pigs.

1. From the conversation, what information did you find out about a hippopotamus?
2. Why does Andrew say 「びっくりしました！」?
3. What birds did Andrew and Emiko see? How many were there?
4. What did Andrew think was a good idea?
5. What counter is used for birds?

I₁ More counters

As you saw in Part H, the counter for birds is わ（羽）. The counter for small animals is ひき（匹）and for large animals it is とう（頭）.

Counters for birds, small animals, large animals

	何羽 (なんわ)	何匹 (なんびき)	何頭 (なんとう)
1	いちわ	いっぴき	いっとう
2	にわ	にひき	にとう
3	さんば	さんびき	さんとう
4	よんわ	よんひき	よんとう
5	ごわ	ごひき	ごとう
6	ろくわ	ろっぴき	ろくとう
7	しちわ	ななひき	しちとう
8	はちわ	はっぴき	はちとう
9	きゅうわ	きゅうひき	きゅうとう
10	じゅうわ	じゅっぴき	じゅっとう
11	じゅういちわ	じゅいっぴき	じゅういっとう
12	じゅうにわ	じゅうにひき	じゅうにとう

I₂ What do these sentences mean?

1. 小さい　2頭のぞうは　かわいいですね。
2. チンパンジーを　6匹　見ました。
3. なごやの　動物園の　2匹の　コアラは　とても　げんきです。
4. 20羽の　フラミンゴは　きれいだと　思います。
5. 5匹の　うるさい　さるは　ピーナツを　食べていました。
6. 10羽の　にわとりは　白いです。
7. 一匹の　ちゃ色の　うさぎは　にんじんを　食べて　水を　のんでいました。
8. 2匹の　黒いうさぎは　レタスを　たべて　ミルクを　のんでいました。
9. 動物園に　ペンギンが　3羽　います。
10. おじさんの　ぼくじょうに　馬は　4頭　います。よく　馬に　のります。

I₃ Put these sentences into Japanese:

1. The black cat ate two birds.
2. The two chimpanzees are noisy.
3. The ten chickens were eating food wraps.
4. The two pigs are smelly.
5. I think that the panda is very cute.
6. I took a photograph of the five deer.
7. Look at this photograph of the three elephants.
8. The six little rabbits were eating carrots.
9. The four monkeys are still sleepy.
10. The six pigs are not very clean.
11. The koala is not very sleepy.
12. The hippopotamus is not at all clean.
13. This area is not new.
14. The bears are not ugly. I think they are cute.
15. Chickens are not intelligent at all.

Feeding deer near Todaiji, Nara

J₁

The past tense

You can already say what something "is" and "is not". Now let's have a look at how to say that something *was* …

For example:

The hippopotamus *was* sleepy.

The zoo *was* clean.

Sentence Pattern 71
True adjectives

おもしろい　です。　It is interesting.

おもしろかったです。It *was* interesting.

Sentence Pattern 72
Adjectival nouns

にぎやか　です。　It is lively.

にぎやかでした。　It *was* lively.

Explanation

To explain what something *was* like (that is, to put an adjective in the past tense), drop the final い and add かった(です).
For example:

It was interesting. おもしろかった(です)。
It was dangerous. あぶなかった(です)。
I was busy. いそがしかった(です)。
He was sleepy. ねむかった(です)。

Remember that the 「です」 is added to each of these endings for politeness.

Explanation

It was mentioned in Unit 9 that でした is the past tense of です. To express the idea that something *was* such-and-such when using either nouns or adjectival nouns, the です is simply replaced by でした.
For example:

It was complicated. ふくざつでした。
It was strange. へんでした。
It was convenient. べんりでした。

J₂ Change each of the following sentences into the past tense. Where appropriate, change 今日 to きのう.

Example:

今日は　あついです。きのうは　あつかったです。 Yesterday it was hot.

1. 今日は　さむいです。
2. 今日は　すずしいです。
3. 今日は　あたたかいです。
4. 今日は　いそがしいです。
5. きれいですね。
6. こわいです。
7. にぎやかです。
8. おそいです。

9. みにくいです。
10. うるさいです。
11. 赤いです。
12. 今日は　げんきです。
13. あおいです。
14. いやです。
15. つまらないです。
16. おっくうです。

J₃ Put these sentences into English:

1. きのう　動物園へ　行って　たのしかったです。
2. きのう　なまけものの　かばを　見ました。

3. お父さんの　あたらしい　くるまは　はやかったですが　今、ふるいから、
　　おそいです。

4. 三匹(びき)の　ぶたは　くさかったです。

5. フラミンゴは　きれいでした。

6. きのう　そうじしました。いそがしかったです。

7. さるは　さるやまに　すんでいます。いつも　にぎやかです。きのうも
　　にぎやかでした。

8. せんしゅう　しゅう学りょ行に　行きました。たのしかったです。

9. とも子さんの　きょ年の　一ばんいいドレスは　きれいでした。でも
　　今年　の　一ばん好きなのは　きれいじゃないと　思います。

10. えいがは　おもしろかったです。

J4 Put these sentences into Japanese:

1. The school excursion was interesting.
2. The monkeys were annoying.
3. That snake is dangerous.
4. The rabbits were cute.
5. I think the hippopotamus is ugly.
6. The pigs were smelly.
7. The little koala was sleepy.
8. The healthy kangaroo was lively.
9. I think the clever monkey is cute.
10. The rhinoceros was dirty.

J5 Make a vertical list of all the true adjectives that you can remember. Add to that list all others that you *should* know (by checking the "new words and expressions" sections from Units 13–18). Then, across the page make the columns as shown and fill all of them in except the last one. (You may be able to guess what would go in this last column!)

True adjectives

Present tense	Past tense	Negative	Past negative
あかいです	あかかったです	あかくないです	

When you have finished the true adjectives, do the same for adjectival nouns, but this time leave *three* lines for each word so that you can write in the three ways of saying "it is not" and "it was not".

Adjectival nouns

Present tense	Past tense	Negative	Past negative
きれいです	きれいでした	きれいじゃありません	1.
		きれいじゃないです	2.
		きれいでは　ありません	3.

K₁ | Past negative

There will be many times in either your daily life in Japan or in writing to your friends that you will need to say that something *was not* such-and-such. Look closely at the following sentence patterns to see how this is done.

True adjectives

Adjectival nouns

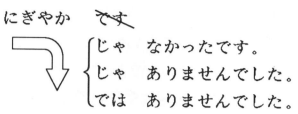

Note: じゃ is less formal or more colloquial than では. Instead of using じゃありませんでした or じゃなかったですit is more polite to say では　ありませんでした.

Sentence Pattern 73a

えいがは　おもしろく　なかったです。

The movie wasn't interesting.

Sentence Pattern 74a

　　パンダは　にぎやか　じゃ　なかったです。
or　パンダは　にぎやか　じゃ　ありませんでした。
or　パンダは　にぎやか　では　ありませんでした。

　　　　The panda wasn't lively.

It would be more likely that you would use such descriptive language in more formal situations or in your writing so では would often be more appropriate.

Sentence Pattern 73b

えいがは　あまり　おもしろく　なかったです。

The movie wasn't very interesting.

Sentence Pattern 74b

　　パンダは　ぜんぜん　にぎやか　じゃ　なかったです。
orパンダは　ぜんぜん　にぎやか　では　ありませんでした。
orパンダは　ぜんぜん　にぎやか　じゃ　ありませんでした。

　パンダは　ぜんぜん　にぎやか The panda wasn't lively at all.

You are now able to complete the grid that you started in J₅.

K₂ Change each of these sentences into the *past* tense.

For example:

カンガルーは　にぎやかじゃ　ないです。

カンガルーは　にぎやかじゃ　なかったです。 The kangaroo was not lively.

1. さるは　ねむくないです。
2. ぶたは　くさくないです。
3. 天気は　あつくないです。
4. かばは　いやじゃないです。
5. らくだは　あぶなくないです。
6. かものはしは　おおくないです。
7. やぎは　ぜんぜん　きれいじゃないです。
8. さいは　ぜんぜん　かわいくないです。

K₃ Put the following sentences into the past tense in a less colloquial way than in K₂

1. こどもの　パーティーは　にぎやかでは　ありません。
2. ぶたは　いやでは　ありません。
3. りこうでは　ありません。
4. 駅は　べんりでは　ありません。
5. ひまでは　ありません。
6. げん気では　ありません。
7. みちは　きれいでは　ありません。
8. あには　なまけものでは　ありません。
9. へんでは　ありません。
10. なっとうが　好きでは　ありません。

A family party

K₄ Answer each of the following questions in the negative. Then be more specific by writing a second sentence using the clues given. Also give the meaning in English of the second sentence.

For example:

かものはしは　みにくいですか。 (not at all)

(a) かものはしは　みにくくないです。

(b) かものはしは　ぜんぜん　みにくくないです。 The platypus is not ugly at all.

1. さるは　ねむいですか。　　　　　　　　　　(not at all)
2. ぶたは　きれいでしたか。　　　　　　　　　(not very)
3. きのうは　さむかったですか。　　　　　　　(not very)
4. せんしゅうは　すずしかったですか。　　　　(not very)
5. さいは　かわいいですか。　　　　　　　　　(not at all)
6. せんしゅう　お母さんは　げん気でしたか。　(not very)
7. おじいさんは　びょう気ですか。　　　　　　(not at all)
8. しゅう学りょ行は　おもしろかったですか。　(yes, very)
9. のうは　つまらなかったですか。　　　　　　(yes, very)
10. あの動物園は　きれいでしたか。　　　　　　(not very)

Put the following sentences into Japanese:

1. That park is not very convenient.
2. The movie was not very interesting.
3. Our school excursion was excellent. It was not boring at all.
4. The pandas were not healthy.
5. The Japanese lessons were not very interesting.
6. The French lessons were not interesting at all.
7. Yesterday was not cold.
8. Last year's summer was not very hot.
9. The house was not very old.
10. The vegetables were not very fresh.

Write a letter in Japanese to your classmates in Australia, telling them about your day at the zoo. Try to:

• Use lots of adjectives and adjectival nouns.
• Use a variety of sentence patterns.
• Use katakana and kanji where appropriate.
• Set out your letter correctly, with date and signature in the usual places.

M Did you know that even the animals in Japan don't speak like those in English-speaking countries?

N When you write a letter to your Japanese friends, never "translate" word-for-word from English to Japanese. Rather, try to think of how to express each idea or sentence or group of sentences in Japanese. Not only do Japanese and English-speaking people speak differently, but in many respects we think about things differently because of the different cultures that have helped make our languages what they are today.

As you put the following letter into Japanese, think of it not as a purely mechanical exercise in translation but as an activity in which you must also be able to transmit the right ideas, showing that you understand how Japanese think and express themselves.

Dear Elizabeth,

How are you? We are all well. The cosmos are blooming. They are beautiful. It is still a little warm here. What is the weather like in Australia?

Yesterday my host mother took me to Ueno Zoo. It was great! I saw lots of animals. The rhinoceros was huge. The little elephant wasn't very clean. His nose is very long. The birds weren't very interesting but the pandas were very cute. We ate lunch at the zoo's restaurant. It wasn't very expensive. One hamburger was ¥300.

The monkeys were noisy. They live in "Monkey Mountain".

Last week I went on a school excursion to Kyoto. It was very enjoyable. I went up Kyoto Tower and I went to the Kinkakuji by bus. The Kinkakuji was beautiful.

I want to go to Tokyo for the winter holidays. I love travelling. On 2 November I am going to Nikko.

Please write soon!

Give my regards to your parents.

Maria

O Andrew received this postcard from his friend Kensuke, who had just been to the Higashiyama Zoo in Nagoya. Read it and answer the questions on page 168.

654－01

神戸市　すま区
ひがし山　しらかわだい
9の6の4
アンドルー・リー　様

名古屋市森山区みなみ山
56の37　　　〒463
田山　けんすけ

アンドルーさんへ
夏休みはたのしいです。おばあさんとおじいさんは元気です。
きのう　ひがし山動物園へ行きました。すてきでした。オーストラリアのコアラとカンガルーを見ました。はじめてでした。かわいいですね。
大きくて黒いゴリラはあまり元気じゃなかったです。しずかでした。でもさるはとてもにぎやかでした。
あぶないへびも見ました。おばあさんはおべんとうをつくってもって行きました。そしてピクニックをしました。たいへんたのしかったです。
九月二十日
さようなら

えい語で　こたえてください。

1. Why do you think Kensuke is in Nagoya?
2. What animals did he see at the zoo and what comments does he make about each one?
3. What did he eat for lunch?
4. Do you think Kensuke has been to Australia? Why do you think this?

P₁

Seeking more information

Sentence Pattern 75

Q. さるは　どんな　食べ物を　食べますか。

What kind of food do monkeys eat?/
What does a monkey feed on?

A. ピーナツを　食べます。

or

A. ピーナツを　食べると　思います。

They eat peanuts.

I think they eat peanuts.

Explanation

どんな is another question word (interrogative) and you can guess because of the な that it can only be used in front of a noun or noun phrase.

どんな is part of a set of similar kinds of words:

  どんな — what kind of

  こんな — this kind of

  そんな — that kind of

In Sentence Pattern 65 you saw how you could give an answer more politely, or express an element of doubt, by using the *plain form of an adjective* + と 思います.

The same can be done with verbs using this pattern:
"plain" or "dictionary" form of verb + と 思います.

Answer each of these questions, using the clues given and following the example below.

Example:

  さるは　どんな　食べ物を　食べますか。　　(Peanuts)

  ピーナツを　食べると思います。

1. わには　どんな　食べ物を　食べますか。　　　(Fish)
2. ねこは　どんな　のみ物を　のみますか。　　　(Milk)
3. かばは　どんな　食べ物を　食べますか。　　　(Food scraps)
4. いぬは　どんな　食べ物を　食べますか。　　　(Meat)
5. さるは　どんな　フルーツを　食べますか。　　(Bananas)
6. ろばは　どんな　食べ物を　食べますか。　　　(Bread)
7. へびは　どんな　のみ物を　のみますか。　　　(Water)
8. ペンギンは　どんな　食べ物を　食べますか。(Fish)
9. コアラは　どんな　食べ物を　食べますか。　(Eucalyptus leaf)
10. ねこは　どんな　食べ物を　食べますか。　　(Mice)

P3 You are applying to become an exchange student in Japan. One of the questions is all about your likes and dislikes. Fill it in, answering each question honestly and in a full sentence.

> 何が　好きですか。
>
> - どんな　食べ物が　好きですか。
>   どんな　食べ物が　きらいですか。
>
> - どんな　のみ物が　好きですか。
>
> - どんな　スポーツが　好きですか。

P4 Put the following sentences into Japanese:

1. I think I'll go back to Japan next year.
2. I think that I'll go to the movies on Sunday.
3. I think I'll do the cleaning.
4. I think snakes eat mice.
5. I think I'll become a teacher of Japanese language.
6. I think I'll play with the dog.
7. I think Mum is going shopping later.
8. I think Dad is working at his company today.
9. I think koalas eat eucalyptus leaves.
10. I think we'll go home soon.

*Students painting during a school
excursion to the zoo*

What do the following sentences mean in English?

1. あしたは　動物園へ　行くと　思います。
2. しんさんは　にいがたに　すんでいると　思います。
3. おじさんと　お父さんは　3時に　目黒駅で　あうと　思います。
4. さるは　バナナを　食べると　思います。
5. すぐ　あさがおは　さくと　思います。
6. 1996年に　日本へ　行くと　思います。
7. あした　せんたくすると　思います。
8. 本を　読むのが　好きだと　思います。
9. この　花は　ゆりと言うと　思います。
10. ゆうれいだと　思います。こわいですよ！

ゆり

Q

Situational dialogue — at the photographers

しゃしんやさん: いらっしゃいませ。

マリア:　　　36まいどりの　カラーフィルムを　1つ　ください。

A roll of colour film of 36 exposures, please.

この　フィルムを　げんぞうしてください。

Could you develop this roll of film, please?

いつ　できますか。or いつ　でき　あがりますか。

When will it be ready?

しゃしんやさん: あしたの　10時で　よろしいですか。

Would 10 o'clock tomorrow be all right?

マリア:　　　はい、いいです。

Yes, that's okay.

What kinds of service does Fuji provide, as advertised on this brochure?

* 当店のカラープリントは、フジカラーサービスの純正仕上げです。

● フジカラーサービス特約

日本最大の総合現像所
株式会社
フジカラーサービス

S With the help of a dictionary, try to work out the meaning of these signs that you would see around a zoo.

The furigana have been given at the bottom to help you.

1,
2,
3.

4. 便所 ▷

5. 大人 ★

6. 小人 ✦

7. 引く

8. 押す

9. 非常口

10. 入場禁止

11. 立入禁止

12.

13. 撮影禁止

14. 禁煙

15. 危険

16. 触れるな

17. 案内所

18. ライオンに注意！

19. ベルを押して下さい。

20. さるに食べさせないで下さい。

1. てあらいじょう
2. だんしよう
3. じょしよう
4. べんじょ
5. おとな
6. こども
7. ひく
8. おす
9. ひじょうぐち
10. にゅうじょうきんし
11. たちいりきんし
12. でぐち
13. さつえいきんし
14. きんえん
15. きけん
16. ふれるな
17. あんないしょ
18. ライオンに　ちゅうい
19. ベルを　おしてください
20. さるに　たべさせないでください

T New words and expressions

Ahiru	あひる	Duck
Anzen	あんぜん	Safe
Benri (na)	べんり（な）	Convenient
Bikkurishimashita	びっくりしました	You surprised me. I am surprised.
Bokujoo	ぼくじょう	Farm (with livestock)
Buta	ぶた	Pig
Chiita	チータ	Cheetah
Chimpanjii	チンパンジー	Chimpanzee
Donna	どんな	What kind of … ?
Doobutsuen	動物園	Zoo
Fuben (na)	ふべん（な）	Inconvenient
Firumu	フィルム	Film
Furamingo	フラミンゴ	Flamingo
Furigana	ふりがな	Hiragana or katakana script attached to Chinese script to show how it's read
Genki (na)	げん気（な）	Well, healthy
Genzoosuru	げんぞうする	To develop (film)
Hana	はな	Nose
Hayai	はやい	Fast (*adjective*)
Hayaku	はやく	Quickly
Hebi	へび	Snake
Hen	へん	Area
Hen (na)	へん（な）	Strange
Hiki	ひき	Counter for small animals
Hima	ひま	(Free) Time
Hiroi	ひろい	Wide
Hitsuji	ひつじ	Sheep
Hiyoko	ひよこ	Chicken
Inko	いんこ	Macaw
Kaba	かば	Hippopotamus
Kamonohashi	かものはし	Platypus
Kamu (kamanai)	かむ（かまない）	To bite (won't bite)
Kangaruu	カンガルー	Kangaroo
Karaa firumu	カラーフィルム	Colour film
Ki o tsukete	きを　つけて	Be careful
Kirei (na)	きれい（な）	Clean, neat, tidy, pretty
Kirin	きりん	Giraffe
Kitanai	きたない	Dirty
Koara	コアラ	Koala
Konna	こんな	This kind of …
Kowai	こわい	Scared, frightened
Kujaku	くじゃく	Peacock
Kusai	くさい	Smelly (awful), stinking

Maidori	まいどり	Exposure
Mezurashii	めずらしい	Rare, uncommon, unusual
Minikui	みにくい	Ugly
Nanika	何か	Something
Nattoo	なっとう	Fermented beans
Nemui	ねむい	Sleepy
Nigiyaka (na)	にぎやか（な）	Lively
Niwatori	にわとり	Fowl, hen
Okkuu (na)	おっくう（な）	Annoying, troublesome
Osoi	おそい	Slow, late
Panda	パンダ	Panda
Pengin	ペンギン	Penguin
Piinatsu	ピーナツ	Peanuts
Raion	ライオン	Lion
Rakuda	らくだ	Camel
Rikoo (na)	りこう（な）	Clever, intelligent
Roba	ろば	Donkey
Sai	さい	Rhinoceros
Saru	さる	Monkey
Saruyama	さるやま	Monkey Mountain
Shashin o toru	しゃしんを　とる	To take a photograph
Shashinyasan	しゃしんやさん	Owner/manager of a camera shop
Shika	しか	Deer
Shimpaishinaidekudasai	しんぱいしないでください	Please don't worry
Shirokuma	白くま	Polar bear
Sonna	そんな	That kind of …
Sore wa yoi kangaedesune	それは　よい　かんがえですね	That's a good idea
Sugoku	すごく	Extremely
Tabemononokuzu	食べ物のくず	Food scraps
Too	とう	Counter for large animals
Tora	とら	Tiger
Tori	とり	Birds
Uma	馬	Horse
Usagi	うさぎ	Rabbit
Ushi	うし	Cow
Wa	わ	Counter for birds
Wani	わに	Alligator
Yagi	やぎ	Goat
Yoi kangae	よいかんがえ	Good idea
Yukai (na)	ゆかい（な）	Delightful
Yuukari	ユーカリ	Eucalyptus tree
Yuukari no ha	ユーカリの　は	Eucalyptus leaves
Yuurei	ゆうれい	Ghost

Kanji studied to the end of Unit 18:

Unit 13:	一	二	三	四	五	六	七	八	九	十	人	何
	1	2	3	4	5	6	7	8	9	10	11	12

Unit 14:	目	口	日	本	母	父	白	赤	黒	色	大	小
	13	14	15	16	17	18	19	20	21	22	23	24

Unit 15:	月	花	木	子	女	好	言	夏	火	秋	春	冬	雨	雲	天
	25	26	27	28	29	30	31	32	33	34	35	36	37	38	39
	気	年													
	40	41													

Unit 16:	上	手	下	語	中	学	校	外	男	生	今	階
	42	43	44	45	46	47	48	49	50	51	52	53

Unit 17:	思	見	聞	行	話	電	買	売	読	入	食
	54	55	56	57	58	59	60	61	62	63	64

Unit 18:	動	物	園	馬	駅	時	青	土	水	金	美
	65	66	67	68	69	70	71	72	73	74	75

Katakana studied to the end of Unit 18:

Unit 14:	ア	ン	ト	ル	ナ	ー	ヒ	ク	オ	レ	シ	リ
	1	2	3	4	5	6	7	8	9	10	11	12

Unit 15:	ハ	イ	マ	テ	ス	ラ	ツ
	13	14	15	16	17	18	19

Unit 16:	コ	ユ	タ	ノ	キ	ニ	カ	フ	ケ	チ	エ	ロ	ミ
	20	21	22	23	24	25	26	27	28	29	30	31	32

Unit 17:	セ	ネ	ウ	ヘ	サ	ホ
	33	34	35	36	37	38

Unit 18:	ヤ	モ	ソ	ヌ	メ	ヨ	ム
	39	40	41	42	43	44	45

Unit 19

Holidays and leisure
休みとレジャー

Topics:
一　Holiday plans
二　Hobbies and interests
三　Catching trains
四　Tourist attractions

A

あとで

* の or ん serves the function of initiating a response by the listener. Although の and ん serve the same purpose it is better to use の with your host family and older people and ん amongst your friends.

B₁ | Making plans

The following sentence pattern is a very useful polite way of telling other people what your plans are or inquiring about their plans.

> ### Sentence Pattern 76
>
> Q. いつ 東京へ 行くよていですか。   When do you plan to go to Tokyo?
>
> A. わたしは 22日に 東京へ   I plan to go to Tokyo on the 22nd.
> 　行くよていです。
>
> **Dictionary form of verb** + よていです = I plan to …

The longer you study Japanese, the more uses you will find for the dictionary form of verbs.

B₂ | Answer each question according to the clue in brackets:

1. 何日に はこねへ 行くよていですか。 (On the 29th)
2. 何時に パーティーは はじまるよていですか。 (At 11.00)
3. 何よう日に あきはばらへ 行くよていですか。 (On Sunday)
4. 何月に オーストラリアへ かえるよていですか。 (In January)
5. 何日に パーティーを ひらくよていですか。 (On the 20th)
6. いつ 動物園へ 行くよていですか。 (On July 25th)
7. いつ ピアノを ひくよていですか。 (Every day before school)
8. 休み中に 何を するよていですか。 (Watch television)
9. 休み中に 何を するよていですか。 (Read many books and magazines)
10. じゅぎょうの あとで 何を するよていですか。 (Go to my guitar lesson)
11. 今しゅうの 日よう日に 何を するよていですか。 (Go shopping in Shinjuku)
12. こどもの 日に 何を するよていですか。 (Visit my grandmother and grandfather)

B₃ | Put these sentences into English:

1. 土よう日に 12時はんまで 学校に いるよていです。
2. 夏休みの 間に 九州を りょ行するよていです。
3. 夏休みの 間に いけばなを ならうよていです。

4. 冬休みの　間に　スキーに　行くよていです。
5. じゅぎょうの　あとで　電車で　びょう気の　おばさんの　家へ　行くよていです。
6. あとで　ともだちに　駅で　あうよていです。
7. そつぎょうごは　大学で　勉強するよていです。
8. あした　おじいさんと　しょうぎを　さすよていです。
9. あした　ともだちの　家を　たずねるよていです。
10. つぎの　たんじょう日に　パーティーを　ひらくよていです。

B₄ Put these sentences into Japanese:

1. I plan to go to Hokkaido next month.
2. What are you planning to do after you graduate?
3. Do you plan to become a teacher?
4. Emiko plans to play tennis with her friends on Sunday.
5. Kensuke plans to come to Australia soon.
6. We are planning to go to the movies on Saturday.
7. I am planning to take my cousins to the zoo on July 15.
8. We are planning to meet at the library after lessons.
9. What are you planning to do tomorrow?
10. We plan to leave at about 6.30.

C　書きましょう・漢字

76.　田　Paddy field

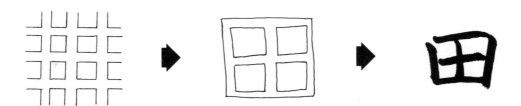

Over time, the very regular *paddy fields* have been reduced to a less detailed grid.

くん　た　おん　でん　いみ　田ぼ paddy field, 田中 Tanaka (a common surname)

かきじゅん　｜　冂　冂　田　田　　　5かく

77. 町　Town

In the early days, *towns* developed around a cluster of paddy fields. A sign was erected near each town to let you know its name.

くん　まち　おん　ちょう　いみ　町(まち)

かきじゅん　｜ 冂 冂 田 田 町 町　　　　　7かく

78. 休　Rest, holiday

Can you see the man with a hat on his head *resting* or taking a break in the shade of a tree? Over time, the character for "man" has moved so that it is now next to the tree rather than under it.

くん　やす(む)　おん　きゅう　いみ　休む(やす) to have a rest or a holiday

かきじゅん　ノ イ 亻 什 休 休　　　　　6かく

79. 車　Car, vehicle, wheel

Early vehicles were hand-drawn carts with two wheels. What remains of this sketch now takes on the meaning of any *vehicle with wheels*.

くん　くるま　おん　しゃ　いみ　車(くるま)、じ動車(どうしゃ) car, じてん車(しゃ) bicycle

かきじゅん　一 厂 冃 戸 自 直 車　　　　　7かく

80.　朝　Morning

Morning comes as the sun rises and the moon starts to disappear.

くん　あさ　おん　ちょう　いみ　朝ごはん、朝、朝食 breakfast

かきじゅん　一 十 十 古 古 古 直 卓 朝 朝 朝 朝　　12かく

81.　家　House

In early times in China, pigs were domesticated animals that lived inside the *house*. (In rural Japan, too, animals occupied the outer areas of a *house*.)

くん　いえ、や　おん　か、け　いみ　家ぞく family, 家

かきじゅん　丶 丶 宀 宀 宀 宇 宇 家 家 家　　10かく

82.　京　Capital, place

A *capital* or large city started with a fortress being built on a high mountain. From this high point, invaders could be easily seen. Gradually more and more people came to live in the area as it offered its citizens protection.

くん　　おん　きょう、けい　いみ　東京 Tokyo, 京都 Kyoto

かきじゅん　丶 亠 宀 古 古 市 京 京　　8かく

83. 東　East

As the sun rises in the east, the ancient Chinese drew a sun rising behind a tree to represent *east*.

くん　ひがし　おん　とう　いみ　東京 とうきょう Tokyo

かきじゅん　一 厂 厂 戸 甶 申 東 東

8かく

84. 都　Capital, big city

The concept of a *capital* or *big city* has three elements:
(a)　Wise men, represented by an old man with a walking stick

(b)　Many people, represented by two mouths

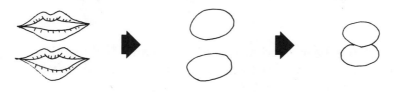

(c)　These people all hold various ranks or positions, as shown by β, the first part of the kanji for "floors". This radical also has a very abstract meaning of "fortification" or "protection", which perhaps came from a sketch of a lookout from where a sentry could watch over the city.

くん　みやこ　おん　と、つ　いみ　京都 きょうと Kyoto

かきじゅん　一 十 土 耂 耂 者 者 者 者゛者 都

11かく

85. 来 Come

The *coming* of each of the seasons represents something significant to the farmer. The rain, for example, affects the rice crop, and life in a country like Japan depends on rice. A sketch of a rice plant ready for harvesting represents the abstract idea of *coming*.

くん　く(る)、きた(る)　おん　らい　いみ　来る(く) come, 来年(らいねん) next year

かきじゅん 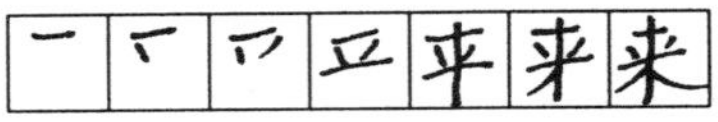 7かく

86. 勉 Endeavour

The first radical shows a rabbit, its burrow and its legs. This represents the belief that through study or one's *endeavours* one's life is "saved" or made "worthwhile". (The rabbit saves its life in times of danger by running on fast legs into its burrow.)

The radical 力 has been used already in the kanji 動 (meaning "move"). As shown in the illustration, it comes from a sketch of the muscles of the arm. Study, too, requires physical energy.

くん　おん　べん　いみ　勉強(べんきょう) study

かきじゅん 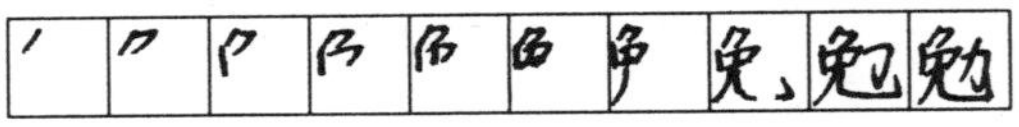 10かく

87. 強 Strong

The first radical is an archer's or warrior's bow— an essential quality of which would be *strength*.

The second radical was derived from a sketch of an insect. One can think of a mosquito that starts buzzing and just won't go away. It's persistent!

The belief expressed in these two radicals is that strength involves not just physical strength but mental strength or persistence — the ability to not give up! The kanji 強 when added to

勉 gives a powerful meaning to the word "study". (It is life-saving, involves mental and physical strength and must be undertaken with persistence!)

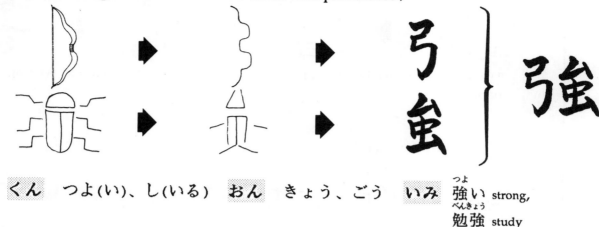

くん	つよ(い)、し(いる)	おん	きょう、ごう	いみ	強い strong,
					勉強 study

かきじゅん

11かく

88. 山 Mountain

It is easy to see how the kanji for *mountain* has evolved.

くん	やま	おん	さん	いみ	山、富士山 Mt Fuji

かきじゅん | 丨 | 凵 | 山 |

3かく

89. 間 Period of time, interval

A *period of time* is measured by noting the position of the sun as it rises higher between the screen doors or gates.

くん	あいだ、ま	おん	かん、けん	いみ	間 during, 時間 hour, time

かきじゅん | 丨 | 冂 | 冂 | 門 | 門 | 門 | 門 | 門 | 閂 | 問 | 間 |

12かく

90. 書 Write

The kanji for *write* is represented by a hand holding a brush and writing on a piece of paper.

くん　か(く)　おん　しょ　いみ　書く

かきじゅん　| フ フ ヨ ヨ ⺺ 聿 事 書 書 書 |　　　　　10かく

D₁ ## Why? Because ...

The following patterns show how to express the reason for doing something. In each case から ("because") is added to the plain form of a noun, adjective or verb. (Sentence 1 below is similar to Sentence Pattern 6.)

Sentence Pattern 77a

1. 休みだから　学校に　行きません。　　　I'm not going to school because it's a holiday.
2. しずかだから　すこし　勉強します。　　　I'll do a bit of study because it's quiet.
3. しずかだったから　すこし　勉強しました。　Because it *was* quiet, I did a bit of study.

Noun or
Adjectival noun + { だから = Because it is
　　　　　　　　　　だったから = Because it was ... }

Sentence Pattern 77b

True adjectives

1. いそがしいから　えみこさんと　　　I won't go with Emiko because I'm busy.
   行きません。

2. いそがしかったから　えみこさんと　　Because I was busy, I didn't go with Emiko.
   行きませんでした。

Plain form of the adjective + { い
　　　　　　　　　　　　　　かった } + から { = Because it is/was ...
　　　　　　　　　　　　　　　　　　　　　　 = Because I am/was ... }

Sentence Pattern 77c

Verbs

1. 来年 日本へ 行くから
   日本語を 勉強しています。

   I am learning Japanese because I am going to Japan next year.

   or

   Because I am going to Japan next year, I am learning Japanese.

2. きのう 行ったから 今日
   行きません。

   I'm not going today because I went yesterday.

Dictionary form or plain past of verbs + から = Because I ...

Explanation

To make the plain past of a verb, simply change the て or で in the て-form to た or だ. Example:

$$みる → みて → みた$$

$$よむ → よんで → よんだ$$

$$かう → かって → かった$$

The plain form at the end of a sentence is not as polite as the more formal ending, but in the middle of a sentence it is usually the only form that can be used.

What does each of the following sentences mean in English?

1. 休みだから おじいさんの家を たずねます。

2. 休みだから おばあさんの家を たずねるよていです。

3. ふくざつだから わかりません。

4. しずかだから しゅくだいを したいです。

5. その みせが べんりだから そこへ よく 行きます。

6. えいがが すてき だったと 思ったから また 見たいです。

7. ゆき子さんは 十六さいだったから さけを のみませんでした。

8. かしはらさんは せんせいだったから こどもが よく わかりました。

9. わたしは いそがしいから タクシーで 行きます。

10. この　ネクタイは　たかいから　買いません。

11. おばあさんの　にもつは　おもいから　おじいさんが　もって行きます。

12. 車は　あたらしいから　とても　きれいです。

13. りょ行を　するのは　たのしいから　まい年　かぞくと　りょ行します。

14. たのしかったから　また　行きました。

15. いぬは　きたなかったから　あらいました。

16. らい年　日本へ　行くから　まい日　日本語を　れんしゅうします。

17. わたしは　ともだちと　えいがを　見に　行くから　ピクニックに
　　かぞくと　行きません。

18. 本を　よんでいるから　でたくないです。

19. 雨が　ふっていたから　およぎに　行きませんでした。

20. 今日　馬に　のっていたから　今　つかれています。

D₃ Put each of these sentences into Japanese:

1. Yukiko Yamada didn't go to school yesterday because she was sick.

2. Because I plan to go to Kyoto with you next week, I won't go with you today.

3. Let's go to the beach because it's hot.

4. Because I took the train, I arrived at 9.05.

5. Because the weather was great, we went on a picnic.

6. Because it's raining, may I go to a movie?

7. I practise the guitar every day because I love playing it.

8. Because the hippopotamus eats a lot, it is very fat.

9. I go to cram school because I want to go to university.

10. Because my brothers and sisters have gone out, the house is quiet.

D₄ Finish off each of the following clauses with a principal clause or the main part of the sentence:

1. いそがしかったから ....。

2. 馬に　のるのが　好きだから ....。

3. あしたは　えいがを　見に　行くから ....。

4. おばあさんが　東京に　すんでいたから ....。

5. わたしは　かいしゃに　入るよていだから......................。

6. りょうりするのが　好きだから ....。

7. 雨が ふっていたから .... 。

8. 勉強したかったから .... 。

9. たかかったから .... 。

10. さむいから .... 。

E₁ Once you've decided on what you are doing, you will need to work out with your friends when you'll meet.

> ### Sentence Pattern 78
>
> - 何時ごろ でますか。   At about what time will we leave?
> - 六時ごろ でましょうか。   Shall we leave at about 6.00?

Just as に is a particle that indicates the *exact* time when something is to happen, ごろ indicates an *approximate* time.

Look at some more examples of how this pattern can be used:

- いま 二時ごろです。   It's about 2 o'clock.

- 今年の 冬ごろから びょうきです。   She has been sick since about winter this year.

- 九時ごろまで ねていました。   I was asleep until about 9.00.

- Q. いつごろ かん国へ 行きますか。   Roughly when are you going to Korea?

- A. 来年の 七月ごろ 行きます。   I'm going there around July of next year.

As you can see, the use of ごろ does not restrict the speaker to the exact minute when an action will occur.

E₂ Your hosts plan to take you on a two-week tour around Honshu. The dates are all a little unclear as your host father is not sure when he'll get off work. Nevertheless, the other family members want to know as much as possible about the trip.

Fill in the dialogue on page 188 according to the clues given. (A photo of the temple referred to is on page 189.)

お母さん: よく　かぞくと　いっしょに　りょ行しませんね。

お父さん: .... (No, we don't, do we.)

じゃ、今年、いっしょに　ほんしゅうの　大きい町を　見ぶつ_{けん}
しましょう。

のぶお: .... (About when will we go/When do you
reckon we'll go?)

お父さん: .... (We'll leave on about the 24th of July.)

あい子: 夏休みですね。 .... (About when will we return?)

お父さん: .... (About the 8th of August.)

のぶお: 奈_な良_らも　見ぶつに　行きますか。

お父さん: はい、とうだいじを　見ぶつに　行きましょうか。

あい子: ええ、とうだいじは　せかいで　一ばん大きい木の　たて物で
すね。

お母さん: ええ、そうです。 .... (About when will we arrive in Nara?)

お父さん: .... (We will arrive on about the 27th.)

のぶお: .... (Will we go to Kyoto too?)

お父さん: .... (Yes, I plan to see Kyoto. I love old places, don't you?)

Todaiji Temple, Nara

E₃ Answer each of the following questions, giving the approximate answer as shown in the example.

Example:

いつ　はくぶつかんに　行くよていですか。(At about 2.30)

二時はんごろ　はくぶつかんに　行くよていです。

1. いつ　さくらの　花が　さきますか。　(In about March)
2. ふつうは　何時ごろ　朝ごはんを　食べますか。(At about 6.45)
3. 何時ごろ　でるよていですか。　(At about 11.30)
4. まい日、いつ　おきますか。　(About 6.00)
5. いつ　ながさきへ　行くよていですか。　(On about the 9th of August)
6. いつごろ　日本人の　ともだちは　つきますか。(On about 10 May)
7. いつごろ　パーティーを　ひらきますか。(About Friday)
8. いつごろから　びょう気ですか。(Since about winter of last year)
9. 日本で　いつ　雨が　よく　ふりますか。(From about June)
10. いつまで　コスモスが　さいていますか。(Until about October)

Leisure-time quiz

How well do you know Japan? On a copy of this puzzle that your teacher gives you, draw a straight line through words matching the clues. Six letters will be left over in the order that they appear in the missing word. What is the word, and where in Japan is it? (There are no diagonal words, but some words are written backwards.)

ら											
く		だ	い	ぶ	つ					や	
ま		く	■	よ	り					ご	
か	ま	く	ら	う	ゆ	■	に		は	な	み
ろ	し	き	く	ゅ	き	ふ	じ	ゅ	く	る	
ば	ろ	よ	だ	き	■	こ	ょ	■	ぶ	ん	き
と	ひ	が	し	や	ま	ど	う	ぶ	つ	え	ん
は	な	な	ん	■	い	も	■	み	か	■	か
り	つ	り	じ	あ	■	し	ぞ	え	ん	そ	く
そ	や	き	ゅ	う	し	ゅ	う	ず	で	う	じ
う	す	た	く	■	な	じ	■	め	い	じ	る
じ	み	き	う	え	の	ん	せ	■	え	す	さ
す	け	ゅ	と	■	が	ち	と	お	■	る	
る	ん	う	う	か	わ	し	な	ば	い		
	ぶ	し	き	わ		い	ら	と			
	つ	ゅ	ょ	い		か	ん	こ	う	り	ょ	こ	う
		う	う	い		い					

(2) indicates that this word is found twice in the puzzle.

1. Once a capital of Japan, 40 km SW of Tokyo. (2)
2. Live in zoos.
3. House.
4. To meet.
5. Japan's largest river.
6. Where one of Tokyo's famous zoos is located.
7. From (in a letter).
8. Snow.
9. You can help out at home during the holidays by doing a lot more of this. (2)
10. Sightseeing tour.
11. Cousin.
12. My aunt.
13. Museum.
14. Flower viewing.
15. Kyushu. (2)
16. Large zoo in Nagoya.
17. Cute.
18. Excursion.
19. Seven. (2)
20. Inland sea.
21. Summer holidays.
22. Elephant.
23. Donkey. (2)
24. Has a hump on its back and is found in a zoo. (2)
25. Fishing. (3)
26. Now.
27. Children.
28. Home of Nagoya Castle.
29. Japan's capital city.
30. Monkey.
31. Husband.
32. To come.
33. Person.
34. Large city on Kyushu.
35. Sightseeing.
36. Flower.
37. One of Tokyo's most important shrines.
38. Big Buddha.
39. Golden Pavilion.
40. You might want to play this sport during the holidays. (2)
41. Tokyo's suburb of tall buildings.
42. Japan's highest mountain.
43. You don't want to go here in the holidays, or would you? (2)
44. Nightingale Castle in Kyoto.
45. City in southern Honshu destroyed by atomic bomb.
46. Currency. (2)

G You received this postcard from your Japanese penpal. (a) What plans will/could you put into action because of this information? (b) Write a short postcard to her in reply.

エリザベスさんへ

わたしは 一人で りょ行するから ちょっと こわいです。わたしの よていを せつめいし す。ジャル771で シドニーの くうこうに 06.45 ごろ つきます。その あとで 08.30ごろ、ブリ スベンまで TN41で 行きます。09.30ごろ ブリ スベンの くうこうに つきます。エリザベス さんに あうのを たのしみに しています。

ゆり子より

H₁ 書きましょう・カタカナ

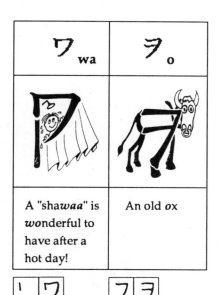

ワ wa	ヲ o
A "sha*waa*" is *wo*nderful to have after a hot day!	An old *ox*
イ ワ	フ ヲ

Can you work out what these telegrams mean?

1. オタンジョウビオメデトウゴザイマス

2. ゴケッコンヲココロカラオイワイモウ シアゲマス

3. ハハノヒオメデトウ、オカアサンホン トウニアリガトウ

4. ツツシンデシンネンヲオイワイモウシ アゲマス

[けっこん = marriage]
[つつしんで = respectfully, humbly]
[おいわいもうしあげる = (lit.) To express congratulations]

H₂ Can you work out how best to put each of the following words into katakana?

1. World series
2. Waffle
3. Wide screen
4. Wax
5. Waltz
6. London
7. Roller skates
8. Yo-yo
9. Monorail
10. Wrestling
11. Europe
12. Motor boat
13. New York
14. Helicopter
15. Bowling

Can you work out what the following words are? Put each of them into a sentence.

1. ロッカー
2. ロケット
3. 東京タワー
4. ロッククライミング
5. ロックンロール
6. ロープウェイ
7. ヨット
8. ユースホステル
9. ゼロ
10. スキージャンプ

Tokyo Tower, Tokyo

What do the following sentences mean in English?

1. 朝　九時ごろ　朝ごはんを　食べます。
2. 十時から　三時ごろまで　本を　読んでいました。
3. 本を　読むのが　好きです。
4. ホンコンへ　買い物に　行きました。
5. その男の人は　車を　売ります。
6. ゆうべは　九時ごろ　ねました。
7. 今日は　朝から　ゆうがたまで　日本語を　勉強していました。
8. ゆうがた　ふつうは　本と　ざっしを　読みます。
9. 日本で　大きい町が　たくさん　あります。
10. 休み中に　何を　するよていですか。
11. 京都の　駅は　いつも　こんでいますね。
12. 東京は　日本の　一ばん　大せつな　としです。
13. この　きれいな　町は　たか山と　言います。
14. 山田さんは　あの　ふるい　家に　すんでいました。

Did you notice when to use particles with 朝, ゆうがた and ゆうべ?

Using as many as possible of the 90 kanji that you know, write a short story about your holiday, basing it on the illustrations below. You may present your story as a diary entry, letter or report.

K ## Situational dialogue — buying tickets and catching trains

A necessary part of any trip to Japan is travelling by train. This section will take you through the steps necessary to get yourself safely on and off this very efficient means of public transport.

Step 1a

To buy a ticket at a vending machine to catch a local train, work out the price. A sign like this will be displayed in the station so that you can work the cost out.

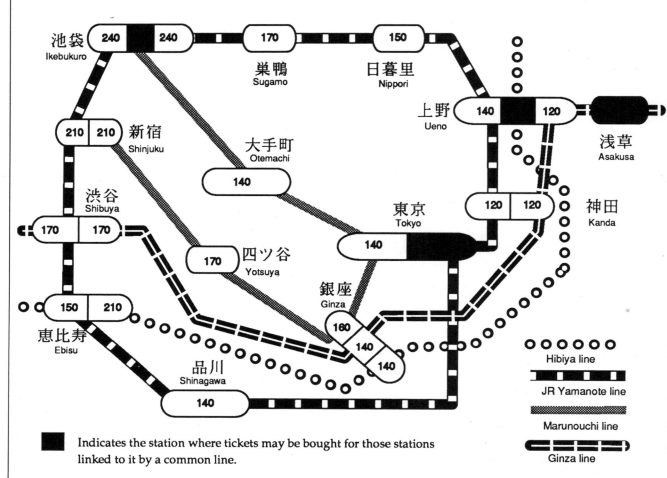

■ Indicates the station where tickets may be bought for those stations linked to it by a common line.

Can you see that it costs ¥140 to travel from Asakusa to the Ginza?

Step 1b

To catch a long-distance train, or to buy a ticket at a manned ticket office, you will need to know how to say the following:

You: なごや行きの　きっぷを　一まい　おねがいします。

One ticket to Nagoya, please.

Ticket seller: 一とうですか　二とうですか。

First or second class?

You: 二とうです。

Second class.

Ticket seller:	片道ですか　往復ですか。
	Single or return (one-way or round-trip)?
You:	片道です。いくらですか。
	Single. How much is it?
Ticket seller:	一まん　三ぜんえんです。
	¥13,000.
You:	なごや行きの　電車は　何ばんせんから　でますか。
	From what track does the train to Nagoya leave?
Ticket seller:	十八ばんせんから　でます。
	It leaves from Track 18.

かたみち (片道)
おうふく (往復)

Step 1c

If you will be using JR trains often (particularly over long distances), you can save both time and money by purchasing a JR rail pass. This can only be obtained by paying for it at a travel agency outside Japan. You will be given a coupon which, once you get to Japan, you exchange for the actual pass at a JR office.

For the price of a rail pass you can travel on any JR train, bus or ferry for a week, two weeks or three weeks, depending on the type of pass. You don't have to worry about buying tickets any more — you can just concentrate on getting on the right train!

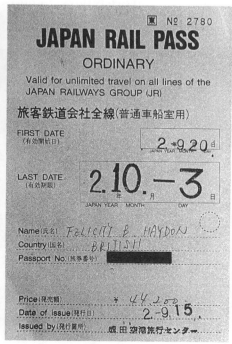

You could exchange your coupon at Narita airport while you are there, so be prepared for the following conversation:

You:	この　JRパス　おねがいします。
	Could I have a JR pass, please.
JR ticket seller:	はい、パスポートを　見せてください。
	Yes, please show me your passport.
	何日から　つかいますか。
	From what date will you use it?
You:	九月の　十六日、月よう日から　おねがいします。
	From Monday the 16th of September.
JR ticket seller:	二しゅう間の　パスですね。
	It's a two-week pass, isn't it?
You:	はい。
	Yes.

Step 2

If you buy your ticket at the vending machine, press the appropriate button — depending on the cost, and whether you are buying a child's ticket or an adult's ticket.

You will receive your change automatically.

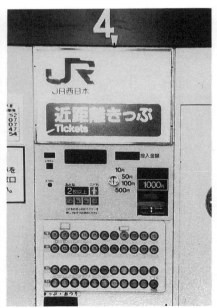

Step 3

Proceed through the ticket wicket (改札口 ^{かいさつぐち}). Either give your ticket to the ticket collector, who will cut it and give it back, or put it in the slot in the automatic gates. If the station you are boarding has automatic gates (as in Kobe) it will soon tell you if you've done something wrong — a buzzer will sound and the gate will lock!

Step 4

Make sure you are on the right platform (ホーム). The tracks are numbered 1番線 ^{ばんせん} (Track No. 1) and so on.

The direction of trains is shown by the station name + 行き ^ゆ (広島行き ^{ひろしまゆ} — Hiroshima-bound) or the station name + 方面 ^{ほうめん} (広島方面 — in the direction of Hiroshima).

It's always much quicker to check the platform with someone than to take the wrong train:

You: すみませんが　大阪 ^{おおさか}行きの　電車は　ここから　でますか。

Excuse me, but does the train for Osaka leave from here?

Japanese person: ええと、そう　思いません。二十ばんせんから　でると　思います。あそこです。

Um, I don't think so. I think it leaves from Track 20. It's over there.

Step 5

Wait for your train on the right or left side of where the train doors will open. Only when everyone has got off should you board.

Step 6

If you are not absolutely sure that you are on the right train, check. Ask someone:

すみませんが　この　電車は　ぎんざ行きですか。

Excuse me, but is this train going to the Ginza? (Is this train Ginza-bound?)

Once you've heard 「はい、そうです。」 you can relax.

Step 7

If you have not reserved a seat, then you will need to sit in one of the carriages displaying this sign:

自由席 means "Unrestricted seating" or "You may sit anywhere".

Signs on the outside of each carriage will tell you whether it is a smoking carriage or not, and whether seating is unrestricted or not.

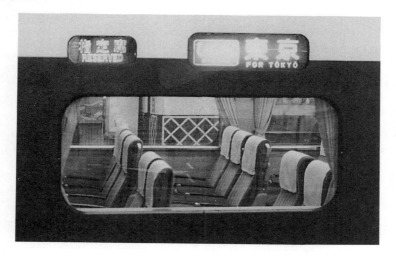

Step 8

Each station is announced through the loudspeaker in the train:

つぎは　ぎんざでございます。

The next (station) is the Ginza.

You will need to hand in your ticket at the ticket wicket or feed it into the automatic gates.

Step 9

You may have to change trains to get to your destination:

You:　　　　　　この　電車は　高山（たかやま）まで　ちょくつうですか。

Is this train direct to Takayama?

Ticket seller:　　なごやで　のりかえてください。

Change (trains) at Nagoya.

By learning these dialogues, you can ensure that you get on the right train and that you get off at the right town.

Length of time

When explaining how long something took to do or how many weeks something will take, or when stating any period or length of time (for example, "a two-week rail pass"), the following patterns are used:

Sentence Pattern 79a

Q. 二しゅう間の　パスですか。　　Is it a two-week pass?/Do you want a two-week pass?

A. いいえ、三しゅう間の　パスです。　　No, a three-week pass.

	なんねんかん **何年間** How many years?	なん　　　　かん **何しゅう間** How many weeks?	なん　じ　かん **何時間** How many hours?	なん **何ぷん** How many minutes?
½	はん年 とし			
1	一年間 ねんかん	一しゅう間	一時間	一ぷん(いっぷん)
1½	一年間はん	一しゅう間はん	一時間はん	
2	二年間	二しゅう間	二時間	二ふん(にふん)
3	三年間	三しゅう間	三時間	三ぷん(さんぷん)
4	四年間	四しゅう間	四時間	四ぷん(よんぷん)
5	五年間	五しゅう間	五時間	五ふん(ごふん)
6	六年間	六しゅう間	六時間	六ぷん(ろっぷん)
7	七年間	七しゅう間	七時間	七ふん(ななふん)
8	八年間	八しゅう間	八時間	八ぷん(はっぷん)
9	九年間	九しゅう間	九時間	九ふん(きゅうふん)
10	十年間	十しゅう間	十時間	十ぷん(じゅっぷん)
11	十一年間	十一しゅう間	十一時間	十一ぷん(じゅういっぷん)
12	十二年間	十二しゅう間	十二時間	十二ふん(じゅうにふん)

Sentence Pattern 79b

Q. どのぐらい　かかりますか。　　Approximately how long will it take?

A. 六しゅう間ぐらい　かかります。　　It will take approximately six weeks.

L₂ Answer these questions according to the clues given:

1. ブリスベンから シドニーまで 車で どのぐらい かかりますか。(14 hours)
2. シドニーから 東京まで どのぐらい かかりますか。(9 hours)
3. うえの駅から あさくさ駅まで どのぐらい かかりますか。(3 minutes)
4. うえのから えびすまで 何ぷんぐらい かかりますか。(12 minutes)
5. 中学校は 日本で 何年間 ですか。(3 years)
6. オーストラリアの 学校で クリスマス休みは 何しゅう間ですか。(6 weeks)
7. オーストラリアの 学校で 冬休みは 何しゅう間ですか。(2 weeks)
8. オーストラリアで どのぐらい 学校に 行きますか。(12 years)
9. まい日、何時間 学校に いますか。(6 hours)
10. メルボルンから パースまで ひ行きで どのぐらい かかりますか。

(3½ hours)

L₃ Answer these questions according to the clues given:

1. 東京から 横浜（よこはま）まで どのぐらい かかりますか。 (26 minutes)
2. 京都から 奈良（なら）まで どのぐらい かかりますか。 (about 1 hour)
3. 東京から 名古屋（なごや）まで ひかりで どのぐらい ですか。 (52 minutes)
4. 東京から 名古屋（なごや）まで こだまで どのぐらい ですか。 (3 hours)
5. 九州への かんこうりょ行は 何しゅう（しゅう）間ですか。 (2 weeks)
6. JRパスは 何しゅう間ですか。 (1 week)
7. どのぐらい 日本に いますか。 (1 year)
8. どのぐらい 日本語を 勉強していますか。 (3 years)
9. なら駅から とう大（だい）じまで あるいて 何ぷんぐらい かかりますか。

(25 minutes)

10. からての じゅぎょうは 何時間ですか。 (1½ hours)

L₄ 聞きましょう

How long does it take to travel between each of the places listed below? Listen to the statements made by your teacher concerning the two places. Also record the means of transport used.

1. Narita airport and Tokyo station
2. Kyoto and Himeji
3. Kobe and Hiroshima
4. Tokyo station and Disneyland (Maihama station)
5. Nagoya and Takayama
6. Osaka and Kobe

M | 聞きましょう

Listen to Maria as she tells you about her holiday plans. Then answer the following questions:

1. What holidays are coming up for Maria? When are they exactly?
2. How long are they?
3. Where is she going?
4. For how long?
5. Why do you think she's going there?
6. What is she planning to do in Beppu?
7. What details does she know about her Nagasaki stay?
8. How long does it take from Nagasaki to Tokyo? Does this pose a problem for her? Explain in detail.

N₁ | Hobbies ...しゅみ

In any exchange of information about yourself with new acquaintances, the discussion of your interests and hobbies would be natural. The next two patterns provide a useful start to your discussion. (ん is used again in Sentence Pattern 80(b) to indicate that the speakers are explaining or asking for an explanation of some information that is of interest to them both.)

Sentence Pattern 80

(a) 日本の　ぶんかに　きょうみが　あります。	I am interested in Japanese culture.
(b) **Q.** なぜ　日本に　来たかったんですか。	Why did you want to come to Japan?
A. 日本の　ぶんかに　きょうみが　あるんです。	Because I am interested in Japanese culture.
(c) 日本の　ぶんかに　きょうみを　もっています。	I have an interest/am interested in Japanese culture.

Sentence Pattern 81

Q. あなたの　しゅみは　何ですか。	What are your hobbies?
A. しゅみは　きってを　あつめることです。	My hobby is stamp collecting.
or more formally:	
しゅみは　きってしゅうしゅうです。	
A. わたしの　しゅみは　レコードを　聞くことです。	My hobby is listening to records.

What hobbies do these people enjoy?

1. サーフィンを　すること

2. りょうりを　すること

3. ひ行きの　モデルを　つくること

4. じょうばを　すること

5. おしゃべりを　すること

6. ぬいものを　すること

7. ローラスケートを　すること

8. スケートボードで　あそぶこと

9. てがみを　書くこと

10. おんがくを　聞くこと

11. きってを　あつめること
　　（きってしゅうしゅう）

12. サインを　あつめること
　　（サインしゅうしゅう）

13. コインを　あつめること
（コインしゅうしゅう）

14. にんぎょうを　あつめること
（にんぎょうしゅうしゅう）

15. はがきを　あつめること
（はがきのしゅうしゅう）

N₃ What do the following sentences mean in English?

1. ヨーロッパの　れきしに　きょうみを　もっています。

2. しゅみは　スプーンしゅうしゅうです。

3. あねは　こけしを　あつめます。

4. ぼくの　しゅみは　はがきを　あつめることです。

5. わたしの　しゅみは　てがみを　書くことです。

6. あにの　しゅみは　ラジオを　聞くことです。

7. おじさんの　しゅみは　りょ行することです。

8. 日本の　ぶんかに　きょうみを　もっています。

9. おばあさんの　しゅみは　おしゃべりです。

10. わたしの　しゅみは　スケート　ボードで　あそぶことです。

N₄ Answer these questions according to the information given in brackets. (Note how ん is used to encourage a response.)

1. なぜ　日本へ　行きたいんですか。 (Because I'm interested in Japanese culture.)

2. なぜ　この　本を　買いたいんですか。 (Because I'm interested in Japanese history.)

3. アメリカの　れきしに　きょうみを
もっていますか。 (No. But I am interested in European history.)

4. あなたの　しゅみは　何ですか。 (Collecting coins)

5. あなたの　しゅみは　何ですか。 (Surfboard riding)

6. にんぎょうを　たくさん　買い
ましたね。 (Yes, my hobby is doll collecting.)

7. そつぎょうごは　大学で　勉強する
よていですか。 (I don't know yet, but I am interested in law.)

8. あなたの　しゅみは　にんぎょう
しゅうしゅうですか。 (No, it's collecting kokeshi.)

9. しゅみは　何ですか。 (Sewing)

10. 何に　きょうみを　もっていますか。 (Japanese cooking)

N₅ If your Japanese friend asked you one of the following questions, how would you answer? Elaborate on *one* of the answers, giving as much detail as possible about your interest or hobby.

1. あなたの　しゅみは　何ですか。

2. 何に　きょうみを　もっていますか。

O₁ **Only ...**

When talking about your recreation or leisure time, you may find this easy pattern useful.

Sentence Pattern 82

* 浅草（あさくさ）から　上野（うえの）まで　5ふんしか
かかりません。 It takes only five minutes from Asakusa to Ueno.

* 奈良（なら）へ　しか　行きませんでした。 I only went to Nara. (I went to nowhere else but Nara.)

* えいがには　日（にち）よう日（び）に　しか
行きません。 I only go to the movies on Sunday.

---

*Note: しか is only used with the negative ending of the verb.

O₂ Put these sentences into English:

1. あしたは　秋葉原（あきはばら）へ　しか　行きません。

2. お母さんは　水よう日と　日よう日に　しか　そうじしません。

3. わたしは　三しゅう間　日本に　いましたが　東京に　しか　いません
でした。

4. 京都に　一しゅう間　しか　いませんでしたが　ふるいところを　たくさん
見ました。

5. 休み中は　いい本を　読むこと　しか　しません。

O₃ **Some particles ... more meanings**

Just as the particle が was used to indicate the object in the sentence "Can you ski?" (スキーが
できますか。), so too is が used with other verbs in the "potential" or "ability" form.

Sentence Pattern 83

(a) ときどき　東京タワーから
　　ふじさんが　見えます。

Sometimes you can see Mt Fuji from Tokyo Tower.

(b) いぬの　なきごえが　聞こえ
　　ますか。

Can you hear the dog?

O4 The particle で, while still retaining the basic meaning "by means of", has other uses that make it a very useful particle to know well.

Sentence Pattern 84

(a) おはしで　すしを　食べました。

I ate with/by means of chopsticks.

(b) 天気よほうを　テレビで　見ました。

I saw the weather report on/by means of TV.

(c) この　たて物は　てつで　でき
　　ています。

This building is made of steel.

O5 Rewrite the following sentences, completing them with the word(s) or phrase given in brackets. Remember to put the verb in the negative form when using しか.

1. さるは　バナナ...............食べます。 (Only)

2. たけしくんは　ピザを　ナイフと　フォーク...................食べました。 (With)

3. その　テーブルは................できています。 (Made from wood)

4. 日本から　オーストラリアまで......................かかります。 (Only 8½ hours)

5. その　えいがは...................見ました。 (On television)

6. ここから　おんがく.................................。 (Can't hear)

7. まどは............................できていました。 (From glass)

8. ニュースは...........................聞きました。 (On the radio)

9. アンドルーさんは........................勉強しています。 (Only Japanese)

10. 日本では　スパゲッティを.........................食べますか。 (With a spoon)

P 聞きましょう

Give as many details as you can about Andrew and Maria's hobbies or interests.

★ Always listen with 100% concentration. Make sure you've got everything ready: exercise book open, pen in working order, and so on.
Although you may hear your teacher or a tape two or three times, in real life you'll usually only have one chance to hear something.

Q

Andrew was keen to find out some facts about a few places. Read the articles he found about Tokyo Tower and Mt Fuji, and make a summary in English of each. Can you work out the meaning of the asterisked words?

東京タワー
東京タワーは 1958年に 東京の しばこう園に
できました。タワーは 大へんゆうめいだから
日本人でも 外人でも、みんな タワーに
のぼります。333メートルです。エレベーターで
タワーの 上まで* のぼります。きっぷは
¥500です。エレベーターで 一ぷんしか かかり
ません。タワーの 上から にぎやかな東京の
町が よく 見えます。天気が いい日に
ふじ山も 見えます。

ふじ山は 日本で 一ばんたかい山です。
それに 一ばんうつくしい山です。この
山の たかさは 三千七百七十六メートル
です。ふじ山の みね*には たいてい
一年中 ゆきが あります。はれた日には
東京からでも ふじ山が 見えます。
ふじ山は 「日本の シンボル」と
言われています。*

R₁ 新しいことば

After you have had a busy day, invariably you (or someone else) will comment on how tired you are.

For example:

| You: | ただいま。 | I'm home. |
| Mother: | おかえりなさい。 | You're back. |

	つかれたでしょう！	You must be tired.
or	おつかれですか。	Are you tired?
You:	はい、すこし　だけ。	Yes, I am a little.
or	いいえ、そんなに。	No, not really.
or	はい、つかれた（です）。	Yes, I'm exhausted.
or	はい、つかれました。	Yes, I'm tired.

Other polite forms of つかれたでしょう are frequently heard. A wife may say to her husband who has just got home from work:「おつかれさま」.

At their destinations, train passengers are told:「おつかれさまでした。」

R₂

Appreciating that you've had an exhausting day and that there's nothing better than a nice hot bath to rejuvenate the body, your host may ask you if you'd like to have a bath:

Host: 今、おふろに　入りたいですか。
Would you like to have a bath now?

You: はい、おさきに、しつれいします。
Yes, excuse me for going first (for having my bath before you).

When you get out of the bath, remember to thank your host:

You: とても　いいゆかげんでした。
The water (temperature) was just right.

S

New words and expressions

Asa	朝	Morning
Atsumeru	あつめる	To gather, collect
Bunka	ぶんか	Culture
Chokutsuu (densha)	ちょくつう（電車）	Direct (train)
Degozaimasu	でございます	Humble form of です
Dekimashita	できました	Was built
Dekiteiru	できている	To be made of
Densha ni noru	電車に　のる	To ride on a train
Donogurai	どのぐらい	About how long?
Eeto	ええと	Um, let me see
Fooku	フォーク	Fork
Ginzasen	ぎんざせん	Ginza line
Goro	ごろ	About (a specific time)
Garasu	ガラス	Glass
Hagakishuushuu	はがきしゅうしゅう	Postcard collecting
Han	はん	Half
Hantoshi	はん年	Six months (half a year)
Hibiya	ひびや（日比谷）	Suburb of Tokyo

Hikari	ひかり	The bullet train that is faster than the Kodama because it stops at fewer stations
Honkon	ホンコン	Hong Kong
… hoomen	方面	… in the direction of
Hoomu	ホーム	Platform
Hooritsu	ほうりつ	Law
Ichiman	一まん	Ten thousand
Ichinenjuu	一年中	Throughout the year
Ie	家	House
Itsugoro	いつごろ	About when?
Ittoo	一とう	First class
Jiyuuseki	じゆうせき（自由席）	Unrestricted seating
Jooba o suru	じょう馬を　する	To ride a horse
Kaisatsuguchi	かいさつぐち（改札口）	Ticket wicket (the place where you show your ticket to the ticket collector)
Kakaru	かかる	To take (a length of time)
Kankoku	かん国	Republic of Korea
Kankooryokoo (suru)	かんこうりょ行（する）	(To go on a) Sightseeing tour
Kankoosuru	かんこうする	To go sightseeing
Katamichi	かたみち	One way, single
Kembutsuni iku	見ぶつに　行く	To go sightseeing (in)
Kembutsusuru	見ぶつする	To sightsee/see the sights
Kikoeru	聞こえる	To be able to hear, can hear
Ki no	木の	Wooden
Kippu	きっぷ	Ticket
Kitteshuushuu	きってしゅうしゅう	Stamp collecting
Kodama	こだま	The bullet train that is slower than the Hikari because it stops at more stations
Koinshuushuu	コインしゅうしゅう	Coin collecting
Komu	こむ	To be crowded
Kyoomi ga aru	きょうみが　ある	To be interested in
Kyoomi o motsu	きょうみを　もつ	To have an interest in
Kyooto	京都	Kyoto (city in Japan)
Mainen	まい年	Every year
Meetoru	メートル	Metre
Mieru	見える	To be able to see, can see
Nakigoe	なきごえ	Barking, whining
Nanbansen	何ばんせん	What track number?
Nanjikan	何時間	How many hours?
Nannenkan	何年間	How many years?
Nanpun	何ぷん	How many minutes?
Nanshuukan	何しゅう間	How many weeks?
Naze	なぜ	Why?
Nekutai	ネクタイ	Necktie

Nimotsu	にもつ	Luggage
Ningyooshuushuu	にんぎょうしゅうしゅう	Doll collecting
Nitoo	二とう	Second class
Noboru	のぼる	To climb
Norikaeru	のりかえる	To change trains
Nuimono o suru	ぬいものを　する	To sew
Omoi	おもい	Heavy
Onegaishimasu	おねがいします	I request, I would like
Oofuku	おうふく	Return/round trip
Onsen	おんせん	Hot spa
Oshaberi o suru	おしゃべりを　する	To chatter
Paatii o hiraku	パーティーを　ひらく	To hold a party
Pasu	パス	Pass (a season ticket, e.g. a JR rail pass)
Pasupooto	パスポート	Passport
Rejaa	レジャー	Leisure
Roorasukeeto o suru	ローラースケートを　する	To rollerskate
Saafin o suru	サーフィンを　する	To surf
Sainshuushuu	サインしゅうしゅう	Collecting autographs
Sekaide	せかいで	In the world
Shi	し	City
Shiba	しば（芝）	Suburb of Tokyo
Shika … masen	しか…ません	Only
Shoogi o sasu	しょうぎを　さす	To play chess (shoogi)
Shuushuu o suru	しゅうしゅうを　する	To collect
Soredemo	それでも	However, nonetheless
Sukeeto boodo o suru	スケートボードを　する	To skate (board)
Takasa	たかさ	Height
Tazuneru	たずねる	To visit
Tenkiyohoo	天気よほう	Weather report
Tetsu	てつ	Steel, iron
Tomaru	とまる	To stay
Tsukareru	つかれる	To be tired/exhausted
Ueno eki no panda	うえの駅の　パンダ	The panda in Ueno station
Yasumi no aida (ni)	休みの　間（に）	During the holidays
Yasumichuu (ni)	休み中（に）	During the holidays
Yoku	よく	Well (skilfully)
Yooroppa	ヨーロッパ	Europe
Yotei	よてい	Programme, schedule, plan
Yukagen	ゆかげん	Water temperature, bath
Yuki	行き	Bound for
Yuube	ゆうべ	Last night
Yuugata	ゆうがた	Evening, nightfall

Kanji studied to the end of Unit 19:

Unit 13:	一	二	三	四	五	六	七	八	九	十	人	何
	1	2	3	4	5	6	7	8	9	10	11	12

Unit 14:	目	口	日	本	母	父	白	赤	黒	色	大	小
	13	14	15	16	17	18	19	20	21	22	23	24

Unit 15:	月	花	木	子	女	好	言	夏	火	秋	春	冬	雨	雲	天
	25	26	27	28	29	30	31	32	33	34	35	36	37	38	39
	気	年													
	40	41													

Unit 16:	上	手	下	語	中	学	校	外	男	生	今	階
	42	43	44	45	46	47	48	49	50	51	52	53

Unit 17:	思	見	聞	行	話	電	買	売	読	入	食
	54	55	56	57	58	59	60	61	62	63	64

Unit 18:	動	物	園	馬	駅	時	青	土	水	金	美
	65	66	67	68	69	70	71	72	73	74	75

Unit 19:	田	町	休	車	朝	家	京	東	都	来	勉	強	山	間	書
	76	77	78	79	80	81	82	83	84	85	86	87	88	89	90

Katakana studied to the end of Unit 19:

Unit 14:	ア	ン	ト	ル	ナ	ー	ヒ	ク	オ	レ	シ	リ
	1	2	3	4	5	6	7	8	9	10	11	12

Unit 15:	ハ	イ	マ	テ	ス	ラ	ツ
	13	14	15	16	17	18	19

Unit 16:	コ	ユ	タ	ノ	キ	ニ	カ	フ	ケ	チ	エ	ロ	ミ
	20	21	22	23	24	25	26	27	28	29	30	31	32

Unit 17:	セ	ネ	ウ	ヘ	サ	ホ
	33	34	35	36	37	38

Unit 18:	ヤ	モ	ソ	ヌ	メ	ヨ	ム
	39	40	41	42	43	44	45

Unit 19:	ワ	ヲ
	46	47

The castle at Himeji is a popular tourist attraction

Unit 20

An awful experience
いや けいけん
嫌な経験

Topics:

A

一　朝に

二

三

四　あとで

* I think I'll go to …

からだ　**The body**

くち(口)

は

へんとうせん

あたま(頭)　みみ(耳)

きんにく

しんぞう

かみ(のけ)

め(目)

かお　はな

かた

むね

おなか

ゆび

くび

て(手)

てくび

せなか

うで

ひじ

ひざ

あし(足)

あしくび

AGOKIBUJ

あたさにいけまゃ

どうしたんですか What's up?

Sentence Pattern 85

Q. どうしたんですか。

What's up?/What's happened?

A. のどが　いたいんです。

I've got a sore throat./My throat is sore.

A. むすこは　のどが　いたいです。

My son has a sore throat.

★ It is easy to remember to use the joshi 「が」 if you think of your throat or other parts of your body as belonging to nature; and, generally, the properties of nature are beyond your control. Remember: 「そらが　あおいです。」— the sky is blue.

Explanation:

Because いたい is a true adjective, its endings change according to the tense.

For example:

きのう　頭が　いたかったです。

Yesterday I had a headache.

今　のどが　いたくないです。

I don't have a sore throat now.

In the question どうしたんですか, ん serves, as it did on page 176, to encourage a response by the listener. When giving a reason for something, in response to a question, ん or の is often used before です.

C₂ How would each of the following sentences be said in English?

1. 冬に　よく　のどが　いたかったです。
2. せんしゅうも　足が　いたかったです。
3. お父さんは　頭が　いたくなかったです。
4. へんとうせんが　いたいです。
5. おばあさんは　ゆびが　いたいです。
6. せなかが　いたくなかったです。
7. 耳が　いたいです。
8. おなかが　いたかったです。
9. 目が　いたくないです。
10. あには　かたが　いたくないですが　せなかが　いたいです。
11. 耳が　いたいから　よく　聞こえません。
12. せなかが　いたいから　今　ねたいです。

C₃ どこが　いたいんですか　　**Where does it hurt?**

Example:

みみ
耳が　いたい(ん)です。

1.

2.

3.

4.

5.

6.

7.

8.

9.

10.

C₄ Express each of these sentences in Japanese:

1. I have a sore throat.
2. Because I took some medicine I don't have a sore throat now.
3. My eyes are sore.
4. My brother had a pain in his stomach.
5. I have an ear ache.
6. I had a headache yesterday.
7. Dad's back is aching.
8. Mum's hand was not sore.
9. My grandmother's wrist was aching.
10. My sister's arm was sore.

In the previous unit you learnt how to express a length of time: a number of minutes, hours, weeks or years. Let's now look at how to express how many days or months something takes.

<ruby>何日<rt>なんにち</rt></ruby> **How many days?**	<ruby>何か月<rt>なん　げつ</rt></ruby> **How many months?**
½　はん日(はんにち)	はん月(はんつき)
1　一日(いちにち)	一か月(いっかげつ)
1½　一日はん(いちにちはん)	一か月はん(いっかげつはん)
2　二日(ふつか)	二か月(にかげつ)
3　三日(みっか)	三か月(さんかげつ)
4　四日(よっか)	四か月(よんかげつ)
5　五日(いつか)	五か月(ごかげつ)
6　六日(むいか)	六か月(ろっかげつ)
7　七日(なのか)	七か月(ななかげつ、しちかげつ)
8　八日(ようか)	八か月(はちかげつ、はっかげつ)
9　九日(ここのか)	九か月(きゅうかげつ)
10　十日(とおか)	十か月(じゅっかげつ)
11　十一日(じゅういちにち)	十一か月(じゅういちかげつ、じゅういっかげつ)
12　十二日(じゅうににち)	十二か月(じゅうにかげつ)

D₂　Answer each question according to the clue in brackets:

1. どのぐらい　<ruby>病院<rt>びょういん</rt></ruby>に　いましたか。　(1 month)

2. 何日　東京に　いましたか。　(5 days)

3. 何日　<ruby>病<rt>びょう</rt></ruby>気でしたか。(8 days)

4. どのぐらい　勉強していましたか。　(12 months)

5. 何年間　学校へ　行っていますか。　(9 years)

6. オーストラリアで　夏休みは　どのぐらい　ですか。(1½ months)

7. 日本で　夏<ruby>休<rt>やす</rt></ruby>みは　どのぐらい　ですか。　(About 40 days)

8. どのぐらい　この　ホテルに　とまるよていですか。　(3 days)

9. 冬は　何か月ですか。(3 months)

10. まいしゅう　日本では　何日　学校へ　行きますか。　(6 days)

D₃

Sentence Pattern 86

Q. いたみ 出^だしてから どのぐらいに なりますか。　　How long have you had this pain?

A. 二日^{ふつか}ぐらいに なります。　　It's been about two days.
(It has become two days since the pain started.)

D₄

Answer the question 「いたみ出^だしてから どのぐらいに なりますか」 using the different words given in each case, as in the example. Give both the kanji and the hiragana reading in your answer.

For example:

いたみ 出^だしてから どのぐらいに なりますか。　About five days.

五日^{いつか}ぐらいに なります。

1. 1 day	8. 2 months	15. Only one day
2. 6 hours	9. A week	16. About 11 days
3. 10 days	10. About 10 days	17. About a month
4. 2 days	11. About 5 days	18. 8 days
5. About 2 weeks	12. About 11 days	19. About 3 months
6. About 4 days	13. About 3 days	20. 7 days
7. 9 days	14. About 6 months	21. 5 months

D₅

Put these sentences into English:

1. 一日 おなかが いたかったです。
2. 五日ぐらい 手が いたいです。
3. 元気^{げん}に なったと 思いましたが 今 また せなかが いたいです。
4. 一か月ぐらい 足^{あし}が いたいです。
5. 頭^{あたま}が いたくなかったです。はが いたかったです。まだ いたいです。
6. 中山さんは 二か月ぐらい 病気^{びょう}でした。インフルエンザだと 思いました。
7. 山田さんは ぜんぜん 病気^{びょう}に なりません。いつも 元気^{げん} です。まい日 ビタミンを たくさん 飲^のみます。
8. 青木さんは 今 きゅうけいしつで ねています。頭^{あたま}が いたいと 思います。
9. 三日ぐらい ねむいです。
10. 木から おちました。今 手が とても いたいです。

Rewrite this travel diary in Japanese:

Last month I went on a sightseeing tour with my family to Kyoto. We arrived in Kyoto at about 5 p.m. on July 25th and stayed at the Kyoto Park Hotel. We were in Kyoto for six days. I saw Nijo Castle. It is very beautiful and interesting. I spent three hours at the Kyoto Handicraft Centre and saw many interesting things there.

It only takes about 25 minutes from Kyoto Station to Uji Station. At Uji, we saw the Byodoin Temple.

We also saw the Kiyomizudera, the Ginkakuji and the Kinkakuji. It takes about 15 minutes by bus from the Ginkakuji to the Kinkakuji! These buildings are made from wood. I think they are beautiful.

We had a very enjoyable time. Next week I am spending two days in Nara and I plan to see the Todaiji.

F 聞きましょう

On the calendar provided by your teacher, mark in all the plans that Maria has for her forthcoming trip. Also write down any other details of the trip that you hear.

日	月	火	水	木	金	土
		1	2	3 *	4	5
6	7	8	9	10	11	12
13	14	15	16	17	18	19
20	21	22	23	24	25	26
27	28	29	30	31		

* 今日

G Can you work out what these "medically related" words are?

1. コレラ
2. ビタミン
3. アルコール
4. カルシウム
5. ホルモン
6. トランキーライザー
7. トラコーマ
8. マラリア
9. アレルギー
10. ガーゼ
11. ラジウム
12. カプセル
13. インシュリン
14. ラノリン
15. アデノイド
16. プラズマ
17. アスピリン
18. バンド　エイド
19. リンパ
20. コーチゾン
21. ペニシリン
22. クリーム
23. ジフテリア
24. ビールス

91.　耳　Ear

When learning Kanji 56, 聞く "listen", we saw an *ear* that was listening through a door. So when writing just "ear" we only need 耳（みみ）.

くん みみ　**おん** じ　**いみ** 耳 (みみ)

かきじゅん ｜ 一 T F F 耳 耳

6かく

92.　足　Leg, foot

The kanji for *leg* or *foot* is represented by a sketch of a foot and the toes, plus a mouth. The mouth here signifies that the leg or foot belongs to a person.

くん あし、た(りる)　**おん** そく　**いみ** 足 (あし)

かきじゅん ｜ 口 口 口 卫 足 足

7かく

93.　出　Leave, come out

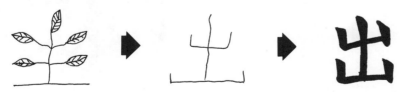

A plant shoots up from the ground; it *comes out* of the soil.

くん で(る)、だ(す)　**おん** しゅつ、すい　**いみ** 出 (で)る、出 (だ)す bring out, post

かきじゅん ｜ 屮 屮 出 出

5かく

94. 立　**Stand, rise**

It is easy to see how the kanji for the verb to *stand* or *rise* was derived.

くん　た(つ)　おん　りつ、りゅう　いみ　立た つ

The Hitachi company writes its name as 日立, meaning "sunrise".

かきじゅん　｜ 丶 亠 十 立 立 ｜　　　5かく

95. 元　**Origin, source, foundation**

In the beginning, there was heaven, earth and man. These three formed the *foundation* on which society was built.

くん　もと　おん　げん、がん　いみ　元気 げんき spirit, energy

かきじゅん　｜ 一 二 テ 元 ｜　　　4かく

96. 飲　**Drink**

You will remember that the first radical on its own means to eat. By addition of the second radical (a now very obscure sketch of a person drinking from a straw), the meaning becomes to *drink*.

くん　の(む)　おん　いん　いみ　飲の む

かきじゅん　｜ ノ ㇒ ㇒ 今 今 今 食 食 食 飲 飲 飲 ｜　　　12かく

97. 病 Sick, disease

The first part of this kanji shows a *sick* person lying down.

The fever or high temperature that afflicts a *sick* person is represented by a sketch of a primitive oven in which the fire is burning either inside a clay structure or under the ground.

くん や(む)、やまい **おん** へい、びょう **いみ** 病気 illness, 病院 hospital

かきじゅん 丶 亠 广 广 广 疒 疒 病 病 病

病

10かく

98. 院 Hall, house, institute

The first radical represents three ideas. (1) A large building such as a hall will consist of several storeys. (2) People in a large organisation are of various ranks. (3) Fortifications or the city walls offer protection.

A *hall* or *house* consists of a roof and people, represented here by one person (the powerful person in charge!).

くん **おん** いん **いみ** 病院 hospital

かきじゅん ⁊ ⻖ ⻖ ⻖' ⻖' ⻖⁻ 院 院 院 院

院

10かく

99. 頭 Head

The first radical is a long, thin object representing both the shape of the body and a hanko or stamp that marks a person's name.

Although the second radical no longer looks like a person's *head*, it is easy to see how it evolved.

頭

くん　あたま、かしら　おん　とう、ず　いみ　頭(あたま)

かきじゅん　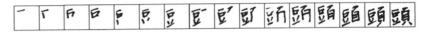　16かく

100. 楽 Enjoyable

A set of bells and drums on a stand represents the idea of something being *enjoyable*, or pleasant, and is also used to mean "music".

くん　たの(しい)　おん　らく、がく　いみ　楽(たの)しい enjoyable、おん楽(がく) music

かきじゅん　　13かく

101. 薬 Medicine

Medicine to the Chinese always consisted of plants or herbs. The top part of this kanji is the same radical used in the kanji for flower (花).

The lower part of this kanji is the same as "enjoyable". In other words, the *medicinal* plants and herbs make life enjoyable again.

薬

くん　くすり　おん　やく　いみ　薬、薬屋 chemist shop

かきじゅん　一 ヤ サ サ ヤ 芦 苩 苩 苩 溄 溄 慹 慹 慹 薬 16かく

102. 屋　House, roof, shop

The top radical, which represents the idea of "permanent abode", originally was a sketch of a person lying down.

The idea contained in the second radical is very abstract. A bird is flying down to its nest. It is arriving *home*.

Together these two radicals convey the idea that a *house*, or permanent dwelling, is the place to which one can always return to rest.

くん　や　おん　おく　いみ　本屋 bookshop, 薬屋 chemist shop

かきじゅん　⼀ ⼆ ⼫ ⼫ 居 居 居 屋 屋 9かく

H₂ Complete the following sentences by inserting appropriate words written in kanji from the frame on page 224. You will need to use some kanji more than once. Where more than one kanji would be appropriate, write out one complete sentence for each different kanji that would be possible.

1. お □□ ですか。おかげさまで、□□ です。
2. □ ごはんは　コーンフレークスを　□ べます。
3. □ み物は　コーヒーが　いいですか。
4. □ で　□ きます。
5. □ は　あけました。
6. □ 時ですか。
7. いいえ、7 □ です。
8. 今日　5□ に　おきました。
9. 6□ に □ べました。
10. 7□ に　□ ました。
11. □□ に　こう園へ　□ きました。

12. 九 ☐ に うちを ☐ ました。

13. ☐と ☐が いたかったです。

14. 一しゅう ☐ ☐☐に いました。

15. ☐☐、☐☐さんは ☐☐に ☐ませんでした。☐☐だと ☐います。

16. ☐み ☐、どこへ ☐くよていですか。

今	食	朝	元	飲	耳	聞	口	六	時	休	中	行
学	間	病	院	山	思	日	頭	来	気	校	出	足

I₁

Needs, wants, desires

You have already seen in Sentence Patterns 40 and 41 how to say that you want *to do* something. This pattern shows how to say "I want *something*".

Sentence Pattern 87a

Present tense:

Q. あなたは 何(なに)が ほしいですか。　　What do you want?

A. わたしは せきどめドロップが ほしい です。　　I want some cough drops.

Past tense:

Q. あなたは 何(なに)が ほしかったですか。　　What did you want?

A. わたしは 薬(くすり)が ほしかったです。　　I wanted some medicine.

The adjective ほしい follows the は … が pattern, where は marks the "experiencer" or the person doing the "wanting", and indicates が, the desired object. Since this pattern expresses a personal feeling, it is usually only used by the first person (I) as in the above answers, or by the second person (you) as in the question shown. If you wish to express the third person's desire (that is, the wish of someone not present during the conversation), then the next pattern is used. (Note that particle を is used with this pattern.) Alternatively, you may wish to use the verb いる (to need) with the particle が, as shown in I₂, number 7.

Sentence Pattern 87b

(a) パムは バンド エイドを もう 一(ひと)つ　　Pam wants another bandaid.
ほしがっています。

(b) パムは バンド エイドを 買(か)いたがって　　Pam wants to buy some bandaids.
います。

The final い in ほしい changes to がっています when talking about another person's needs. が is used with ほしい and を with ほしがっている.

I₂ What do the following sentences mean in English?

1. のどが　いたいから　せきどめドロップが　ほしいです。
2. きのう、頭が　いたかったから　薬が　ほしいです。
3. のどが　かわきました。飲み物が　ほしいです。
4. 頭が　いたいです。アスピリンが　ほしいです。
5. きのう　サッカーを　しました。今、足が　いたいです。マッサージに　行きたいです。
6. ジェニーは　ぜんそくの　ほっさを　おこしましたから　薬を　ほしがっています。
7. お父さんは　足が　いたいです。サロンパスが　いります。
8. 青木さんは　木から　おちました。だいじょうぶですが　バンド　エイドを　ほしがっています。
9. 山田さんは　頭が　いたいです。薬を　ほしがっています。
10. マリアナさんは　のどが　いたいから　せきどめドロップを　ほしがっています。

I₃ Finish off each statement with an appropriate word. Using katakana for foreign names would be appropriate if your host family knew what you were talking about!

1.

耳が　いたいです。
…………が　ほしいです。

2.

お父さんは　頭が　いたいです。
………………を　買いたがっています。

3. せなかが　いたいです。
.... が　ほしいです。

4. きのう　おなかが　いたかったです。
.... が　ほしかったです。

5. せんしゅう　気もちが　わるかったです。
かぜを　ひいていました。
.... が　ほしかったです。

6. ジェニーは　足が　いたいです。
.... を　ほしがっています。

7. さくばん　お父さんは　よく　ねませんでした。
今日　からだが　わるいです。................. を
ほしがっています。

8. 手つだってください。
ゆびを　きりました。
.... が　いります。

9. ぜんそくを　おこしています。
.... が　ほしいです。

10. マリアナは　のどが　いたいです。
.... を　買いたがっています。

I₄ For each item illustrated below, answer the following two questions. Answer the first question as if the person in the centre is you and answer the second question as if the person is Maria (your friend).

1. あなたは　何が　ほしいですか。　　　　2. マリアさんは　何を　ほしがっていますか。

I₅ Put each of the following sentences into Japanese, carefully considering whether to use …たい, …たがっています、ほしい or ほしがっています.

1. I want a drink.
2. Aiko wants a new piano.
3. I want to play with the dog.
4. Dad wants to buy another computer.
5. Mum wants a new table.
6. I want a shirt.
7. I want to watch television
8. I want to spend a week in Nagasaki.
9. I want a television.
10. Mum wants to buy some medicine at the chemist.

J₁ # Doubt ... Probability ...

In English, when we wish to express doubt we use words such as "probably", "maybe", "might", "possibly", "perhaps". In Japanese, the words たぶん ("perhaps") or きっと ("surely") can be used in such sentences, but the "probable" or "tentative" form of the verb must also be used.

Study the following sentence pattern carefully:

Sentence Pattern 88

- あの　アパートは { たかい　　でしょう。 / たかかった }   That apartment { is probably expensive (isn't it?). / was }

- あの　人(ひと)は { せんせい　　　でしょう。 / せんせいだった }   That person { is probably a teacher (don't you think?). / was }

でしょう expresses doubt or uncertainty. It may also be intended to convey an effect of politeness by inviting the listener to react in some way. It adds the meaning "isn't it/wasn't it/don't you/don't you think?".

A summary of some forms of the verb です:

   …です it is (polite form).   … だ it is (plain form — see Sentence Pattern 65.)

   …でしょう it probably is (plain form).   … だったでしょう it probably was.

   …でした it was (polite form).

J₂ Express these sentences in English:

1. あした　あついでしょう。
2. けんいちくんの　しけんは　むずかしかったでしょう。
3. ゆうれいだったでしょう。
4. この　おみやげは　たぶん　ふろしきでしょう。
5. ぜんそくだったでしょう。

A furoshiki

J₃ Put each of the following sentences into the "probable" form and write out the meaning of the new sentence:

1. さむかったです。
2. この　えいがは　おもしろいです。
3. そうですか。
4. くうこうは　きっと　うるさかったです。
5. きのうの　えんそくは　たのしかったです。
6. お母さんの　一ばん好きな　ようふくは　赤いです。
7. この　本は　山口さんの　です。
8. ねこです。
9. これは　スカート　でした。
10. 美しい　けしきでした。
11. それは　何ですか。
12. けんすけちゃんは　カンガルー　が　好きです。

J₄ Put each of these sentences into Japanese:

1. He is probably sick.
2. It's probably a cold.
3. It's probably asthma.
4. It might be a book.
5. She is probably very busy.

6. That girl is probably Toshio's younger sister.
7. His leg probably aches.
8. That man is probably a doctor.
9. The word processor was probably expensive.
10. It was probably hot.

K₁ To put a verb into the "probable" form, simply add でしょう to the plain or dictionary form of the verb.

Sentence Pattern 89

(a) <ruby>田中<rt>た なか</rt></ruby>さんは <ruby>病院<rt>びょういん</rt></ruby>に <ruby>行<rt>い</rt></ruby>くでしょう。   Mr Tanaka will probably go to the hospital.

(b) <ruby>田中<rt>た なか</rt></ruby>さんは <ruby>病院<rt>びょういん</rt></ruby>に <ruby>行<rt>い</rt></ruby>ったでしょう。   Mr Tanaka probably went to the hospital.

You probably noticed that the *plain past* of any verb is the same as the て form, but using た instead of て. The following rules detail how to put a verb in the て or た (plain past) form.

Step 1:

Decide if the verb is <ruby>一<rt>いち</rt></ruby>だん (one level), <ruby>五<rt>ご</rt></ruby>だん (five levels) or irregular (する or くる).

Step 2a:

<ruby>一<rt>いち</rt></ruby>だん verbs end in る and are preceded by the い or え sound, for example:

みる, たべる, おしえる   (m*iru*, tab*eru*, oshi*eru*)

If the verbs are <ruby>一<rt>いち</rt></ruby>だん: take off the ending and add て or た as shown:

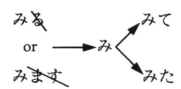

> The only verbs used in Isshoni 1 and 2 which are exceptions to this rule are はしる、はいる、かえる、しる、きる (cut) and いる (need). They end in る and are preceded by い or え sounds but they are *godan* verbs. If you are in doubt, check the verb summary on pages 324–26.

Step 2b:

A 五だん verb is one whose meaning and purpose change depending on which of the five levels of the final syllable is used. For example, in the verb "to read" the five final syllables could be ま, み, む, め or も:

よまない—not read, よみます—read, よむ—to read,

よめます—can read, よもう—will read.

The way of making the て or た form of a 五だん verb varies depending on the final syllable in the … ます form.

In summary, there are nine rules for making the て or た form of a 五だん verb.

When the ます base is:

1. …います　　い is replaced by って as in かいます→ かって or かった
2. …きます　　き is replaced by いて as in かきます→ かいて or かいた
3. …ぎます　　ぎ is replaced by いで as in およぎます→ およいで or およいだ
4. …ちます　　ち is replaced by って as in まちます→ まって or まった
5. …ります　　り is replaced by って as in かえります→ かえって or かえった
6. …します　　し is replaced by して as in はなします→ はなして or はなした
7. …びます　　び is replaced by んで as in あそびます→ あそんで or あそんだ
8. …にます　　に is replaced by んで as in しにます→ しんで or しんだ
9. …みます　　み is replaced by んで as in よみます→ よんで or よんだ

Step 2c:

The て or た forms for the irregular verbs are as follows:

1. くる or きます becomes きて or きた
2. する or します becomes して or した

Complete the following verb grid with the ます form and the "probable" form in both the present and the past tense of each verb. Be careful of those verbs listed in K1 that are exceptions to the 一だん rule. You should know that they are 五だん anyway because of the ます form. For example, はしる becomes はしります, not はします as it would be if it were 一だん.

	Verb	ます -form	Present probable	Past probable
1.	食べる	食べます	食べるでしょう	食べたでしょう
2.	見る			
3.	おしえる			
4.	食べる			
5.	人る			
6.	読む			
7.	話す			
8.	売る			
9.	聞く			
10.	およぐ			
11.	見せる			
12.	立つ			
13.	勉強する			
14.	書く			
15.	出る			
16.	ふる			

17.	はしる			
18.	行く			
19.	言う			
20.	思う			
21.	来る			
22.	おちる			
23.	もつ			
24.	つれて行く			
25.	電話する			

K₃ Put these sentences into Japanese:

1. It is probably chickenpox.
2. Mr Tanaka probably caught a cold.
3. Miss Yamada's arm is probably broken.
4. Martin probably had appendicitis.
5. It was probably asthma.
6. The cat probably fell from the tree.
7. Hanako is not coming today. She probably has a cold.
8. Hanako Yamamoto probably has tonsillitis.
9. It was probably the flu.
10. Andrew may have had an asthma attack.

K₄ The following sentences are all very definite statements. However, Japanese tend to be not as direct in their speech as Australians and even if they are sure of something they often use the "probable" form. The "probable" form is also considered to be more polite in many circumstances — you are saying what you believe to be true, rather than expressing absolute certainty.

Change these sentences to the "probable" form so that they make a less abrupt and direct statement. Check that you know the meaning of each sentence.

1. 来しゅう　おじいさんと　二日　とまります。
2. その　女の人は　べんごしです。
3. あの　男の人は　ディズニーランドから　かえっています。
4. 今日、病気だから　あした　おいしゃさんに　行きます。
5. 八月の　七日に　電車は　たぶん　こみますね。
6. ベトナム人も　中ごく人も　おはしで　食べます。
7. 今年、ほっかいどうの　冬は　きびしい　です。
8. きのうは　せと口せんせいが　ぶんかさいの　デコレーションを　買いました。

9. 今朝　ともだちは　電車に　のりました。

10. その　本を　読むのは　二時間　かかります。

11. きょうしに　なりたいです。

12. まりこさんは　べんごしに　なりたかったです。

L₁
In Sentence Patterns 40 and 65 you saw how to say "I think it's ...". The pattern ...と　思います can be used with verbs in the same way as でしょう (that is, by adding it to the plain form) to mean "I think I'll ...". This is another pattern that is extremely useful because it shows politeness (you are being less direct). Compare the sentences in the next pattern with the two sentences below them, with which you are already familiar.

Sentence Pattern 90

(a) 来年、さとうさんは　日本へ　行くと　　　I think Mr Satoo will go to Japan next year.
　　思います。

(b) きのう　さとうさんは　かんこう　　　　I think that Mr Satoo went on a sightseeing
　　りょ行に　箱根へ　行ったと　思います。 trip to Hakone yesterday.

Compare with:

• 来年、さとうさんは　日本へ　行きます。

• 来年、さとうさんは　日本へ　行くでしょう。

Can you work out what this sentence might mean?

　　　来年、さとうさんは　日本へ　行くだろうと思います。

L₂
Rewrite these sentences in full and give their meanings:

1. わたなべさんは　もう　オーストラリアへ ⎰来ました、
　　　　　　　　　　　　　　　　　　　　　⎨来たと　思います。
　　　　　　　　　　　　　　　　　　　　　⎱来たでしょう。

2. マリアさんは　つきみだんごを　食べるのが　好き ⎰です。
　　　　　　　　　　　　　　　　　　　　　　　　　⎨でしょう。
　　　　　　　　　　　　　　　　　　　　　　　　　⎱だと　思います。

3. あの　男の人は　いかを ⎰売ります。
　　　　　　　　　　　　　⎨売ると　思います。
　　　　　　　　　　　　　⎱売るでしょう。

4. お母さんは　今朝　{
そうじしました。
そうじしたと　思います。
そうじしたでしょう。

5. アンドルーさんは　オーストラリアへ　{
かえりたがっています。
かえりたがって　いるでしょう。
かえりたがっていると　思います。

L₃ How could you express these sentences in Japanese?

1. I think that Shin had a fever.
2. Mr Yamaguchi probably went to Sapporo yesterday at 11.00 a.m.
3. After graduating, Michiko will probably go to university.
4. I think that Ayano is going skiing in Niigata during the holidays.
5. You probably need a nap.
6. Toshio's father probably works for a company.
7. I think that Kyoto is the prettiest town in Japan.
8. I wonder what that is.
9. This street was probably very crowded too.
10. You will probably be well tomorrow.
11. Jenny probably wants to buy the new dress today.
12. Jenny will probably meet me at Ueno station.
13. Mrs Nakayama might have written that letter.
14. Maria probably had asthma.
15. I think that Hitomi had a sore foot.

M Read the entries that Andrew made in his diary on 29 July and 4 August and answer the questions that follow.

　　日よう日、7月29日

今日　はこねへ　家ぞくと　かんこうりょ行に　行きたかったですが
ぼくは病気に　なりました。気もちが　わるいです。かぜを　ひいたん
でしょう。来しゅうの　日よう日に　行くでしょう。
今日　一日中　休むと　思います。

> 土よう日、8月4日
>
> 今朝、はこねへ　行くよていです。気もちが　いいです。夏、はこねは
> 美しい　ところです。八時はんごろ　出るでしょう。電車に　のると
> 思います。
>
> 九時ごろ　かえりました。たいへん　楽しかったです。きれいな　みどりの
> 木が　たくさん　ありました。人が　たくさん　いました。　ロープウェイ
> から　けしきは　すばらしかったです。
> ふじ山が　よく　見えました。

1. What were Andrew's plans for 29 July?

2. What eventuated, and why?

3. How did things change over the next week?

4. What preconceived idea of Hakone did Andrew have? Do you think it was correct? Explain.

5. What seems to have been the highlight of his trip? Explain.

N どうしたんですか

Can you diagnose what illness these people are suffering from? Is their self-diagnosis correct?

1. 気もちが　わるかったです。のどが　いたかったです。はなが　出ていまし
   た。ねつが　ありました。もうちょうに　なったんでしょう。 _____
   病気

2. からだが　とても　かゆいです。ねつが　あります。のどが　いたいです
   かぜを　ひいたんでしょう。 _____
   病気

3. マリアさんは　今朝　はきました。おなかは　すごく　いたかったです。
   もうちょうに　なったんでしょう。 _____
   病気

4. きのう　あそこの　ユーカリの　木に　のぼりました。でも、おちました。
   今、手が　いたいです。たぶん　手のほねが　おれたんでしょう。 _____
   病気

5. 頭が　いたいんです。足が　いたいんです。手が　いたいんです。せなかが　いたいんです。気もちが　わるいです。水ぼうそうでしょう。

病気

On doctor's orders

A visit to the doctor will surely require an understanding of the next two patterns, "Please don't ..." and "You must ...". Both are formed from the same "negative" stem of the verb. Once you understand how to make this ending, you'll be able to use these patterns often in your daily life in Japan.

Step 1:   **Identify the type of verb**

(a) In Part **K₁** you saw how there was a pattern in forming the endings of verbs and the endings were formed depending on whether or not the verb was 一だん or 五だん.

With ichidan (one level) verbs the stem never changes:

*tabe*ru	to eat
*tabe*masu	(I) eat
*tabe*nai	not eat
*tabe*te	eat

(b) There are the irregular verbs:

1. kuru or kimasu → konai (not come)

2. suru or shimasu → shinai (not do)

You saw how there are five possible basic endings for the 五だん verbs and how the first level is the "negative" ending.

For example: よみます (second level) よまない (first level)

Step 2:   **Know how to make the negative endings**

* With ichidan verbs it's easy! Simply add *nai* to the base:

    TABE + NAI

    MI + NAI

* As there are only two irregular verbs, they don't pose a problem either:

    SU RU → SHI + NAI

    KU RU → KO + NAI

* When putting the 五だん verbs into the negative form, change the final sound into its "A" (あ) or first-level base.

    For example:

"To write"	KAKU →	KAKA + NAI
"To read"	YOMU →	YOMA + NAI
"To speak"	HANASU →	HANASA + NAI

"To wait"   MATSU → MATA + NAI

Notice the change in verbs ending in *u* to make pronunciation easier:

"To buy"   KAU → KAWA + NAI

"To wash"   ARAU → ARAWA + NAI

Step 3:   **Remember the endings**

 To help you remember the endings, regularly read aloud all the negative bases of the verbs in the verb appendix on pages 324–26. Practise them with the two endings explained in the next two sentence patterns.

O₂ If you visit a doctor in Japan you will have to listen carefully for any instructions he or she gives you, particularly if they mean you *must* do something.

Sentence Pattern 91

フルーツを　食(た)べなければ　なりません。   You must eat fruit.

休(やす)まなければ　なりません。   You must rest.

Negative base + なければ　なりません = You must …

O₃ What else could the doctor say? What do these instructions mean?

1. 何かを　食べなければ　なりません。
2. 水を　たくさん　飲まなければ　なりません。
3. この　せきどめシロップを　飲まなければ　なりません。
4. この　カプセルを　飲まなければ　なりません。
5. まい日　2キロぐらい　あるかなければ　なりません。
6. この　薬で　からだを　あらわなければ　なりません。
7. ぎゅうにゅうを　飲まなければ　なりません。
8. はやく　ねなければ　なりません。
9. それを　薬やで　買わなければ　なりません。
10. すぐ　おじいさんは　病院へ　行かなければ　なりません。

O₄ Put each of these sentences into Japanese:

1. You must drink this medicine every day at 8 o'clock.
2. You must drink six glasses of water every day.
3. You must go to the doctor straight away.
4. You must eat plenty of vegetables.

5. You must wash your foot.

6. You must wash this every day.

7. You must sit down.

8. You must have a very cold bath.

9. You must eat red meat.

10. You have to drink this.

Chemist shops in Japan are as cluttered as many Australian ones

P₁ More instructions

Sentence Pattern 92

ぎゅうにゅうを　飲まないでください。　　Please don't drink milk.

Negative base + ないでください = Please don't ...

P₂

What is the doctor saying this time?

1. りょ行しないでください。

2. さけを　飲まないでください。

3. 話さないでください。

4. まだ　あるかないでください。

5. その　手を　まだ　つかわない
でください。

6. しんぱいしないでください。

7. 小さいサイズを　買わないでください。

8. 赤にくを　食べないでください。

9. 8時まで　食べないでください。

10. 来しゅうまで　またないでください。
今　はじめてください。

P₃

Put each of these instructions into Japanese:

1. You must sleep for eight hours every night.

2. You must eat vegetables.

3. You must drink this medicine.

4. You have to eat breakfast.

5. You must not eat red meat.

6. You must not run.

7. Please don't travel yet.

8. You must not go outside.

9. Please don't drink sake.

10. You must drink water.

What does this sign say?

聞きましょう

Listen to the doctor's conversations with the three patients.

(a)   What is wrong with each of the three people?

(b)   What remedies or instructions does the doctor give?

R   Who could have written each of the following messages? What do they mean?

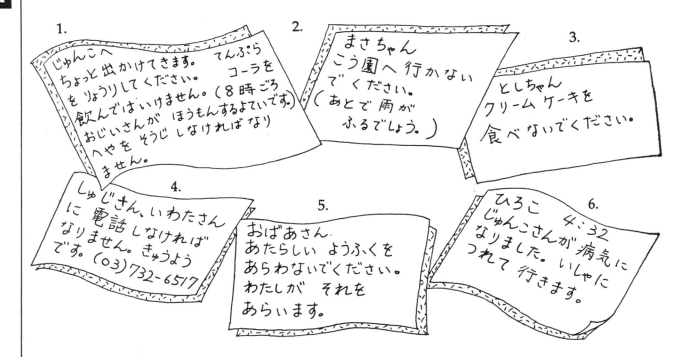

1.
じゅんこへ
ちょっと出かけてきます。　てんぷら
をりょうりしてください。　コーラを
飲んではいけません。（8時ごろ
おじいさんが　ほうもんするよていです。）
へやを　そうじ　しなければなり
ません。

2.
まさちゃん
こう園へ　行かない
でください。
（あとで　雨が
ふるでしょう。）

3.
としちゃん
クリームケーキを
食べ　ないでください。

4.
しゅじさん、いわたさん
に　電話しなければ
なりません。きゅうよう
です。（03）732-6517

5.
おばあさん。
あたらしい　ようふくを
あらわないでください。
わたしが　それを
あらいます。

6.
ひろこ　　4:32
じゅんこさんが病気に
なりました。いしゃに
つれて　行きます。

S   Can you work out what you are to do in this activity? Once you've worked out the task, test your katakana!

カタカナの　書きかたで　よいほうに「○」　を　つけましょう。

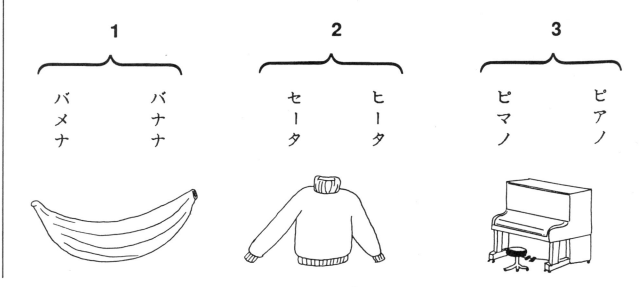

1	2	3
バメナ　　バナナ	セータ　　ヒータ	ピマノ　　ピアノ

4

パンダ　　パソダ

5

ヌフィンクス　　スフィンクス

6

ソックス　　ンックス

T | ## Situational dialogue — at the bank

ぎんこういん
銀行員：おまたせいたしました。

ごようけんを　どうぞ。
I'm sorry to have kept you waiting.
How can I help you?

外人：トラベラーズ　チェックを　げんきんに

かえてください。
Could I please cash these traveller's cheques.

ぎんこういん
銀行員：はい、ちょっと　まってください。
Yes, just a moment, please.

このようしに　きにゅうしてください。
Could you fill in this form, please.

ここに　サインしてください。
Please sign here.

せんえんさつが　よろしい　ですか。
Are ¥1000 notes okay?

外人：ええ、いいです。ありがとうございました。
Yes, fine thanks. Thank you very much.

New words and expressions

Akaniku	赤にく	Red meat
Apaato	アパート	Apartment
Ashi	足	Leg, foot
Ashikubi	足くび	Ankle
Asupirin	アスピリン	Aspirin
Atama	頭	Head
Bando eido	バンド　エイド	Bandaid
Benpisuru	べんぴする	To be constipated
Bitamin	ビタミン	Vitamin
Dake	だけ	Only
Dekakeru	出かける	To go out
Doko ga itai n desuka	どこが　いたいんですか	Where does it hurt?
Dooshitandesuka	どうしたんですか	What's up? What's happened?
Furoshiki	ふろしき	A square cloth used to wrap goods
Genkin	げんきん	Cash, ready money
Geri o suru	げりを　する	To have diarrhoea
Goyooken o doozo	ごようけんを　どうぞ	How can I help you?
Gyuunyuu	ぎゅうにゅう	Milk
Ha	は	Teeth
Haku	はく	To vomit
Hana ga deru	はなが　出る	To have a runny nose
Hentoosen	へんとうせん	Tonsils
Hentoosenen (desu)	へんとうせんえん（です）	Tonsillitis
Hiji	ひじ	Elbow
Hiza	ひざ	Knee
Hone	ほね	Bone
Hoomonsuru	ほうもんする	To visit
Hoshigatteiru	ほしがっている	To want, desire, wish to have (3rd person)
Hoshii	ほしい	Want, desire, wish to have (1st, 2nd person)
Hoteru	ホテル	Hotel
Ichinichijuu	一日中	For/During one day
Ika	いか	Squid
Ikagadesuka	いかがですか	How is it?
Ikoo	行こう	I will go (volitional form of 行く)
Iru	いる	To want, to need, to require
Itai	いたい	Hurting, painful (*adjective*)
Itami	いたみ	A pain, an ache (*noun*)
Infuruenza	インフルエンザ	Influenza
Kapuseru	カプセル	Capsule
Karada	からだ	Body
Kata	かた	Shoulder
Kayui	かゆい	Itchy

Kaze	かぜ	Cold, influenza
Kazegusuri	かぜぐすり	Medicine for a cold
Kaze o hiiteiru	かぜを　ひいている	To have a cold
Kaze o hiku	かぜを　ひく	To catch a cold
Keiken	けいけん	Experience (*noun*)
Kesa	今朝	This morning
Keshiki	けしき	Scenery
Kimochi ga waruidesu	気もちが　わるいです	Feel sick (out of sorts)
Kinniku	きんにく	Muscle
Kinyuusuru	きにゅうする	To fill in (the blanks)
Kiro	キロ	Kilometre
Kitto	きっと	Surely, very likely
Kowareteiru	こわれている	To be broken
Kubi	くび	Neck
Kusuri	薬	Medicine
Kusuri o nomu	薬を　飲む	To take/have/drink medicine
Kyuuyoo	きゅうよう	Urgent business
Maru	まる	Circle
Massaaji	マッサージ	Massage
Mimi	耳	Ear
Mizuboosoo (ni naru)	水ぼうそう(に　なる)	(To have) chickenpox
Moochoo	もうちょう	Appendix
Moochoo (ni naru)	もうちょう(に　なる)	(To have) appendicitis
Mooichimai	もういちまい	One more (flat thing)
Motsu	もつ	To hold (in one's hand)
Mune	むね	Chest (of the body)
… naidekudasai	… ないでください	Please don't …
… nakereba narimasen	… なければなりません	You must …
Nankagetsu	何か月	How many months?
Nannichi	何日	How many days?
Nemuri	ねむり	Sleep, nap (*noun*)
Netsu ga aru	ねつが　ある	To have a fever
Nodo	のど	Throat
(Kara) Ochiru	(から)おちる	To fall (from)
Okosu	おこす	To be seized with, fall ill with
Omiyage	おみやげ	Souvenir
Onaka	おなか	Belly, stomach
Oreru	おれる	To break (a bone)
Roopuuei	ロープウェイ	Ropeway
Sainsuru	サインする	To sign
Sakuban	さくばん	Last night
Saronpasu	サロンパス	Liniment-treated stick-on bandages used to relieve muscular pain
Satsu	さつ	Paper money
Sekidomedoroppu	せきどめドロップ	Cough drop
Sekidomeshiroppu	せきどめシロップ	Cough syrup

Sekinokusuri	せきの薬	Medicine for a cough
Seki o suru	せきを　する	To have a cough
Senaka	せなか	Back
Shinzoo	しんぞう	Heart
Sugosu	すごす	To spend (time)
Tabun	たぶん	Perhaps
…tagatteiru	…たがっている	(Someone else) wants
Tanoshiku sugoshimashita	楽しく　すごしました	I had an enjoyable time
Te	手	Hand
Tekubi	手くび	Wrist
Toraberaazu chekku	トラベラーズ　チェック	Traveller's cheques
Ude	うで	Arm
Warui	わるい	Bad
Yakkyoku	薬局	Pharmacy
Yasai	やさい	Vegetables
Yoi, ii	よい、いい	Good
Yooshi	ようし	(Blank) Form
Yubi	ゆび	Finger
Zensoku	ぜんそく	Asthma
Zensoku no hossa ga aru	ぜんそくの　ほっさが　ある	To have an asthma attack
Zensoku no hossa (o okosu)	ぜんそくの　ほっさ(を　おこす)	(To be seized by) an asthma attack

V₁ Kanji studied to the end of Unit 20:

Unit 13: 一 二 三 四 五 六 七 八 九 十 人 何
1 2 3 4 5 6 7 8 9 10 11 12

Unit 14: 目 口 日 本 母 父 白 赤 黒 色 大 小
13 14 15 16 17 18 19 20 21 22 23 24

Unit 15: 月 花 木 子 女 好 言 夏 火 秋 春 冬
25 26 27 28 29 30 31 32 33 34 35 36

雨 雲 天 気 年
37 38 39 40 41

Unit 16: 上 手 下 語 中 学 校 外 男 生 今 階
42 43 44 45 46 47 48 49 50 51 52 53

Unit 17: 思 見 聞 行 話 電 買 売 読 入 食
54 55 56 57 58 59 60 61 62 63 64

Unit 18: 動 物 園 馬 駅 時 青 土 水 金 美
65 66 67 68 69 70 71 72 73 74 75

Unit 19: 田 町 休 車 朝 家 京 東 都 来 勉 強 山 間 書
76 77 78 79 80 81 82 83 84 85 86 87 88 89 90

Unit 20: 耳　足　出　立　元　飲　病　院　頭　楽　薬　屋
91　92　93　94　95　96　97　98　99　100　101　102

V₂

The unit in which each katakana was introduced:

Unit 14: ア　ン　ト　ル　ナ　ー　ヒ　ク　オ　レ　シ　リ
1　2　3　4　5　6　7　8　9　10　11　12

Unit 15: ハ　イ　マ　テ　ス　ラ　ツ
13　14　15　16　17　18　19

Unit 16: コ　ユ　タ　ノ　キ　ニ　カ　フ　ケ　チ　エ　ロ　ミ
20　21　22　23　24　25　26　27　28　29　30　31　32

Unit 17: セ　ネ　ウ　ヘ　サ　ホ
33　34　35　36　37　38

Unit 18: ヤ　モ　ソ　ヌ　メ　ヨ　ム
39　40　41　42　43　44　45

Unit 19: ワ　ヲ
46　47

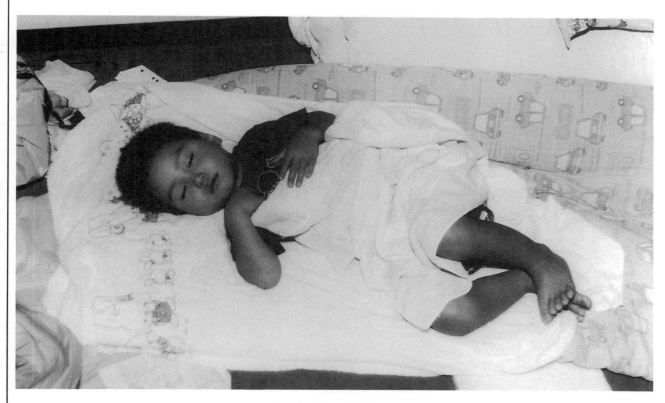

Sound asleep on his futon

Unit 21

Home and neighbourhood
いえ きんじょ
家と近所

A

本田まり子　という　ともだちは　むこうの
だんちに　すんでいます。

へやが　せまいから　はやく　そうじすること
が　できます。あとで　お母さんを　手つだうこと
が　できます。

物ほしざおを　つかったことが　ありません。
はじめてです。

この　通りのおわりに　みせが　あります。

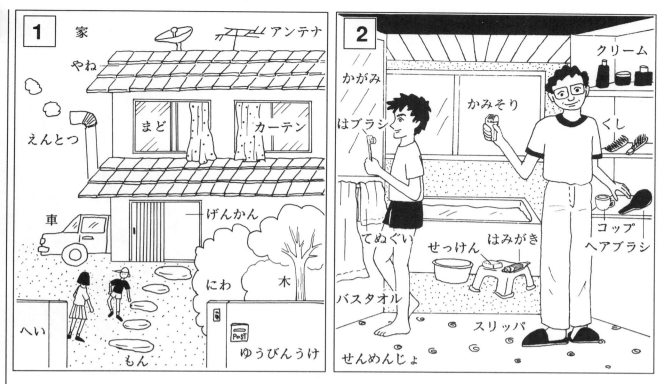

1. Read the statements on the following page about where certain things are in the pictures above or what could happen in each place.

2. Work out what each sentence means.

3. Work out your own rules for explaining where something is located.

How similar are your rules to those on pages 247–48?

Picture 1:

1. 家の外に　郵便<ruby>うけ<rt>ゆうびん</rt></ruby>が　あります。
2. 家の上に　やねが　あります。
3. まどの<ruby>前<rt>まえ</rt></ruby>に　カーテンが　あります。
4. 家の上に　えんとつが　あります。
5. 家のむこうに　車が　あります。
6. 家の外に　にわが　あります。
7. 家の外で　子どもは　あそんでいます。

What is where in this kitchen?

Picture 2:

1. せんめんじょの中に　人が　二人　います。
2. くしのそばに　ヘアブラシが　あります。
3. お父さんのうしろに　むすこが　います。

Picture 3:

1. お<ruby>兄<rt>にい</rt></ruby>さんは　スーパーの前　です。
2. ハムは　ソーセージのそば　です。
3. スーパーの中で. たくさんの　人は　話しています。

Picture 4:

1. お母さんは　だい<ruby>所<rt>どころ</rt></ruby>に　います。
2. 電しレンジは　れいぞうこのとなり　です。
3. しょうゆは　テーブルの上に　あります。
4. しょっきだなは　ながしの上に　あります。

B₂

Sentence Pattern 93

Q. 家_{いえ}の前_{まえ}に 何_{なに}が ありますか。   What is in front of the house?

A. 家_{いえ}の前_{まえ}に にわが あります。   In front of the house there is a garden.

Location					
Landmark	の	Position	に	Subject of the sentence	が あります／います。

The location of a particular thing (for example, "a garden") is given by showing its position in relation to some other landmark (for example, "in front of (*position*) the house (*landmark*)").

Particle に is used with the verbs あります and います, which indicate the location or existence of something.

B₃

Sentence Pattern 94

Q. このへんに ポストは ありますか。   Is there a post box around here/in this area?

A. ええ、ポストは 駅_{えき}の前_{まえ}に あります。   The post box is in front of the station.

		Location				
Topic は	Landmark	の	Position	に	あります／います。	

In this pattern, because the subject (the post box) is being emphasised, particle は is used.

B₄

Sentence Pattern 95

Q. すみませんが みつこしを しっていますか。   Excuse me, but do you know where the Mitsukoshi is?

or すみませんが みつこしは どこでしょうか。   Excuse me, but where is the Mitsukoshi?

A. （ええ、しっています。） この 通_{とお}りの おわりです。   (Yes, I do.) It's at the end of this street.

		Location			
Topic は	Landmark	の	Position	です	

です can be used in this pattern instead of に あります. The question みつこしは どこでしょうか is a politer way of saying みつこしは どこですか.

Sentence Pattern 96

家の外で　こどもは　あそんでいます。

The children are playing in front of the house.

Location				
Landmark	の	Position	で	Action

Just as in Sentence Pattern 25, で is used if there is an action occurring at the location referred to.

C₁

You have already learnt the location words ここ, そこ, あそこ and how to use them to make sentences like おふろばは　ここです (Sentence Pattern 31).

You will also find the other location words in this list very useful.

Location words

ここ	Here		近く(ちかく)	Close
そこ	There		となり	Next (door) to
あそこ	Over there		よこ	Side
こっち	Here, this direction		前(まえ)	In front of
そっち	There, that direction		うしろ	Behind
あっち	Over there, in that direction		中(なか)	Inside
			下(した)	Underneath
右がわ(みぎがわ)	Right side		上(うえ)	On top
左がわ(ひだりがわ)	Left side		外(そと)	Outside
そば	Near, next to		ならび	On the same side
			むかいがわ	Across the street
Extension words ...			おわり	The end
こっちがわ	This side			
そっちがわ	That side			
あっちがわ	That side over there			

C₂

Answer these questions as they relate to the illustrations:

1 a. ねこは　どこに　いますか。

　b. いぬは　どこに　いますか。

　c. 車は　どこに　ありますか。

　d. えんとつは　どこですか。

　e. カーテンは　どこですか。

2 a. せんたくきの上に　何が　ありますか。
  b. アイロンだいの上に　何が　ありますか。
  c. たなの上に　何が　ありますか。
  d. せんたくかごのそばに　何が　ありますか。
  e. ドライヤーの下に　何が　ありますか。

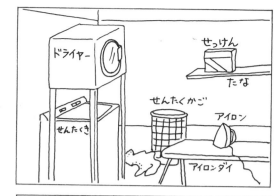

3 a. リビングの中で　お母さんは　何を
     していますか。
  b. くずかごの中に　何が　ありますか。
  c. バケツの中に　何が　あるでしょうか。
  d. バケツのそばに　何が　ありまか。
  e. そうじきのそばに　だれが　いますか。

4 a. たなの上に　何が　ありますか。
  b. おきどけいの下に　何が　ありますか。
  c. 本ばこの上に　何が　ありますか。
  d. コアラは　どこに　ありますか。
  e. にんぎょうは　どこに　ありますか。

5. Answer these questions as appropriate for the two
   people talking in front of the Yamadas' yard. They are
   facing the park.

  a. 山口さんは　山田さんのとなりですか。
  b. こう園は　田中さんの家のならびですか。
  c. 木は　どこですか。
  d. 山口さんの家は　右がわですか。
  e. じてん車は　どこですか。
  f. この通りのおわりに　何が　ありますか。

D

Read the dialogues on pages 250–51.

• Note the use of certain idioms and words — for example, いいえ.

• Also observe the useful strategy of confirming that you've understood everything by repeating it.

1. アンドルー： すみませんが　このへんに
　　　　　　　　ポストは　ありますか。

　日本人： ポストですか。
　　　　　　まっすぐ　行って　左がわに
　　　　　　郵便局が　あります。
　　　　　　ポストは　郵便局の前
　　　　　　です。

　アンドルー： 郵便局は　ふじ銀行のそば
　　　　　　　ですか。

　日本人： ええ、そうです。

　アンドルー： ありがとうございました。

　日本人： いいえ。

2. マリア： すみません。

　日本人： はい。

　マリア： まるぜんへ
　　　　　　行きたい（ん）ですが…

　日本人： まるぜん本屋ですね。

　マリア： ええ、そうです。

　日本人： じゃ、この通りを　わたって、
　　　　　　まっすぐ
　　　　　　行ってください。
　　　　　　二つ目の　しんごうを
　　　　　　左がわへ　まがってください。
　　　　　　つぎの　かどに　しんごうが
　　　　　　あります。その通りを
　　　　　　わたってください。目の前に
　　　　　　まるぜんの本屋が
　　　　　　あります。

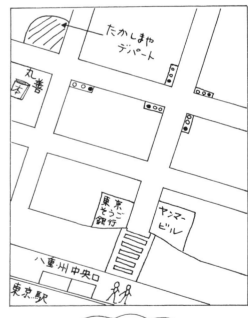

マリア： ちょっと　わかりません。
この　通りを　わたって、
まっすぐ　行って　二つ目の
かどを　左がわへ　まがるん
ですね。すると　一つ目の
かどに　まるぜんが　あるん
ですね。

日本人： ええ、そうです。

マリア： どうも　ありがとうございま
した。

日本人： いいえ。

3.

アンドルー： すみませんが　きょうわ銀行は
どこでしょうか。

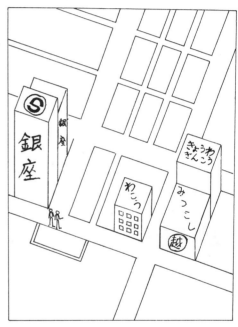

日本人： みつこしデパートを　しって
いますか。

アンドルー： いいえ、しりませんが...

日本人： じゃあ、この通りを　まっすぐ
行ってください。そうすると
左がわに　わこうデパートが
あります。その　かどを　左が
わへ　まがってください。わこ
うの　前に　みつこしデパート
が　あります。みつこしの
そばに　きょうわ銀行が　あり
ます。

アンドルー： どうも　ありがとうござい
ました。

日本人： どういたしまして。

In each of the following cases, *you* are being asked by a Japanese how to get to certain locations marked with a question mark. Write a set of instructions for the Japanese person to get to the required destinations.

1.

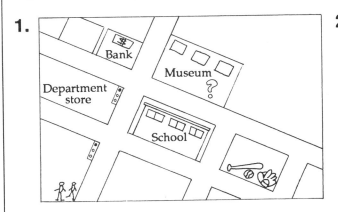

2.

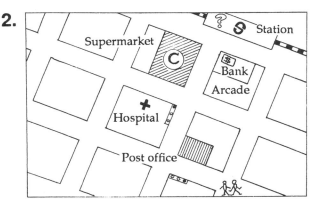

3.

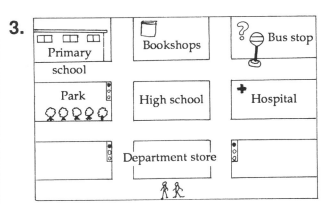

4.

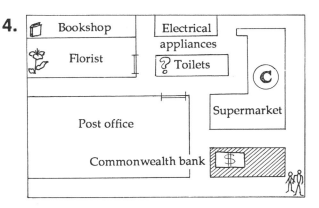

Because of the seemingly haphazard way in which many Japanese cities have grown, it is not easy to find your way around. The おまわりさん (and there are many of them) are vital in providing directions.

The following expressions could be very useful:

- みちに まよいました。

  I'm lost.

- ちずを 書いてくださいませんか。

  Would you please draw a map!

- もういちど せつめいしてくださいませんか。

  Would you please explain that again.

- たすけて（下さいませんか。）

  (Would you please) help me!

- きを つけて。

  Be careful. Take care.

The Kaminarimon Police Box, Asakusa

G

With a partner, prepare a dialogue between a policeman and someone who is lost.

Remember, in this instance you should try to be polite. Therefore you might choose ください ませんか ("won't you please"), which is more polite than just ください ("please").

H₁ Street signs

Street signs are numerous in Japan. Study the twelve road signs below and work out what each could mean. (An explanation is given in Japanese to help you.)

1. 人と　じてん車だけ
   とおれます。車は、
   入れません。

2. いったん止（と）まって、右（みぎ）と
   左（ひだり）を、よく見ましょう。

3. じてん車は、いったん止（と）まって、
   右（みぎ）と　左（ひだり）を、よく見ましょう。

4. 車が、入ることは
   できません。

5. 右（みぎ）と左（ひだり）を、よく見てわたり
   ましょう。ほどうきょうが
   あるときは、ほどうきょうを
   わたりましょう。

6. ここでわたってはいけません。

7. あるく人も、じてん車の
   人も　車も、入れません。

8. 青はすすめ、赤は止（と）まれ。

9. 車のさいこうそくどは　50キロです。

10. さきに、ふみきりが
    あります。きを　つけて。

11. いったん止（と）まって、右（みぎ）と左（ひだり）を、
    よく見ましょう。

12. じてん車も、車も　入れません。
    あるく人だけとおれます。

What happens where these two boys are walking?

I Complete each of the dialogues with appropriate sentences and idioms as shown in the example.

Example:

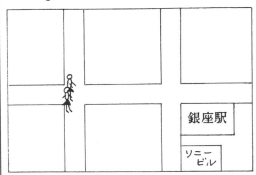

A. ソニービルは　どこに　ありますか。
B. あっちです。
　　ぎんざ駅のそば　です。
A. 駅のそばですね。
B. ええ、そうです。
A. どうも　ありがとうございます。

1. A. すみませんが　このへんに　ポストは
　　　ありますか。
　　B. ....。
　　A. ....。
　　B. ええ、そうです。
　　A. どうも。

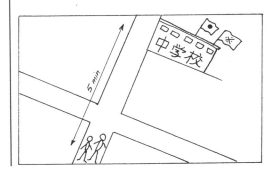

2. A. すみませんが　中学校は　ちかく
　　　に　ありますか。
　　B. ....。
　　A. どのぐらい　かかりますか。
　　B. ....。
　　A. どうも。

3. A. 郵便局は　左がわですか。

   B. ....。

   A. 郵便局は　スーパーの　前ですか。

   B. ....。

銀行		郵便局	
スーパー		本屋	
デパート			

J 聞きましょう

You will hear ten sentences stating where certain things are. In your exercise book, write down whether the object really is there or not. If it is, write ある. If it's not there, write ない.

K₁ 書きましょう・漢字

103. 左　Left

When you build anything, the *left* hand always helps the right hand by holding tools such as the carpenter's square shown in this kanji.

くん　ひだり　おん　さ　いみ　左

かきじゅん　一　ナ　ナ　左　左

5かく

104. 右 Right

Because we put food into our mouth with our right hand, the kanji for *right* is shown as a sketch of both a mouth and a right hand.

くん みぎ　おん ゆう、う　いみ 右

かきじゅん 一ナオ右右

5かく

105. 前 In front of, before

There are three parts to this rather abstract kanji. The top radical shows a chopping board on which meat is put to be cut up. The left-hand radical is a sketch of a pork chop *before* it is put on the chopping board. The radical on the right shows the chop after it has had the meat cut off. Together, the three radicals represent the idea of *in front of* or *before*.

くん まえ　おん ぜん　いみ 前

かきじゅん 丶丷丷广首首首前前

9かく

106. 名 Name

When the moon rises and night falls it becomes harder to see people's faces. People then have to call out their *names* to identify themselves. The kanji for *name*, then, consists of a sketch of the moon and the mouth used to call out one's name.

くん な　おん めい、みょう　いみ 名前 name

かきじゅん ノクタタ名名

6かく

107.　止　Stop

A picture of a foot that is flat on the ground means *stop*.

くん　と（まる）、と（める）　おん　し　いみ　止まる

かきじゅん　| １ | ト | 止 | 止 |

4かく

108.　高　High, costly

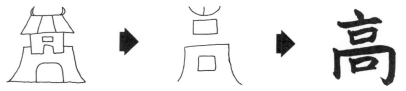

A castle is built **high** on a hill. It is also **costly** to build. Both meanings ("high" and "costly") are represented by this kanji.

くん　たか（い）　おん　こう　いみ　高い high, expensive

かきじゅん　| ` | 亠 | 宀 | 古 | 古 | 户 | 高 | 高 | 高 | 高 |

10かく

109.　銀　Silver

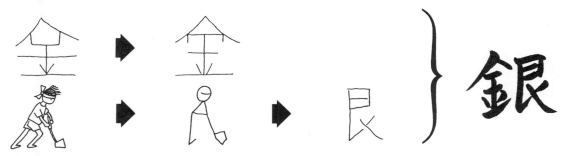

The kanji for *silver* consists of two parts; the first is the same as "gold" but when it is added to the second part — a person digging for *silver* — it takes on the meaning "silver".

くん　　おん　ぎん　いみ　銀行 bank

かきじゅん　| ノ | 人 | ト | 仝 | 仝 | 合 | 金 | 金 | 金 | 釘 | 釘 | 銀 | 銀 | 銀 |

14かく

110. 所 Place

The first radical represents a door — so simplified that it is barely recognisable.

The second half of this kanji shows an axe cutting the branches off a tree. The wood from the tree makes the *place* (including the door) where one lives or works.

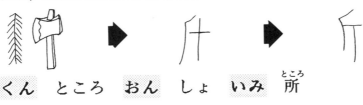

くん　ところ　おん　しょ　いみ　所(ところ)

かきじゅん　一 ラ ヨ 戸 戸 斦 所 所

8かく

111. 近 Near, close

Near consists of two radicals: the first (辶) means "advance, proceed or go forward" and the second (斤) means "axe". The idea conveyed is that one's progress is cut short so that one is still *near* or *close* to where one started.

The radical meaning "advance" or "go forward" shows the crossroads and a foot indicating that someone is travelling on foot.

The axe cutting the tree symbolises the cutting short of one's progress.

くん　ちか(い)　おん　きん　いみ　近(ちか)い、近所(きんじょ) neighbourhood

かきじゅん　ノ 亻 亇 斤 斤 近 近

7かく

112. 通　Go along, pass through

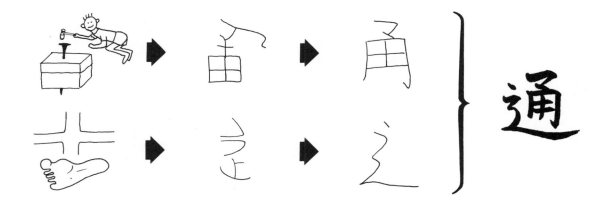

The idea of *to go along* or *to pass through* is represented by a nail being hammered until it passes through the wood. It is used in conjunction with 辶 to add to the idea of progressing and moving along.

くん　とお(る)、かよ(う)　**おん**　つう、つ　**いみ**　通る[とお]

かきじゅん　｜ フ ｜ マ ｜ ア ｜ 厃 ｜ 厈 ｜ 甬 ｜ 甬 ｜ 涌 ｜ 涌 ｜ 通 ｜

10かく

113. 郵　Collection and delivery of goods, letters

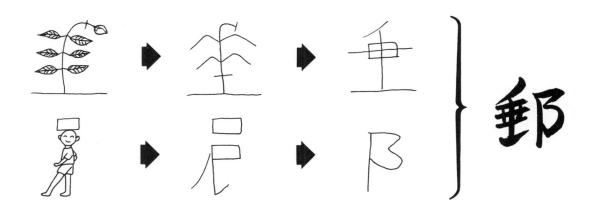

In this kanji, the first radical represents the collection of goods — in this case the picking of a flower. The second radical shows a person carrying goods on his or her head. Together they represent the *collection and delivery of goods, letters, etc.*

くん　　**おん**　ゆう　**いみ**　郵便[ゆうびん] post, mail

かきじゅん　ノ ｜ ┗ ｜ ╘ ｜ ┢ ｜ 弁 ｜ 乒 ｜ 乗 ｜ 垂 ｜ 郵 ｜ 郵 ｜ 郵 ｜

11かく

114. 便 Mail, convenience

Mail is sent and delivered by someone so the first radical shows a person.

In the second radical we see an oven with the fire under it, and a hand holding a fire poker. The idea is that, when a fire is poked, bright new sparks are formed. Receiving a letter from someone can make us bright, and the letter sparks or rejuvenates our friendship.

くん　たよ(り)　おん　べん、びん　いみ　^{ゆうびん}郵便 post, mail, ^{べんじょ}便所 toilet

かきじゅん　｜ノ｜イ｜イ｜仁｜佰｜佰｜佰｜便｜便

9かく

115. 局 Office

An *office* consists of people sitting down working and visitors coming into the office. (The visitors are represented by the mouth.)

くん　　おん　きょく　いみ　^{ゆうびんきょく}郵便局 post office

かきじゅん　｜フ｜コ｜尸｜月｜局｜局｜局

7かく

116. 紙 Paper

The first radical shows a loom spinning cotton. Many kanji that have the idea of something being developed include this as one of the radicals.

Paper was made from the reeds near the river, so this radical showing the lotus plant on the water was used to represent the material used for writing.

The two radicals together give the idea that friendships are spun or developed in letters on *paper*.

くん　かみ　おん　し　いみ　紙 paper, 手紙 letter

かきじゅん | 〈 | 纟 | 纟 | 纟 | 糸 | 糸 | 糸 | 紅 | 紅 | 紙 |

10かく

117. 私　Self, I, privacy

Each person is given his or her own bowl of rice — hence the first part of *self* is a rice stalk.

Combined with the rice stalk is a sketch of a nose — to further emphasise **I**, *self*, *privacy*.

くん　わたくし、わたし　おん　し　いみ　私

かきじゅん | 丿 | 二 | 千 | 千 | 禾 | 私 | 私 |

7かく

118. 待　Wait

The first radical represents the notion of someone going somewhere but stopping briefly at the crossroads.

By itself the second radical means "temple". The hand represents "measurement" (because the wrist is where one's pulse is taken). The laws of the land were drawn up by the monks in the temples. This fact is represented by a sketch of a plant — meaning "earth".

The stopping (at the intersection) before the temple meant *waiting*.

くん　ま(つ)　おん　たい　いみ　待つ

かきじゅん | 丿 | ク | 彳 | 彳 | 待 | 待 | 待 | 待 | 待 |

9かく

119. 兄 Older brother

Older brothers, because of their superior status within the family in ancient China, had the privilege of being able to use their big mouths to give orders to younger siblings. Their fast legs would obviously have helped out!

くん あに おん けい、きょう いみ 兄(あに)

かきじゅん ｜ 丨口口尸兄 5かく

120. 回 Turn, circle

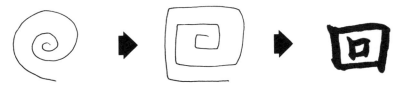

The circular form of a whirlpool gave the original idea for this kanji meaning to *go around in circles*, or *turn*.

くん まわ(す) おん かい、え いみ 回(かい) counter for a number of times

かきじゅん ｜ 冂冂冋回回 6かく

121. 安 Cheap, safe

A home with a roof above and a woman (mother) inside could ensure that other occupants (children) felt *safe* and *protected*. This kanji also means *cheap*. Perhaps the designer of this kanji was a man who also thought it would be cheaper for him if his wife stayed indoors rather than going out shopping!

くん やす(い) おん あん いみ 安(やす)い

かきじゅん ｀ 丶宀宀安安 6かく

122. 帰 Return

This kanji consists of three parts:

(a) In *returning,* one would have to go back down the road again.

(b) The hand would be used by a mother to signal to a child to come home.

(c) When a visitor is *returning* or *going home,* one gets a back view of the person. In Japan in years gone by, that would have meant getting a view of the obi at the back of the kimono.

くん　かえ(る)　おん　き　いみ　^{かえ}帰る

かきじゅん　｜　リ　リフ　リヲ　リヨ　リヨ゚　リヨ゚　帰　帰　帰

10かく

K₂ Make a list of all the kanji you know that contain the following radicals:

1. 言　2. 辶　3. イ　4. 女　5. 儿　6. 阝　7. 斤　8. 口　9. 艹　10. イ

K₃ Write out each of the following words or phrases three times and give the English meanings or names. The last one is for those who like a challenge!

1. 家の前に
2. 高山
3. 近くの薬局
4. 郵便局
5. 中学校
6. 花屋
7. じ動車

8. 名前
9. 銀行
10. 便所
11. 手紙
12. 夏休み
13. 本屋
14. 赤い花

15. 出入口
16. 元気
17. 食べ物
18. 目黒駅
19. 薬屋
20. 病院
21. 安売り

Naming people and places

Sentence Pattern 97

まつや　というデパートは
高_{たか}いでしょう。

The Matsuya department store is probably expensive.
(The department store called Matsuya)

Proper noun	という	General noun		=	a ... called ...

Explanation

You will find this pattern particularly useful when you wish to use the proper name for something with which your listener or reader may not be familiar.

Look at these examples:

- 「まつや」というデパートは　「みつこし」というデパートの　ならびです。

- 中山というかぞくは　となりです。

- 「サンシャイン60」というビルの　上まで　行きました。

- なっとうという食べ物は　まずいと　思います。

- べっぷという町に　すんでいます。

- プリンスホテルというホテルに　とまりました。

Answer the following questions as shown in the example.

Example:

Q. 休み中、どこに　とまりましたか。(At the place called Higashiyama Youth Hostel)

A. ひがし山ユース　ホステルという所に　とまりました。

1. ふつう　食べ物は　どこで　買いますか。(At a place called Benri Suupaa)
2. さくばん　どこで　食べましたか。(At a restaurant called Sushiro)
3. だれと　九州_{しゅう}に　かんこうりょ行するよていですか。 (With a friend called Tomoko Honda)
4. 一ばん　好きな　所は　どこですか。(A temple called the Byodoin)

5. となりの人は　何といいますか。(Setoguchi)

6. えい語の　せん生は　何といいますか。(Mr McKenzie)

7. 日本で　一ばんおもしろい　動物園は　何といいますか。(Ueno)

8. どこで　はたらいていますか。(At a company called Sony)

9. どの　大学に　入りたいですか。(A university called Waseda)

10. どこで　ばんごはんを　食べましょうか。(What about at the restaurant "With You"?)

L3 Put these sentences into Japanese:

1. I saw a movie called "Frantic".

2. Dogs eat food called "Pal".

3. The Sogo department store was busy yesterday.

4. I plan on going to a beautiful town called Takayama.

5. My next-door neighbours, who are the Watanabes, will probably buy a new car soon.

6. You must wait at the coffee shop called "Coffee and Cake".

7. I think that the food called "nattoo" is awful.

8. I must buy a toy called a "kendama".

9. May I go to the place called Hakone?

10. Turn left at the supermarket called "My Super".

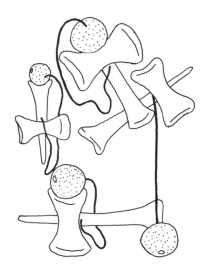

けんだま

L4 調べましょう

By asking questions of your penpal, by reading and by researching, can you complete the following phrases as shown in the example?

Example:

まつや　という...　　　→　　まつや　というデパート

1. ながさき　という...

2. そごう　という...

3. まるぜん　という...

4. わせだ　という...

5. 本田　という...

6. オーストラリア　という...

7. スミス　という...

8. マリア　という...

9. 高山　という...

10. たろう　という...

11. マクドナルド　という...

12. 「ゴースト」　という...

13. ヒルトン　という...

14. すう学　という...

₅

How would you refer to each of the following places if you didn't think your listener had heard of them before?

Example:

みつこし　というデパート

1.

2.

3.

4.

5.

6.

If you will be staying with a host family in Japan, it is likely that they will write a letter to you introducing themselves. There will usually be something in any letter that you won't understand. Don't panic. Concentrate first on what you *do* know and then get out your dictionary!

Read this letter that Elizabeth received from the family with whom she would be spending a week. Then put it into good English and write a reply.

エリサベスさんへ

お手紙を　はい見いたしました。私たちは　エリザベスさんに
あうことを　とても　たのしみに　しています。かぞくは
5人です。父と　母と　しゅ人と　むすめが　います。むすめは
11さいです。むすめのとも子は　小学校の　5年生です。しゅ人
は　えぼし中学校というハイ　スクールで　びじゅつを　おしえ
ています。私は　しごとを　していません。いつも　家に
います。母が　病気だからです。

四国の　こうちという町で　うまれました。23年間ぐらい　こう
ちに　すんでいました。そのあとで、こうべへ　来ました。

エリザベスさんの　学校は　つついだい中学校です。うちから
つついだい中学校まで　10分ぐらい　かかります。日よう日に
三のみやという所へ　行きましょう。三のみやに　みせが
たくさん　あります。だいまるというデパートへ　買い物に
行きましょう。だいまるは　13階だての　たて物です。まるぜん
という本屋を　しっていますか。ここで　いいじしょと　日本
についての本を　買うことが　できます。ざんねんですが
私たちは　えい語が　しゃべれません。いつも　えい語を
勉強したいと　思っています。私たちは　とても　安心してい
ます。エリザベスさんは　日本語が　できるからです。
いろいろ　おしえてください。どうぞ　よろしく　おねがい
します。

それでは、9月19日を　楽しみに　しています。お元気で、
ごかぞくの　みなさんに　よろしく。

　　　　　　　　　　　　　　さようなら

1993.8.04
中山　じゅん子

N | I'm okay

Your Japanese hosts will be very concerned that your stay in Japan is as enjoyable as possible. When they seem particularly worried, you could put their minds at rest with:

しんぱいしないでください。　　　　　Please don't worry.

You will also find だいじょうぶです and よろしいです two very useful expressions. They can be used in many circumstances, as shown below.

Both translate in English as "I'm/It's okay". However, they have different meanings and so are used in different situations.

- だいじょうぶ literally means "safe" or "secure". You can use it to indicate that you haven't hurt yourself, or that you can manage on your own without any help.

  In other words, you are not experiencing any physical trauma.

- よろしい, on the other hand, means "good, right, suitable or proper". It may be used by a shop assistant to confirm that a customer really does want the particular item in question.

  It may also be used to check if the listener really does understand what is being said.

The adverb — a tool for better communication

Without realising it, you have probably been displaying excellent understanding of adverbs ever since you started learning Japanese. Do you know what the following sentences or expressions mean? "Adverbs" have been used in each.

1. しずかに（してください）！

2. たのしみに しています。

3.

かきなさい = かいてください

4.

5.

6. よく　聞いてください。

7. どうぞ　よろしく。

8. はやく！

9.

かんがえる = to consider, think

Can you see the way in which adverbs are constructed?

Look at how an adverb works!

ADJECTIVAL NOUNS → ADVERB

- しずかな　所に　すんでいます。 *(adjective)*　　　I live in a quiet area.
  しずかに　してください。　　*(adverb)*　　　Please do it quiet*ly*.

- きれいな　花は　ふじと言います。 *(adjective)*　　The beautiful flower is called wisteria.

  ふじは　きれいに　見えます。　　*(adverb)*　　The wisteria looks beautiful.
  へやは　きれいに　してください。　　*(adverb)*　　Tidy your room.
  (Do your room neatly.)

TRUE ADJECTIVES → ADVERB

- {いい　せいとは　たくさん　います。 *(adjective)*　There are many good students.
  {よい

  せいとは　よく　勉強しています。 *(adverb)*　　Many students study well.

- チータは　はやい　動物です。　　*(adjective)*　　A cheetah is a fast animal.
  チータは　はやく　はしります。 *(adverb)*　　The cheetah runs fast.

In each of the sentences shown, the adjective describes a person, place or thing. The adverb in Japanese describes *how* something is, is done, looks or sounds.

For example:

How does a cheetah run? *Fast* → はやく

How are you to make your room? *Tidy/clean/neat* → きれいに

Sentence Pattern 98

(a) チータは　はやく　はしります。　　　　The cheetah runs quickly.

(b) しずかに　あそんでください。　　　　Please play quietly.

(c) エリザベスさんに　あうことを　楽しみに　　I am waiting happily/excitedly to meet Elizabeth.
　　待っています。

Explanation

To make an adjectival noun into an adverb, just add に: しずか → しずかに, きれい → きれいに, たのしみ → たのしみに. To change a true adjective into an adverb, change the final い into く: はやい → はやく, よい／いい → よく.

270　Isshoni 2

O₄ Change these adjectives or adjectival nouns into their adverbial forms:

1. はやい
2. 大きい
3. おそい
4. 上手
5. 下手
6. きれい
7. いい（よい）
8. ねむい
9. 小さい
10. あつい
11. しずか
12. 病気
13. 美しい
14. おもしろい
15. いそがしい

O₅ What does each of the following sentences mean?

1. 先生が　いませんでしたから　生とは　うるさく　話しました。
2. まり子さんは　いつも　きれいに　へやを　そうじします。
3. その　生とは　いっしょうけんめいに　勉強しないでしょう。
4. せと口先生は　上手に　えい語を　話します。
5. おじいさんは　えを　すごく　上手に　書きました。
6. 一しゅう間　東京で　楽しく　すごしました。
7. かれは　あまり　よく　できませんでした。
8. トムさんは　上手に　ピアノを　ひきません。
9. 12月25日を　楽しみに　待っています。
10. 子どもは　しずかに　あそんでいました。
11. おばあさんは　はやく　あるきません。
12. コーヒーを　あつく　してください。
13. この　みちを　よく　おぼえています。
14. とも子さんは　はやく　はしります。
15. ひとみさんは　おそく　おきました。

When the teacher's away — at a senior high school

O₆ The verbs します (do, act, behave), みえます (can see, look) and きこえます (can hear, sounds) can be used with adverbs to make a variety of interesting and useful sentences.

します　•　おとを　もうすこし　小さく　してください。

　　　　　Turn the volume down. (Please make the noise a little more small.)

　　　　•　つくえを　きれいに　してください。

　　　　　Please tidy your desk. (Please do/make your desk neatly.)

　　　　•　へやを　もうすこし　あかるく　してください。

　　　　　Please make the room brighter. (Please make your room a little more bright.)

Unit 21　**271**

みえます　　•　その　えは　きれいに　見えます。

The painting looks beautiful.

•　ここから　山は　近く　見えます。

From here, the mountain looks close.

•　この　へんは　きたなく　見えますね。

This area looks dirty, doesn't it.

きこえます　•　あなたのこえは　へんに　聞こえます。病気ですか。

Your voice sounds strange. Are you sick?

•　いぬの　こえは　大きく　聞こえます。どこに　いますか。

The dog('s voice) sounds loud. Where is it?

 Put the following sentences into Japanese. (Remember: when putting English into Japanese, think how the Japanese might express the *idea* that is expressed in English. Don't try to translate word for word.)

1. You look sick. Are you okay?
2. This hospital looks busy.
3. The children sound happy. They are playing noisily.
4. Turn the volume down, please.
5. That dress looks strange.
6. Please don't mess up your room.
7. These students always work very conscientiously.
8. This railway station looks dirty, doesn't it.
9. My grandparents live close by.
10. From the top of the New Shinjuku Building, you can sometimes see Mt Fuji.

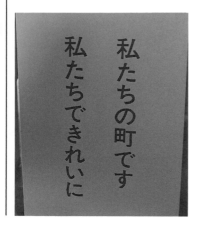 Can you work out what this sign is asking of everybody?

私たちの町です
私たちできれいに

Can you?

In Sentence Patterns 59 and 60 you saw how to express the ability to do particular things — for example, "I can play (do) the piano." In each of the sentences practised, the verb was always できます ("can do"). However, in many instances there will be a need to say that someone can or cannot do other things — for example, "can study", "can't go", "can't eat", "can visit". In all such cases the following pattern is used.

This girl can play the koto

Sentence Pattern 99

Q. くだ物を　安く　買うことが　出来ますか。　　Can you buy fruit cheaply?

A. はい、近くの　マーケットで。　　Yes, at the nearby market.

Explanation

By adding ことが　出来ます to the dictionary ending you can express any verb in the "potential" or "ability" form. Note also that 近くの is more commonly used than 近い.

Look at how Maria used the "potential" form when she jotted in her diary some of the things she could and could not do during her stay in Japan. What does she say?

- よる　おそくまで　一人で　ちかてつに　のることが　出来ます。
  安ぜんだからです。

- まい日、ともだちと　学校へ　あるく　ことが　出来ます。おなじ　マンションに　すんでいるからです。

- 木の　下で　ひるごはんを　食べることが　出来ません。日本で　せいとは　きょうしつの中で　ひるごはんを　食べなければ　ならないからです。

- 書どうを　ならうことが　出来ます。でも　私の　中学校で　フランス語を　ならうことが　出来ません。

- うちから　駅まで　あるくことが　出来ます。7分しか　かかりません。

- きのう　ちゃのゆへ　行くことが　出来ませんでした。ソックスを　もって　行くのを　わすれたからです。

P₃ Make a statement about what the people in each of the following photographs can or can't do. Include an adverb in at least five of your statements.

Q₁ | But ...

There are ways of showing contrast or contradiction other than が or でも. You will frequently hear these three words:

けど, けれども (or its shortened version けれど) and しかし

Like が, both けど and けれども can be used at the end of a statement. As well, like でも, they can be placed at the beginning of a sentence. しかし is, however, used only at the beginning of the qualifying statement and is somewhat more formal than でも and けれど(も).

Sentence Pattern 100

(a) きものは　きれいです。

でも
けれど(も)
けど
しかし
} とても　高いですね。

Kimono are beautiful. However, they are very expensive, aren't they?

(b) 秋_{あき}は　いいきせつだと思_{おも}います

が
けど
けれど(も)
} よく　雨_{あめ}が　ふりますね。

I think autumn is a good season, but it rains often.

Q₂ |

Using しかし, けど or けれど(も), add a contradictory or qualifying statement to each of the following sentences, in accordance with the clues given.

Example:

きのう　あつかったです。　(But it got cool at night.)

• しかし、よる　すずしく　なりました。

1. 銀_{ぎん}ざは　高い　所です。　　(But it is interesting.)

2. きのう　あたらしい　レストランで　食べました。　(But the food was awful.)

3. 7時まで　待ちました。　　(But Miss Suzuki didn't come.)

4. きのう　このビルの上から　ふじ山が　見えました。　(But we can't see it at all today.)

5. 駅まで　あるくことが　出来ます。(But it takes a long time.)

Answer each of the following questions in the negative and then add more information, as shown in the example.

Example:

Q. 上手に　うたうことが　出来ますか。

A. いいえ、上手に　うたうことが　出来ません。

けれども　おんがくを　聞くことが　好きです。

1. じてん車に　のることが　出来ますか。
2. コンピューターを　つかうことが　出来ますか。
3. はやく　はしることが　出来ますか。
4. 日本語で　手紙を　ただしく　書くことが　出来ますか。
5. 東京の　ちかてつに　一人で　のることが　出来ると　思いますか。
6. 来年　メキシコへ　行くことが　出来ますか。
7. 学校の　ダンスパーティーへ　行くことが　出来ますか。
8. とても　おそくまで　勉強することが　出来ますか。
9. 二さいの　子どもは　みちを　一人で　わたることが　出来ますか。
10. 日本語のざっしを　読むことが　出来ますか。

R

Imagine you are a nurse and the doctor describes a patient's state to you.

- The patient is not able to eat any food, but can drink water, tea and miso soup.

- The patient must not get out of bed.

- Visitors are not allowed in this patient's room.

- The patient is not able to watch TV.

Design the sign that you would place above the patient's bed.

S₁

As you wander around the streets of any Japanese city there will be many things that you have never seen or experienced before. Your Japanese hosts will take great delight in this. If it is the first time you've seen or done something, say so. It will make your hosts feel good and it will also demonstrate yet again how polite you are to communicate with them.

The following patterns will be useful in expressing the idea that you have never seen or done something before.

Sentence Pattern 101

(a)

Q. 前に　たたみ屋へ　行った
ことが　ありますか。

Have you ever been to a tatami shop before? (Do you have the experience of having been to a tatami shop before?)

A. いいえ、（前に　たたみ屋へ）
行ったことが　ありません。
今　はじめてです。

No, I haven't ever been to a tatami shop before. (No, I have not had the experience of having been to a tatami shop before.)

This is the first time.

(b)

Q. 日本へ　行ったことが
ありますか。

Have you ever been to Japan? (Do you have the experience of having been to Japan?)

A. いいえ、（日本へ）行った
ことが　ありません。

No, I have never been to Japan. (No, I don't have the experience of having been to Japan.)

(c)

Q. 東京タワーに　のぼったこと
が　ありますか。

Have you ever been up Tokyo Tower? (Do you have the experience of having been up/climbed Tokyo Tower?)

A. はい、二回　のぼったことが
あります。

Yes, I have been up twice. (Yes, I have had the experience of going up twice.)

Explanations

• A たたみや is the place (usually very small) where tatami mats are made, recovered or repaired. It is also possible to have the tatami mat cover turned over (once only) to renew its appearance. (See the photograph on page 274.)

• You may find it easier to understand the above patterns if you can think of them as meaning the following:

…た　ことが　ありますか	as	Do you have the experience (up to the present) of ever having (done) ...?
…た　ことが　あります	as	I have the experience of having (done) ...?
…た　ことが　ありません	as	I don't have the experience of having (done) ...

• To express the number of times something has occurred, the counter 回（かい） is used, as shown in the table on page 278.

何回　なんかい		How many times?
一回	いっかい	Once
二回	にかい	Twice
三回	さんかい	Three times
四回	よんかい	Four times

S₂ Answer each of the following questions in the manner shown, using the clues given. As you work through this exercise, make sure that you know what the questions and answers mean.

Example:

ほっかいどうへ　行ったことが　ありますか。(No)
いいえ、ほっかいどうへ　行ったことが　ありません。

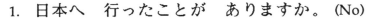

1. 日本へ　行ったことが　ありますか。(No)
2. オーストラリアへ　来たことが　ありますか。(No)
3. 東京へ　行ったことが　ありますか。(Yes, once)
4. あさくさかんのんを　見たことが　ありますか。(Yes)
5. おまわりさんと　話したことが　ありますか。(Yes, often)
6. ふじ山の　上まで　のぼったことが　ありますか。(No, but I'm looking forward to it.)
7. わしきの　おふろに　入ったことが　ありますか。(No, this is the first time.)
8. あきはばらへ　買い物に　行ったことが　ありますか。(No)
9. よる　学校から　うちまで　一人で　帰ったことが　ありますか。

   (Yes, but I got lost.)

10. ユースホステルで　とまったことが　ありますか。

    (Yes, at Higashiyama Youth Hostel in Kyoto. It was wonderful.)

11. 日本りょうりを　食べたことが　ありますか。(No)
12. 日本人と　話したことが　ありますか。(Yes, but not very often)

S₃ Imagine that you will be hosting a Japanese student in your Australian home in the near future. You want to plan a very exciting time for your friend and you want to make sure that it will be the first time he or she has experienced at least five things.

Write a letter in which, apart from including pleasantries and sharing information, you ask questions that will help you plan his or her stay with you. For example, you might ask questions like "Have you ever ridden a horse before?"

S4 Put these sentences into Japanese:

1. Can you play the piano well?

2. Have you ever been to Shikoku?

3. I am looking forward to meeting you.

4. Dad will meet you at a little shop called "The Silver Bell".

5. Excuse me, but do you know where the Tamaya department store is?

6. There is a beautiful garden in front of the Nakayamas' house.

7. Where is the dishcloth?

8. I think I'll stay at a youth hostel.

9. My hobby is stamp collecting.

10. It only takes seven minutes from home to the station.

T Read this culturally informative extract from a letter from your Japanese friend and rewrite it in English. Then write a reply in Japanese with similarly culturally informative details of life in Australia.

日本には きせつが 四つ あります。今 日本は 夏です。春は とても よいきせつです。じつは 春は 私の 一ばん好きな きせつ です。3月3日は ひなまつりでした。まい年 とても きれいな ひなにんぎょうを かざります。今年 とこのまに おばあさんと いっしょに にんぎょうを かざりました。ほんとうに きれいに 見えました。4月には たくさんの花が さきます。さくらの 花が とても きれいだから 花見に 行きます。今年も さくらの 花が とても きれいでしたから、さくらの木の下で かぞくの みんなと おべんとうを 食べました。

そして 4月5日に 学校が はじまりました。

5月5日は 子どもの日 でした。私は おとうとが 一人 います から、おじいさんと おばあさんが こいのぼりと かぶとを 買いま した。高かったです。

夏は とても あついから、学校は 40日間 夏休みです。

でも、夏休みの　前に　つゆが　あります。毎日　雨が　ふります。

7月20日から　夏休みですが、しゅくだいが　たくさん あります。
だから　毎日　勉強しなければ　なりません。

秋は　くだ物が　とても　おいしいですから、この　きせつが　大好き
です。まい年　みんなは　たくさん　食べて　ふとります。　とても
いい天気ですから、うんどうかいと　ぶんかさいが　あります。

冬は　とても　さむいから　きらいです。けれども　スキーは　好き
です。上手に　できませんが　楽しいと　思います。毎年　雪が　たく
さん　ふります。でも　きょ年の　12月と今年の　1月は　あたたか
かったです。雪が　すくなくて　スキーが　出来ませんでした。
ざんねんでした。

Situational dialogue — at the post office

- オーストラリアまで　手紙を　六まい　出したいの*ですが...

  I would like to send these six letters to Australia.

- きっては　いくらですか。

  How much is each stamp?

- こうくう便ですね。

  That's by airmail, isn't it?

- はい、そうです。

  Yes, please.

- オーストラリアまで　こうくう便で...

  To Australia by airmail ...

  80円です。ぜんぶで　480円に　なります。

  That's ¥80. In all that comes to ¥480.

- それに、この　こづつみを　ふな便で　おくり
たいの*ですが...

  As well, I'd like to send this parcel by seamail.

- はい、ぜいかんしんこくしょを　書いてく
ださい。

  Yes, fill in this customs declaration, please.

*The の is making the request a little politer, and is also encouraging the listener to respond.

- 2870グラムですから、4500円に　なります。ぜんぶで　4980円です。

  It's 2870 grams so that'll be ¥4500. That'll be ¥4980 in all.

- こづつみは　よろしいです　けど　手紙は　外の　ポストに　入れ
  てください。

  The parcel is okay but please put the letters in the post box outside.

V New words and expressions (words with an asterisk (*) are for recognition only)

Airondai	アイロンだい	Ironing board
Akarui	あかるい	Light, bright
Anshin	安しん	Peace of mind, relief
Antena	アンテナ	TV antenna
Aruku	あるく	To walk
Asuparagasu	アスパラガス	Asparagus
Atchi	あっち	Over there, that direction
Baketsu	バケツ	Bucket
Basutaoru	バスタオル	Bath towel
Chikai	近い	Nearby, close
Chizu	ちず	Map
Daidokoro	だい所	Kitchen
Daijoobu	だいじょうぶ	Okay, all right
Daimaru	だいまる	Large department store chain
Danchi	だんち	Housing development (high rise)
Dasu	出す	To post, to mail
Denshirenji	電しレンジ	Microwave oven
Disuko	ディスコ	Disco
Doraiyaa	ドライヤー	Clothes dryer
Entotsu	えんとつ	Chimney
Fuji ginkoo	富士銀行	Fuji Bank
Fujisan	富士山	Mt Fuji
Fukin	ふきん	Dishcloth
Fukinkake	ふきんかけ	Dishcloth rack
Fumikiri *	ふみきり	Railway crossing
Funabin de	ふなびんで	By seamail
Furaipan	フライパン	Frying pan
Futatsume (no)	二つ目(の)	The second (in a sequence)
Gasurenji	ガスレンジ	Gas stove
Gawa	がわ	Side
Genkan	げんかん	Entrance
Ginkoo	銀行	Bank
Guramu	グラム	Gram
Haburashi	はブラシ	Toothbrush
Hajimete	はじめて	First time
Hamigaki	はみがき	Toothpaste

Hamu	ハム	Ham
Heaburashi	ヘアブラシ	Hair brush
Hei	へい	Fence
Heya	へや	Room
Hidarigawa	左がわ	Left side
Hitotsume (no)	一つ目（の）	The first (in a sequence)
Hodoo kyoo	ほどうきょう	Pedestrian crossing
Honbako	本ばこ	Bookcase
Honya	本屋	Bookshop
Isshookenmei (ni)	いっしょうけんめい（に）	With all one's might
Ittan*	いったん	Once (e.g. "Once you've stopped")
Jitsu wa	じつは	As a matter of fact
Kaaten	カーテン	Curtain
Kado	かど	Corner
Kagami	かがみ	Mirror
Kai	回	Counter for times
Kamisori	かみそり	Razor
Kare	かれ	He
Karifurawaa	カリフラワー	Cauliflower
Kazaru	かざる	To display
Keizai*	けいざい	Economics
Keredo	けれど	However (less formal than keredomo)
Kinjo	近所	Neighbourhood
Kotchi	こっち	Here, this direction
Koogyoo*	こうぎょう	Industry
Kookuubin de	こうくう便で	By airmail
Koppu	コップ	Cup
… koto ga aru	… ことが　ある	To have the experience of …
Kozutsumi	こづつみ	A package
Kuriimu (kurenjingu kuriimu)	クリーム（クレンジング クリーム）	Cold cream (cleansing cream)
Kushi	くし	Comb
Kuzukago	くずかご	Waste paper basket
Kyoowa ginkoo	協和銀行	Kyowa Bank
Mae	前	In front of, before
Magaru	まがる	To turn, go around
Manshon	マンション	Apartment ("mansion")
Massugu	まっすぐ	Straight up
Matsuya depaato	まつやデパート	Matsuya department store
Mekishiko	メキシコ	Mexico
Me no mae ni	目の前に	Right in front of your eyes
Michinimayoimashita	みちにまよいました	I'm lost
Migigawa	右がわ	Right side
Mukaigawa	むかいがわ	Across the street
Mittsume (no)	三つ目（の）	The third (in a sequence)

Mon	もん	Gate
Moo sukoshi	もうすこし	A little more
Mukoo	むこう	Other (or opposite) side
Nabe	なべ	Saucepan
Nagashi	ながし	Sink (in the kitchen)
Naka	中	Inside, in
Nankai	何回	How many times?
Narabi	ならび	On the same side
… ni narimasu	… に　なります	That comes to …
… nen mae ni	…年前に	… years ago
Ningyoo	人ぎょう	Doll
Nihongo de kaitearu	日本語で　かいてある	… written in Japanese
Noogyoo *	のうぎょう	Agriculture
Okidokei	おきどけい	Clock (table clock)
Onaji	おなじ	Same
Owan	おわん	Wooden bowl
Owari	おわり	End
Painappuru	パイナップル	Pineapple
Posuto	ポスト	Post box (a red-orange colour)
Potto	ポット	Airpot/Vacuum flask filled with hot or cold drink
Reizooko	れいぞうこ	Refrigerator
Rejisutaa	レジスター	Cash register
Ribingu	リビング	Living room
Saikoo sokudo *	さいこうそくど	Maximum speed
Sakini	さきに	Soon, before long
… san ni yoroshiku	…さんに　よろしく	Give my regards to …
Sara	さら	Plates
Seifu *	せいふ	Government
Semai	せまい	Narrow, pokey, confined
Senmenjo	せんめん所	Bathroom
Sentakukago	せんたくかご	Clothes basket
Sentakuki	せんたくき	Washing machine
Serorii	セロリー	Celery
Shamoji	しゃもじ	Large wooden spoon
Shikashi	しかし	However
Shingoo	しんごう	Traffic lights
Shiru	しる	To know
Shita	下	Under, underneath
Shokkidana	しょっきだな	Kitchen cupboard
Shooyu	しょうゆ	Soy sauce
Soba	そば	Next to, beside
Soniibiru	ソニービル	Sony building
Soojiki	そうじき	Vacuum cleaner
Sooseeji	ソーセージ	Sausage
Soosuruto	そうすると	When you've done that, then

Sorezore (no)	それぞれ（の）	Each
Sotchi	そっち	There, that direction
Soto	外	Outside
Suru to	すると	Whereupon, on doing that
Susume*	すすめ	Go forward
Tadashii	ただしい	Correct, right, proper
Tana	たな	Shelf
Tatamiya	たたみ屋	Tatami mat shop
Tenugui	手ぬぐい	Towel
Tetsudau	手つだう	To help, to assist someone with their work
Toiretto peepaa	トイレットペーパー	Toilet paper
Tomaru	止まる	To stop
Tonari	となり	Next door, next door neighbour's house
Toori	とおり	Street, road
Ue	上	On top of, above
Ushiro	うしろ	Behind
Utau	うたう	To sing
Wakoo depaato	わこうデパート	Wako department store
(o) Wataru	（を）わたる	To cross (the street)
Yane	やね	Roof
Yoko	よこ	Side
Yuubinkyoku	郵便局	Post office
Yuubinuke	郵便うけ	Letterbox
Yuusuhosuteru	ユースホステル	Youth hostel
Zannendesu ga …	ざんねんですが …	Unfortunately, it is unfortunate
Zeikan shinkokusho	ぜいかんしんこくしょ	Customs declaration form

W₁

Kanji studied to the end of Unit 21:

Unit 13:	一	二	三	四	五	六	七	八	九	十	人	何			
	1	2	3	4	5	6	7	8	9	10	11	12			
Unit 14:	目	口	日	本	母	父	白	赤	黒	色	大	小			
	13	14	15	16	17	18	19	20	21	22	23	24			
Unit 15:	月	花	木	子	女	好	言	夏	火	秋	春	冬	雨	雲	天
	25	26	27	28	29	30	31	32	33	34	35	36	37	38	39
	気	年													
	40	41													
Unit 16:	上	手	下	語	中	学	校	外	男	生	今	階			
	42	43	44	45	46	47	48	49	50	51	52	53			

Unit 17:	思	見	聞	行	話	電	買	売	読	入	食			
	54	55	56	57	58	59	60	61	62	63	64			
Unit 18:	動	物	園	馬	駅	時	青	土	水	金	美			
	65	66	67	68	69	70	71	72	73	74	75			
Unit 19:	田	町	休	車	朝	家	京	東	都	来	勉	強	山	間	書
	76	77	78	79	80	81	82	83	84	85	86	87	88	89	90
Unit 20:	耳	足	出	立	元	飲	病	院	頭	楽	薬	屋			
	91	92	93	94	95	96	97	98	99	100	101	102			
Unit 21:	左	右	前	名	止	高	銀	所	近	通	郵	便	局	紙	私
	103	104	105	106	107	108	109	110	111	112	113	114	115	116	117
	待	兄	回	安	帰										
	118	119	120	121	122										

The unit in which each katakana was introduced:

Unit 14:	ア	ン	ト	ル	ナ	ー	ヒ	ク	オ	レ	シ	リ
	1	2	3	4	5	6	7	8	9	10	11	12
Unit 15:	ハ	イ	マ	テ	ス	ラ	ツ					
	13	14	15	16	17	18	19					
Unit 16:	コ	ユ	タ	ノ	キ	ニ	カ	フ	ケ	チ	エ	ロ	ミ
	20	21	22	23	24	25	26	27	28	29	30	31	32
Unit 17:	セ	ネ	ウ	ヘ	サ	ホ						
	33	34	35	36	37	38						
Unit 18:	ヤ	モ	ソ	ヌ	メ	ヨ	ム					
	39	40	41	42	43	44	45					
Unit 19:	ワ	ヲ										
	46	47										

Mothers usually carry their babies in slings rather than use strollers, which are too cumbersome going up and down the steps in railway stations

Topics:

Offering assistance ...

It is easy to look up a word in a dictionary, but when the word has different meanings it is often difficult to choose the correct form from the range given. The verb "help" is certainly one of these words.

There'll be many times during a homestay when you will want to offer assistance, but do you use 手つだう or たすける ?

- たすける means to rescue someone who is in trouble. So you might hear someone being attacked yelling:

  たすけてくれ！(*males*) たすけて！(*females*) — meaning "Help!"

- 手つだう, on the other hand, means to assist someone with his or her work.

Therefore, when offering to help people with what they are doing, you could say 手つだいしましょう ("I shall help you") or, even more politely, お手つだいしましょう ("Can I help you?").

What would it mean if you said this to someone who was standing precariously on the side of a bridge?

「手つだいしましょう」

How to ...

While staying with a Japanese family there will be many opportunities for you to do things together. You'll learn how to do many things and, likewise, you'll be wanting to show your new friends how to do various things. The next pattern will prove very useful.

Sentence Pattern 102

(a) この そうじきの つかい方が 分かりません。

I don't understand how to use this vacuum cleaner.

(b) 書どうのし方を 知りません。

I don't know how to do calligraphy.

(c) てんぷらの りょうりのし方を わすれました。

I have forgotten how to cook tempura.

Explanation

1. To change a verb into the "how to ..." form, add かた（方）to the ます base and notice the change of particle を to の.

　　さらを　あらいます　→　さらの　あらい方（かた）= how to wash the dishes

　　きっぷを　かいます　→　きっぷの　かい方（かた）= how to buy a ticket

2. The する verbs such as 勉強する, 電話する, そうじする, りょうりする, せつめいする also need particle の before し方.

C₂ What does each of these sentences mean?

1. この　かんじの　書き方（かた）が　分（わ）かりません。
2. あの　男の人の　あるき方（かた）は　おもしろいですね。
3. 日本語の　勉強のし方（かた）を　教（おし）えて下さい。
4. この　そうじきの　つかい方（かた）を　教（おし）えて下さい。
5. あの　さるは　木の　のぼり方（かた）が　すごいですね。
6. この　かんじの　読み方（かた）が　分（わ）かりません。
7. ちかてつの　のり方（かた）を　ならいたいです。
8. すしの　作（つく）り方（かた）を　教（おし）えて下さい。
9. 車の　うんてんのし方（かた）を　知（し）っています。
10. ふとんの　しき方（かた）を　教（おし）えて下さいませんか。

C₃ Put these sentences into Japanese:

1. I like the way he teaches Japanese.
2. Please show me how to use the washing machine.
3. I don't understand how to put my futon out. Would you please show me?
4. Would you please show me how to clean the lacquer ware?
5. Would you please show me how to eat these long noodles?
6. The way my little brother walks is funny.
7. Please show me how to cook inari zushi.
8. Do you know how to explain this in English?
9. Do you know how to cook chawanmushi?
10. It is interesting to watch how she skilfully cuts the paper.

Inari zushi and chawanmushi

C₄ A very useful expression using the 方 pattern is:

し方が　ない。   It can't be helped.

This literally means "There is no way to handle this situation." It is, therefore, used to express resignation at an outcome. For example, if your host parents were being very apologetic about having to cancel your trip to Tokyo Disneyland because of a bad storm, you could show that you understand that it is beyond their control by saying し方が　ない.

C₅ What does each of the following dialogues mean?

1. • ぼんおどりのし方を　知っていますか。

   • ええ、知っていますけど　あまり　上手に　出来ません。

Bon odori

2. • うちへの　帰り方を　おぼえていますか。

   • はい、17ばんの　バスに　のって　クリスタル　マンションで
     おります。すぐ　うちが　見えます。

3. • おり紙で　かえるの　おり方を　知っていますか。

   • ええ、やさしいです。

4. • 今日、何を　ならいましたか。

   • 日本語で　じこしょうかいのし方を　ならいました。

5. • じゅぎょうの　あとで　何を　しましたか。

   • イングリシュ　スピーキング　クラブで　アドバンス　オーストラリア
     フェアと言ううたの　うたい方を　教えました。楽しかったです。

123. 百　Hundred

One (一) bag of rice weighed **one hundred** pounds so the kanji for a hundred consists of the kanji for "one" and a grain of rice, which represents a full bag of 100 pounds.

くん　　おん　ひゃく　いみ　百ひゃく

かきじゅん　｜一｜ｱ｜ｱ｜丙｜百｜百｜　　　　　　　6かく

124. 千　Thousand

When a **thousand** people stand to attention in a row, only the first one can be seen clearly.

くん　ち　おん　せん　いみ　千せん、千人せんにん thousand people

かきじゅん　｜ノ｜ノ｜千｜　　　　　　　3かく

125. 円　Yen

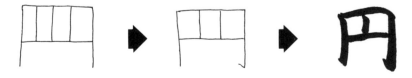

The new, simplified kanji for **yen** must have come from a sketch of a bank-teller's cage!

くん　まる(い)　おん　えん　いみ　円えん

かきじゅん　｜｜｜冂｜冂｜円｜　　　　　　　4かく

126. 市 Market, city

The kanji for *city* or *market place* is a sketch of the gate at the entrance to the market place and of the road that leads through it.

くん いち　おん し　いみ 市（し）

かきじゅん ｀ 亠 广 市 市　　　　5かく

127. 国 Country

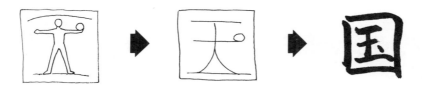

A *country* consists of a border and many people (both represented by the radical 口), and a king holding a national treasure. The king and all his subjects have the heavens above and earth below them, as represented by the two horizontal lines.

くん くに　おん こく　いみ 国（くに）、外国人（がいこくじん）foreigner

かきじゅん 丨 冂 冂 冂 同 国 国 国　　　　8かく

128. 広 Wide, spacious

The cliffs along the coastline offer a *wide*, expansive view of the ocean for any person (symbolised by the nose) wanting such a view.

くん ひろ(い)　おん こう　いみ 広（ひろ）い

かきじゅん ｀ 亠 广 広 広　　　　5かく

129. 洗 Wash

The first radical shows the sparkling water as it flows down the waterfall.

People go to the river (which is surrounded by reeds) to wash their feet.

Together the two radicals have the meaning *wash*.

くん　あら(う)　おん　せん　いみ　^{あら}洗う、洗たくき washing machine

かきじゅん 　`　 ⁏　氵　汀　沪　汫　汫　洗 　　　　　9かく

130. 毎 Every

Every person (represented by the top radical) has a mother.

くん　　おん　まい　いみ　毎^{まいにち}日 every day

かきじゅん ノ ⺅ ⺈ 女 毎 毎 　　　　　6かく

131. 先 Previous, ahead

The top radical shows the plants growing along the river bed while the second radical shows a person running to the river to wash his feet. You will use this kanji mostly in the word for teacher, 先生 . The idea being expressed is that just as the water gives life to the plants, and as the river refreshes and revitalises the body, it is your teacher whose lessons help you learn and whose ideas stimulate your brain to help you get *ahead* in life.

くん　さき　おん　せん　いみ　先生 teacher, 先月 last month

かきじゅん　┃ノ┃┝┃ﾉ┤┃生┃牛┃先┃　6かく

132. 分　Division, part, minute

A stick is *divided* into two *parts* by a sword. Time is divided into *minutes*. When something is divided into small pieces or parts it can be analysed. It is then easier to *understand*.

くん　わ(ける)　おん　ぶん、ふん、ぶ　いみ　分 minute, 分かる understand

かきじゅん　┃ノ┃八┃分┃分┃　4かく

133. 知　Know

To say that you *know* something is to be particularly direct. Hence the kanji for "know" consists of a straight arrow and a mouth.

くん　し(る)　おん　ち　いみ　知る 、知らせる to inform

かきじゅん　┃ノ┃┝┃┝┃ﾄ┃矢┃知┃知┃知┃　8かく

134. 作　Make

The inspiration for this kanji was a man building or *making* his house.

くん　つく(る)　おん　さく、さ　いみ　作る

かきじゅん　┃ノ┃亻┃亻┃作┃作┃作┃作┃　7かく

135. 方 Direction, way, means, person, suffix indicating plurality

It is possible to tell the *way* the wind is blowing, or its *direction,* by watching which way the boats are moving.

くん かた おん ほう いみ あなた方 (あながた) you (plural), し方 (しかた) how to do ...

かきじゅん `丶 亠 方 方` 4かく

136. 新 New

New branches grow in spring after the tree has been pruned with an axe. The kanji consists of a tree with lots of growth, and the axe next to another tree.

くん あたら(しい)、あら(た)、にい おん しん いみ 新しい (あたらしい) new, fresh
新聞 (しんぶん) newspaper

かきじゅん `丶 亠 十 立 立 产 辛 亲 亲 釒 剃 新 新` 13かく

137. 泊 Stay, one night's stay, lodge

Staying the night somewhere usually also means having something to eat and drink. Therefore the kanji for *stay* contains the radicals for both water and rice.

くん と おん はく いみ 泊まる (とまる) pass a night, stay, 一泊 (いっぱく) one night's stay

かきじゅん `丶 冫 氵 氵 汋 泊 泊 泊` 8かく

138. 教 Teach, educate

The kanji for *teaching* consists of three parts:

(a) The first radical is an old man on a walking stick, representing a learned teacher.

(b) The second radical represents a child.

(c) A whip is used if necessary to ensure that the child does as he or she is told.

くん　おし(える)　おん　きょう　いみ　教える、教し teacher

かきじゅん　｜一　十　土　ナ　芦　考　孝　孝　郏　教　教｜　　11かく

D2 Put these words into kanji:

1. Newspaper	6. Teacher	11. School	16. Chemist shop
2. How to make	7. Name	12. Park	17. Zoo
3. Takayama city	8. Chinese people	13. Foreigners	18. Nine minutes
4. Each year	9. University	14. Last month	19. How to understand
5. A telephone	10. Letter	15. Animal's legs	20. One thousand, two hundred and twenty

E1 Answer each of the following questions in an extended manner, as shown in the example. Try to make your answers as creative but as realistic as possible.

Example:

Q. ソフトテニスの　やり方を　知っていますか。

A. はい、ソフトテニスの　やり方を　知っていますが　あまり　上手じゃないです。

1. JRじこくひょうの　読み方が　分かりますか。
2. オーストラリアの　ラミントンの　作り方を　知っていますか。
3. きものの　き方を　知っていますか。
4. 日本の　ふろの入り方を　おぼえていますか。
5. 日本の　ちかてつの　のり方を　知っていますか。

E₂

Before your first visit to Japan it would be a good idea if you could answer each of these questions in the affirmative!!!

1. わしきの　おふろの　入り方が　分かりますか。

2. わしきの　お手洗いの　つかい方が　分かりますか。

3. ふとんの　しまい方が　分かりますか。

4. ふろしきの　つつみ方が　分かりますか。

5. めいしの　出し方が　分かりますか。

6. 電車の　きっぷの　買い方が　分かりますか。

Life in Japan revolves around people doing things together as a group. In fact, Japanese see themselves more as members of a group than as individuals. They believe that it is when working well as a group that people work best and improve as individuals, and when each individual is working to the best of his or her ability the group (company/community/nation) is most effective.

Japan's success in the world economy is often attributed to the effectiveness of this philosophy.

Schools are perfect examples of where we see everyone working together.

• Read the following dialogue that could take place before a ぶんかさい and act it out.

• Then, in small groups, write similar dialogues showing a group of people working together.

G1 In many discussions involving groups of people doing things together, people quote either directly or indirectly what others have said. The Japanese way of quoting is much simpler grammatically than the way we do it in English. See how useful you would find the following sentence patterns.

Sentence Pattern 103

(Direct speech)

お母さんは 「おきてください」と言いました。　　Mum said "Get up!"

Person who says something	は	Actual statement made	と言う

Sentence Pattern 104

(Indirect speech)

1. お母さんは おきる と言いました。　　Mum said that she will get up.

2. まりこさんは アンドルーさんが りゅう学生だ と言いました。　　Mariko said that Andrew is an exchange student.

3. アンドルーさんは たいいくさいが おもしろかった と言いました。　　Andrew said that the Sports Festival was interesting.

4. マリアさんは 日本の 中学校が 楽しい と言っています。　　Maria says that Japanese junior high schools are fun.

Person who says something not being quoted directly	は	Summary of statement made in the plain form	と言う

G2 What does each of these sentences mean in English?

1. いもうとは 「チョコレート ケーキを 作って下さい」と 言いました。

2. 毎日 お母さんは 「あけみちゃん、ふとんを しまってください」と言います。

3. 毎日 大きいこえで こうちょう先生に 「おはようございます。」と 言わなければ なりません。

4. 車しょうは 「つぎは 池袋、つぎは 池袋、しゅうてんでございます。ご注意下さい。」と 言いました。

5. みせの人は　「いらっしゃいませ。」と　言いました。

6. ふつうは　じゅぎょうのあとで　生とは　いっしょに　「先生、ありがとう　ございました。」と　言います。

7. ていねいな　銀行いんは　「おまたせいたしました。」と　言います。

8. エレベーターの　女の人は　「しょうしょう　お待ちください。」と　言います。

9. ひょうしきに　「お足元に　ご注意下さい。」と　書いてあります。*
   <small>あしもと</small>　<small>ちゅうい</small>

10. ひょうしきに　「ディスカウントショップ」と　書いてあります。

    *書いてある means "reads" or "is written" and it is used in the same way as と言う.

G₃ On a day out in Japan with your Japanese friends, they read or repeat directly all the signs and announcements that you see or hear. You are to tell them what the equivalent is in English. (You may need to use a dictionary to look up some words.) Write down what they say to you and then give the English meaning.

Example:

禁煙

- ひょうしきに　「きんえん」と　書いてあります。
- The sign says "No smoking".

1. あしもとに　注意
   <small>ちゅうい</small>

2. つぎは　しんじゅくでございます。

3. お出口は　左がわでございます。

4. まもなく、はらじゅく、はらじゅく。

5.

2	電車が来ます

6.

出口⇨

7.

東京駅

8.

コインロッカー

9.

タクシーのりば

10. These are for those of you who like a challenge. You will need your kanji and a Japanese–English dictionary to work them out!

What does each of these sentences mean in English?

1. お母さんは　私たちが　おばあさんと　二日ぐらい　泊まると　言います。
2. 先生は　たいふうが　強くないと　思っています。
3. 八百屋（やおや）は　赤いりんごが　安いと　言いました。
4. となりの人は　むすこが　それを　してはいけないと　言いました。
5. ともだちは　毎日　家の前で　私を　待つと　言いました。
6. お母さんは　オーストラリアへ　行ったことが　ないと　言いましたけれど　ヨーロッパへ　行ったことが　あると　言いました。
7. ともだちは　スイスが　一ばん美しい国だと　思うと　言いました。
8. お父さんは　新しい車を　買いたいと　言いました。
9. すずきさんの　お母さんは　みこしの　作り方を　知っていると　言いました。
10. けんたろうくんは　けっして　学校を　休まないと　言いました。

G₅ Put these sentences into Japanese:

1. The teacher said, "Shall we go to Kyoto for our school excursion this year?"

2. Mum always says, "You must eat your vegetables."

3. Akemi said, "Please don't use the white paper. It's mine."

4. The principal said, "You must not eat chewing gum at this school."

5. "Please turn the volume down," said Dad.

6. Akemi said, "Today my legs are aching because yesterday I climbed Mt Fuji."

7. In Japan, dogs say "Wan wan."

8. Mum said to go to the shop.

9. The teacher said to write the story in our notebooks.

10. My grandmother said that she won't shut the windows.

11. Hitomi said that she won't cook meat pies again.

12. She said, "These are awful!"

H₁ Quote indirectly what the following people have said. Remember to use the "plain form" before と言う.

こうちょう先生

あしたの朝、八時に 出ます。

Example:

こうちょう先生は あしたの 朝、
八時に 出ると 言いました。
The principal said that we would leave at 8 o'clock.

1. お母さん

銀ざの みつこしの前で 10時30に
待っていてください。

2. ゆう子

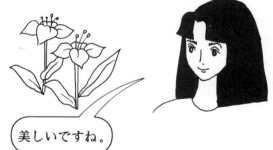

美しいですね。

3. としお

ゆう名な タワーです。

4. 先生

生とは、毎日、しゅくだいを しなければ
なりません。

5. ひでみさんの　お父さん

東京銀行に　つとめています。

6. 駅ちょう

その　電車は　ひめじ行きです。

7. あなた。

おります。

8. 車しょう

しゅうてんです。

つぎは　いけぶくろ、しゅうてんです。

9. 先生

よく　出来ました。

10. お父さん

日よう日に　おばあさんを　ほうもんするよていです。

H2 Express these sentences in Japanese:

1. The train conductor said, "Be careful not to leave anything behind."

2. Yoshiyuki said that the move called "Ghost" was very funny.

3. Dad said that I must study every day during the holidays.

4. My aunt said that the weather in Kyushu was fine.

5. The radio announcer said that it snowed in Sapporo yesterday.

6. The doctor said that I have a fever.

7. Mr Setoguchi said, "Always carry your rail pass!"

8. Michiko said that the history exam was easy.

9. The teacher said that your painting was beautiful.

10. The little girl said that she was lost.

What is this?

If it rains ... (The conditional tense)

Involving others in your plans, as you will during any homestay, means that there'll be negotiations and compromises; as well, you'll be seeking information before making decisions.

Understanding the conditional tense ("if ...") allows you to be much better at doing all of the above. It allows you to have greater control over arrangements that involve you, and it allows you to understand more fully the consequences of choosing to do one thing rather than another.

There are several ways of expressing the idea "if ...". They are sometimes interchangeable and sometimes not. In this course, the たら form (the more colloquial) will be studied.

This form will allow you to make plans with others and organise alternative activities — and generally express yourself even better.

Sentence Pattern 105

(a) あした　雨が　ふったら　　行きません。　　　If it rains tomorrow I won't go.

たら is used to mean "if". It is commonly used in the pattern

If ... then { I will (volition)
            { I won't

The verb is always in the plain past + たら.

(b) 安かったら　買って下さい。　　　　　　If it's cheap, please buy it.

たら is also the conditional form used when "if" is followed by an order, command, instruction or request. A true adjective is also put in plain past form + ら.

(c) しごとが　はやく　おわったら　わたしの
うちに　来て下さい。

If you finish your work early, please come to my place.

If the principal clause is an invitation, the たら form may be used to mean "if".

(d) Q.　ひまが　あったら　どう　しますか。

What will you do if you get/when you get some free time?

A.　もし　ひまが　あったら　いい本を
読みたいです。

If I get some free time, I want to read a good book.

たら may also be used to mean "if" in questions or in sentences when the time is in the future. もし in the answer serves to emphasise "if" rather than "when". It is also used in a conditional sentence when the possibility of the event happening is fairly remote.

Sentence Pattern 105 (continued)

(e) 車だったら　15分　かかります。　　　If (you go by) car, it will take 15 minutes.

たら can be used to mean "if" if the second clause will happen as a result of the first clause happening. The たら form of an adjectival noun or a noun is formed by adding ら to the だった (the plain past form).

(f) もし　私は　大学を　そつぎょう　　　If can graduate from university, I'll be an
出来たら　先生に　なりたいです。　　　　elementary school teacher.

In this example, もし further emphasises the meaning "if" as in (d). Note how you can use できる with する verbs.

(g) お金が　あったら　こんな　うちには　　If I had money, I wouldn't be in this kind of
いません。　　　　　　　　　　　　　　house.

Notice the use of the particle が in the above sentences.

There are other ways of expressing the idea "if" and there are other meanings of the suffix たら. However, you will probably find the seven uses in the above pattern quite enough for now.

I₂

What does each of the following sentences mean in English?

1. しゅくだいが　はやく　おわったら　おばあさんの　うちに　行きましょう。
2. 雨が　ふったら　えいがに　行きましょうか。
3. 知っていたら　教えて下さい。
4. 日本へ　行ったら　浅草へ　買い物に　行きたいです。
5. もし　雨が　ふったら、ハイキングは　やめます。
6. もし　時間が　あったら　チョコレート　ケーキを　作りましょう。
7. いそがしくなかったら、あそびに　行きましょうか。
8. 分からなかったら　私に　言って下さい。
9. ゆう名な　所だったら　そこへ　行きましょう。
10. ともだちの　電話ばんごうを　知っていたら　教えて下さい。
11. まい日　日本語を　れんしゅうしたら　きっと　上手に　なるでしょう。
12. はやく　そうじ出来たら　買い物に　行きましょう。

I₃ Put these sentences into Japanese:

1. If you have time, do you want to come to Kyoto with me to see the Byodoin?
2. If it rains, may we go to Ikebukuro to do some shopping?
3. If it's hot in your room, please open the windows.
4. If it doesn't rain, do you want to go hiking?
5. If the Ginza is crowded, let's go to Shinjuku.
6. If I'm not at home, please wait outside for me.
7. If the weather is fine, let's go fishing.
8. If it's quiet later, I'll write some letters.
9. If it rains, do you want to play shogi with me?
10. If you don't understand, please tell me.

In front of Seibu Ikebukuro station

J Write a dialogue between yourself and a Japanese exchange student who is staying with you. In the dialogue you try to plan the first couple of days and generally try to make him or her feel at home. You may wish to say things like:

- If you want to do any washing, I'll show you how to use the washing machine.
- If you don't understand my English, please tell me.
- If it doesn't rain, would you like to walk to my friend's house with me?
- This is your room. Please make yourself at home. If it gets cold, please shut the window.

Use at least five "conditional" sentences in your dialogue.

K Answer the following questions as in Sentence Pattern 104(g), using all of the activities listed below each question.

しつもん **A**: もし お金が たくさん あったら どう しますか。
こたえ:　　　I'd like to (I want to) buy a big house.
　　　　　　I'd like to go to Japan.
　　　　　　I'd like to buy a new car.
　　　　　　I'd like to buy a bike.
　　　　　　I'd like to travel the world.

しつもん **B**: もし ひまが あったら どう しますか。
こたえ:　　　I'd like to travel around Japan.
　　　　　　I'd like to travel around Australia.
　　　　　　I'd like to read lots of good books.
　　　　　　I'd like to visit my friends often.
　　　　　　I'd like to learn how to do calligraphy.

L₁ What do these sentences mean in English?

1. そんな物を　食べたら、病気に　なります。
2. きょうしつが　しずかだったら　勉強しましょう。
3. 先生に　聞いたら　分かりますよ。
4. 学校が　おわったら　およぎに　行きましょう。
5. そんな　あまい　おかしを　たくさん　食べたら　ふとるでしょう。

L₂ How is each of the following sentences expressed in Japanese?

1. I plan to travel to Kyushu in the winter. (That is, "When it becomes winter, I plan to travel to Kyushu.")
2. If it's not expensive, I'll buy it.
3. If you're hot, please take off your jacket.
4. If the teacher is talking, students must not talk.
5. If it rains tomorrow, you aren't going, are you?

Would you pay this much for a rockmelon?

M たら is also used in certain idiomatic expressions such as:

...たら　いいです。
いいでしょう。 } It would be nice/good if ...

...たら　だめです。　　It'll be bad if ...

...たら　たいへんです。It'll be dreadful if ...

...たら　どうですか。　What about if (we) ...

Even in such sentences, there is still a sequence of first and then second.

What do the following sentences mean in English?

1. あなたも　いっしょに　行ったら　いいでしょう。
2. ここで　すこし　休んだら　どうですか。
3. 近くの　こう園で　あそんだら　どうでしょうか。
4. この　コップを　おくったら　いいでしょう。
5. あしたは　うんどうかいですね。雨が　ふったら　たいへんですね。
6. 毎日、しゅくだいを　しなかったら　だめです。

Andrew and Maria are coming towards the end of their twelve months in Japan and are now starting to make plans to come home.

Read Andrew's letter to his parents (who can now understand his Japanese) and put it into English so that his grandparents will also know the news.

お母さんと　お父さんへ

お元気ですか。来月の　27日に　ブリスベンへ　帰るよていです。土よう日の　20:15に　しゅっぱつすると　思います。ジャルです。日よう日の　7時ごろ　ブリスベンの　国さい　くうこうに　つきます。もし　ちがったら　電話します。

ちょっこうびんです。

すずきさんは　なりたくうこうまで　車で　つれて行くと　言いました。でも　雨が　ふったら　電車に　のるでしょう。わけは　みちが　大へん　こんでいるからです。

今年は　とても　楽しかったですが　オーストラリアへ　帰ることを　楽しみに　しています。また　土よう日は　休みに　なります。

来しゅう、ともだちと　一しゅう間　かんこうりょ行するよていです。京都に　ある　「うたの」　と言う　ユースホステルに　泊まります。もう　よやく　しました。　京都に　おもしろい所が　たくさん　あります。金かくじを　見た　ことが　ありますが　りょうあんじへ　行ったことが　ありません。　行きたいです。ひまが　あったら　奈良へも　行きたいです。「お母さん」は　奈良の　とう大じは　せかいで　一ばん　大きい木のたてものだと　言いました。

じゃ、すぐ　あいましょう。

Andrew

O₁ ユースホステル Youth hostels

Staying at youth hostels is an excellent way to travel around Japan fairly cheaply and at the same time meet lots of young people. As long as you become a member of the Youth Hostel Association and you are over 14 years of age (if travelling without an adult), you are able to use the Japanese hostels. They vary in price, but for bed/futon, dinner and breakfast you could expect to pay about $35.

Remember to take your own bath towel and to observe the youth hostels' "Lights out!" and "Doors locked" rules. These are strictly observed!

You will need to make a reservation. (You can obtain names and addresses of youth hostels in Japan from any Youth Hostel Association office.)

Make your reservation by sending a letter something like this to the ペアレント.

YOUTH HOSTEL APPLICATION FORM

ペアレントさんへ

名前 .... Print name in block letters

じゅうしょ
住所 .... Print address in block letters

....

....

しゅくはく
宿泊月日　　　月　日から　　月　日まで（　泊）　　Dates and number of nights stay

　　　　　　　　男　　　名　　　　Number of males
　　　　　　　　女　　　名　　　　Number of females
　　　　　　　ごうけい
　　　　　　　合計　　　名　　　　Total number

しょくじ　うちわけ　つぎ　　　　ねが
食事の内訳 ... 次のようにお願いします。　　Breakdown of meals requested

　　　　　　　　　　　　　　　ちょうしょく
　　　　　　　月　　　日　　　朝食　　　Date(s) for breakfast
　　　　　　　　　　　　　　　ゆうしょく
　　　　　　　月　　　日　　　夕食　　　Date(s) for evening meal

とうちゃく
到着は　から　　月　　日　　時ごろ　　Arrival date and time
しっぱつ
出発は　まで　　月　　日　　時ごろ　　Departure date and time

308　Isshoni 2

O₂ Hostels — what you can expect

Utano Youth Hostel, Kyoto — this one has double-decker beds.

Tenshoji Youth Hostel, Takayama — this hostel offers large and small "dormitory"-style rooms, complete with ふとん .

Most hostels have large dining halls with either tables and chairs or Japanese-style furniture, like this one at Tenshoji Youth Hostel. A requirement of hostels is that you help clean up after your meal!

... and don't forget to get all the soap off yourself *before* getting into the hostel's baths — which are single sexed but communal.

P₁ How long will you be staying?

If you have not pre-booked, one question you will need to answer at a hotel or youth hostel will be this one:

どのぐらい　ごたいざいに　なりますか。

To which you could answer:

1泊　たいざい　したい(ん)　です。　I would like to stay one night.

(The ん is optional, but it does make the sentence politer and encourages the listener to make a comment.)

何泊　なんぱく	How many nights?	
1	一泊	いっぱく
2	二泊	にはく
3	三泊	さんぱく
4	四泊	よんはく
5	五泊	ごはく
6	六泊	ろっぱく
7	七泊	ななはく

P₂ What does each of these sentences mean in English?

1. 1泊　たいざいしたいんですが...
2. 1泊　だけ　たいざいしたいんです。
3. 2泊　よやく　しました。
4. 3泊　たいざいしても　いいですか。
5. 京都に　一しゅう間　たいざいするよていです。
6. 4泊　たいざいします。
7. 3泊　よやく　しました。

Q Situational dialogue — at the youth hostel

あなた：　　　　　今ばんは。わたしは　アンドルー　ジョーンズです。先月
　　　　　　　　　手紙で　二泊　よやく　しました。

ペアレント：　　　はい、わたしたちの　ユースホステルへ　ようこそ
　　　　　　　　　いらっしゃいました。

　　　　　　　　　へやは　17ばんごうです。2階です。かいだんは　あちら

です。男の人の　おふろは　一階です。おふろの　時間は
7時から　8時まで　です。夕食時間は　5:30–6:30です。

どうぞ　ごゆっくりしてください。

あなた:　　　　はい、ありがとうござます。

R₁ | Cooking together

You and your Japanese friends can learn much when cooking, by teaching one another how to cook something. It is not too difficult to learn lots of vocabulary by helping out in the kitchen because we tend to repeat certain words and phrases, for example, にく "meat", きる "cut", あらう "wash", いためる "fry", 火に　かける "put on the fire/stove", まぜる "stir, mix".

Try cooking this recipe at home or at school with a couple of friends from your Japanese class. Each of you should try to learn off the names of the ingredients as you work. Try to communicate only in Japanese.

すきやき どんぶり

どうぐ

はし　まないた　ほうちょう　ざる　大さじ
アルミの　あついなべ　(なければ　フライパン)

ざいりょう　(3人ぶん)

ごはん:	3人ぶん
ぎゅうにく:	250 g
ねぎ:	2ほん
しらたき:	1わ
しょうゆ:	大さじ　3ばい
さとう:	大さじ　2はい
水:	大さじ　3ばい
サラダオイル:	大さじ　1ぽい

作り方

1. にくを　ほそく　きります。

2.

しらたきを　まないたに　ひろげて、5–7 cm に　きります。よく　洗って、ざるに　あげて　おきます。

3. ねぎを　洗います。
ねを　きりおとして、3 cm くらいの
ながさに　きっていきます。さらに
たてはんぶんに　きります。

4.

アルミの　あついなべに　サラダオイル
を　大さじ　1ぱいと、ねぎを
入れて、火に　かけます。(ガスの
火は　中くらいです。)

5. なべが　あつくなったら　はしを　つかって、ねぎを　いためます。ねぎが
やわらかく　なって　きたら、ぎゅうにくと　しらたきを　入れます。

6. さとうを　大さじ　2はい、しょうゆ
を　大さじ　3ばいと　水を　大さじ
3ばい　入れて　よく　まぜます。
5ふんぐらい　にたら　ガスの火を
けします。

7. あたたかい　ごはんを、どんぶりに
もりつけ、その　上に、すきやきと
おなべに　のこったしるを　かけます。

R₂ Using a dictionary, try putting one of your favourite recipes into Japanese. Give your recipe to someone else in the class, get them to cook it and see if it tastes the same!

You may like to swap a recipe with your penfriend and see if you can follow his or her instructions.

S₁ ## Review

Put these sentences into Japanese:

1. When I graduate, I want to be a lawyer.
2. My new black shoes are expensive.
3. This dress was not very expensive.
4. It will soon be winter.
5. The dance is on the 12th of November.
6. I was born on 6 August 1975.
7. Our school has two floors.
8. I like visiting my grandparents.
9. The animals at the zoo were lively.
10. I want to stay with my friend for two weeks.
11. Let's meet at the restaurant "Everyone's Favourite" at about 6 o'clock.
12. I am not interested in European history.
13. Our house is made of wood.
14. The meat was probably expensive.
15. You must drink this medicine.
16. Our house is near a little shop.
17. Is there a post box around here?
18. We will stay in a youth hostel in Takayama but we'll stay in a hotel in Nara.
19. I have forgotten how to cook lamingtons.
20. Andrew says that life in Japan is fun.
21. Mum said, "Clean up your room now!"
22. If you study hard, you will understand.
23. If you finish your homework early, do you want to come to the movies with me?
24. You must not come in.
25. I don't want to work in a bank.
26. In winter I usually go skiing in Sendai with my family.
27. Hitomi has brown eyes and black hair.
28. My father is a teacher and my mother is a nurse.
29. When is your birthday, Kentaro?
30. I can play the piano well.
31. I think cricket is boring but I enjoy watching football.
32. This blue shirt is my favourite.
33. I plan on going to Shikoku this year.
34. I'll stay at the youth hostel for two nights.
36. I don't want to go on the 16th of June because I have an exam on the 17th.
37. My hobby is collecting stamps.
38. Jenny has a sore throat. I think she has a cold.
39. Please don't eat the cakes.
40. May I go with you too?
41. There is a pretty garden in front of the house.
42. The exam was not difficult.
43. The shop nearby is very convenient.
44. Have you ever been to Nagasaki?
45. I can't study properly here. It is very noisy, isn't it?
46. If it rains, we'll stay home.

Put these sentences into English:

1. のうは　ふくざつだと　思います。
2. 私は　ひしょに　なりたいと　思います。
3. この　へびは　かまないから　大じょうぶです。
4. ピアノを　あまり　上手に　ひくことが　できません。
5. きものの　き方を　教えて下さいませんか。
6. いとこの　ジェニーは　来年　日本へ　来るよていです。
7. 赤い　りんごは　一ばん　おいしいと　思います。
8. お母さんは　「今、ステレオの　おとを　小さく　して　下さい」と　言いました。
9. ビデオは　おもしろくなかったです。
10. 東京から　大阪まで　3時間ぐらい　かかります。
11. すてきな　えいがを　テレビで　見ました。
12. ディビッド　ジョーンズと　いうデパートは　5階だての　たて物です。
13. 12月の24日に　りょうあんじを　見に　行くよていです。
14. しゅくだいを　わすれたことが　ありません。あなたは？
15. えい語を　上手に　話すことが　できますね。
16. 日本でも　学校は　3時に　おわります。
17. 日本では　12月は　さむいです。
18. しゅう学りょ行は　楽しかったです。
19. お父さんは　十時ごろ　帰ります。
20. あそこに　ぞうが　二頭　います。
21. この　動物園は　きれいですね。
22. しょうしょう　お待ち下さい。
23. ケーキを　もって来ましたか。
24. ごかぞくは　何人ですか。
25. さるは　うるさかったです。
26. おばあさんは　白が　です。
27. すぐ　夏に　なります。
28. むしあついですね。
29. じょうだんだろう！
30. シチューを　まぜて　下さい。
31. きれいに　なしを　きって　下さい。

Stone garden at Ryoanji Temple, Kyoto

32. その　ひょうしきを　読むことが　出来ますか。
33. 日本では　つりに　行ったことが　ありません。
34. あした　はれでしょう。
35. この　電しレンジの　つかい方が　分かりません。
36. 休みを　楽しみに　しています。
37. 薬局は　郵便局の　そばです。
38. きのう　マリアさんは　足が　いたいと言っていました。
39. かの女は　薬を　ほしがっていました。
40. おふろの　中で　せっけんを　つかっては　いけません。
41. 日本では　土よう日にも　学校へ　行かなければなりません。
42. 神戸の　ユースホステルで　2泊　泊まるよていでした。けれども　病気に
　　なりました。
43. オーストラリアでは　生とは　教しつで　サンドイッチを　食べてはいけ
　　ません。
44. ねこは　木の上で　ねずみを　食べています。
45. どのぐらい　ごたいざいに　なりますか。
46. 3泊　たいざいしたいんですが...

S₃ What would you say in each of the following situations?

1. When you greet your host parents first thing in the morning.
2. When you have finished your breakfast.
3. When you farewell your host mother in the morning before you go to school.
4. When you see your teacher first thing in the morning.
5. When you want to check if your friend is okay—he has just tripped over!
6. When you don't want any more of the drink that your friend is offering you.
7. When you say goodbye to your teacher at the end of the day.
8. When you get home.
9. When your host parent suggests that you look very tired.
10. When your host parent suggests that you have a bath—before the rest of the family.
11. When you get out of a very relaxing bath.
12. When you go to bed.
13. When you answer the telephone.
14. When you ask your host parents if you could help them do something.
15. When someone frightens you.

Answer each of these questions that your host family could ask you. Develop your answers as much as possible.

1. 馬に　のったことが　ありますか。
2. お父さんの　ごしょくぎょうは　何ですか。
3. 一ばん　好きな　食べ物は　何ですか。
4. おたん生日は　何月何日ですか。
5. ピアノを　ひくことが　出来ますか。
6. あなたの　学校は　何階だてですか。
7. 何を　するのが　好きですか。
8. コアラは　どんな　食べ物を　食べますか。
9. 来年　何を　するよていですか。
10. あなたの　しゅみは　何ですか。
11. あなたの　家は　何で　出来ていますか。
12. 学校は　あなたの　家の　近くですか。
13. オーストラリアに　たいふうが　きますか。
14. ミートパイの　作り方が　分かりますか。
15. ペットが　いますか。
16. おちゃを　もう　いっぱい　いかがですか。
17. ふつうは　何時ごろに　ねますか。
18. 日本語の新聞を　読むことが　出来ますか。

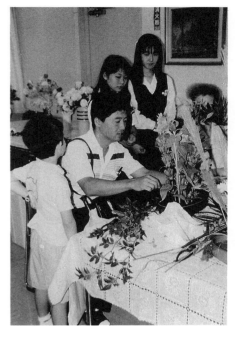

Learning how to do ikebana

New words and expressions (words with an asterisk (*) are for recognition only)

Arumi no atsui nabe	アルミの　あついなべ	Deep aluminium saucepan
Ashimoto	足元	Step (gait)
Bangoo	ばんごう	Number
Bideo	ビデオ	Video
Bonodori	ぼんおどり	Bon Festival dance
Chawanmushi	ちゃわんむし	Steamed egg custard with chicken and prawn
Chokkoo bin	ちょっこうびん	Direct flight
Chooshoku	朝食	Breakfast
Chuuingamu	チューインガム	Chewing gum
Damedesu	だめです	It's bad/wrong. Don't do that, it'll be no good
Densha	電車	Electric train
Domburi	どんぶり	(Deep) bowl
Doogu	どうぐ	Utensils
Doo suru	どうする	What to do

Ekichoo	駅ちょう	Station master
Futon o shiku	ふとんを　しく	To lay out the bedding
Ginkooin	銀行いん	Bank clerk
Gochuuikudasai	ご注意下さい	Please be careful
(Go)yukkurishitekudasai	（ご）ゆっくりして下さい	Make yourself at home
Gyuuniku	ぎゅうにく	Beef
Hajimeni	はじめに	Firstly
Haku, paku	泊	Counter for night's stay
Hambun	はんぶん	Half
Harajuku	原宿	Suburb of Tokyo
Hi ni kakeru	ひにかける	To put on the fire/heat/stove
Hirogeru	広げる	To spread out, unfold
Hoochoo	ほうちょう	Kitchen knife
Hosoi	ほそい	Thin, slender
Hyooshiki	ひょうしき	Sign, signpost
Ikebukuro	池袋	Suburb of Tokyo
Inari zushi	いなりずし	Rice wrapped in fried bean curd
Ippaku	一泊	One night's stay
Irasshai	いらっしゃい	Welcome
Ireru	入れる	To put in, insert
Itameru	いためる	To stir fry
Jikokuhyoo	じこくひょう	Timetable
Kaeru	かえる	To convert to, change
Kaeru	かえる	Frog
Kaidan	階だん	Stairs
Kaite aru	書いてある	To be/is written
Kakeru*	かける	To pour on
Kata	方	How to, way of
Kesu	けす	To turn off
Kinen	きんえん	No smoking
Kokunai (no)	国ない（の）	Domestic
Kokusai (no)	国さい（の）	International
Kondeiru	こんでいる	To be crowded
Konoyooni	このように	Like this
Kuni	国	Country
Mamonaku	まもなく	Soon
Manaita	まないた	Chopping board
Mazeru	まぜる	To stir, mix, blend
Meishi o dasu	めいしを　出す	To give one's name card
Mikoshi	みこし	Portable shrine
Monogatari	ものがたり	Tale, story
Moritsukeru	もりつける	To dish up, dish out
Moshi	もし	If
Nampaku	何泊	How many nights?
Ne*	ね	Roots
Negi	ねぎ	Eschallots

Nihonjuu ryokoosuru	日本中りょ行する	To travel around Japan
Niku	にく	Meat
Niru	にる	To boil, cook
Nokoru *	のこる	To be left over
Noseru	のせる	To place (a thing) on
Nugu	ぬぐ	To take off (jacket)
Odori	おどり	Dance
Odoru	おどる	To dance
Okashii	おかしい	Funny, strange
Oosaji	大さじ	Tablespoon
Oriru	おりる	To get off, to get down from, descend
Oru	おる	To fold
Otemawarihin	お手回りひん	One's personal effects
Otosu*	おとす	To clean off the dirt
Owaru	おわる	To end, finish
Owasuremono	おわすれもの	Belongings left behind
Pearento	ペアレント	Manager of a youth hostel
Ryooanji	りょうあんじ	Temple with stone garden in Kyoto
Ryuugakusei	りゅう学生	Exchange student
Saji	さじ	Spoon
Satoo	さとう	Sugar
Sekaijuu ryokoosuru	せかい中りょ行する	To travel the world
Sentakuki	洗たくき	Washing machine
Shashoo	車しょう	Conductor, guard (of a train)
Shichuu	シチュー	Stew
Shikata	し方	Way of doing
Shikataganai	し方がない	Can't be helped
Shiku	しく	To make, lay out a bed (a futon)
Shimau	しまう	To put away
Shinjuku	新宿	Suburb of Tokyo
Shirataki	しらたき	Clear Japanese noodles
Shiru	しる	Juices, broth
Shiru	知る	To know
Shooshoo omachikudasai	しょうしょうお待ちください	Please wait a moment
Shuppatsusuru	しゅっぱつする	To depart
Shuuten	しゅうてん	Terminus, terminal
Sofuto tenisu	ソフトテニス	Soft tennis
Sorede wa	それでは	Well, in that case
Suisu	スイス	Switzerland
Sumimasen	すみません	Said to a waitress to indicate that you want service: "Excuse me ..."
(ni) suru	(に) する	To decide on
Taizaisuru	たいざいする	To stay (at a place)
Tasukeru	たすける	To help someone who is in trouble
Tokoro	所	Place

Toodaiji	とう大じ	A temple in Nara
Tsukuru	作る	To make
Tsutsumu	つつむ	To wrap, tie up (a furoshiki)
Ukagau	うかがう	To call (on a person at the person's house), visit
Wa	わ	Counter for a bundle of something
Wake	わけ	Reason
Yameru	やめる	Not do, to cancel
Yaoya	八百屋	Greengrocer, vegetable shop
Yaru	やる	To play, act, perform, do
Yasashii	やさしい	Easy, simple
Yawaraka (na)	やわらか（な）	Tender, soft
Yookoso irasshaimashita	ようこそいらっしゃいました	Welcome, we are glad that you have come
Yoyakusuru	よやくする	To book, make a reservation
Yuushoku	ゆう食	Dinner, evening meal
Zairyoo	ざいりょう	Ingredients
Zaru	ざる	Bamboo plate
Zaru ni ageru	ざるに　あげる	To put on a bamboo plate

U₁ Kanji studied to the end of Unit 22:

Unit 13:
一	二	三	四	五	六	七	八	九	十	人	何
1	2	3	4	5	6	7	8	9	10	11	12

Unit 14:
目	口	日	本	母	父	白	赤	黒	色	大	小
13	14	15	16	17	18	19	20	21	22	23	24

Unit 15:
月	花	木	子	女	好	言	夏	火	秋	春	冬	雨	雲	天
25	26	27	28	29	30	31	32	33	34	35	36	37	38	39

気	年
40	41

Unit 16:
上	手	下	語	中	学	校	外	男	生	今	階
42	43	44	45	46	47	48	49	50	51	52	53

Unit 17:
思	見	聞	行	話	電	買	売	読	入	食
54	55	56	57	58	59	60	61	62	63	64

Unit 18:
動	物	園	馬	駅	時	青	土	水	金	美
65	66	67	68	69	70	71	72	73	74	75

Unit 19:
田	町	休	車	朝	家	京	東	都	来	勉	強	山	間	書
76	77	78	79	80	81	82	83	84	85	86	87	88	89	90

Unit 20:	耳	足	出	立	元	飲	病	院	頭	楽	薬	屋			
	91	92	93	94	95	96	97	98	99	100	101	102			
Unit 21:	左	右	前	名	止	高	銀	所	近	通	郵	便	局	紙	私
	103	104	105	106	107	108	109	110	111	112	113	114	115	116	117
	待	兄	回	安	帰										
	118	119	120	121	122										
Unit 22:	百	千	円	市	国	広	洗	毎	先	分	知	作	方	新	泊
	123	124	125	126	127	128	129	130	131	132	133	134	135	136	137
	教														
	138														

The unit in which each katakana was introduced:

Unit 14:	ア	ン	ト	ル	ナ	ー	ヒ	ク	オ	レ	シ	リ
	1	2	3	4	5	6	7	8	9	10	11	12
Unit 15:	ハ	イ	マ	テ	ス	ラ	ツ					
	13	14	15	16	17	18	19					
Unit 16:	コ	ユ	タ	ノ	キ	ニ	カ	フ	ケ	チ	エ	ロ	ミ
	20	21	22	23	24	25	26	27	28	29	30	31	32
Unit 17:	セ	ネ	ウ	ヘ	サ	ホ						
	33	34	35	36	37	38						
Unit 18:	ヤ	モ	ソ	ヌ	メ	ヨ	ム					
	39	40	41	42	43	44	45					
Unit 19:	ワ	ヲ										
	46	47										

Appendix A
Map of Japan

1. さっぽろ
2. はこだて
3. あおもり
4. あきた
5. せんだい
6. ふくしま
7. にいがた
8. にっこう
9. とやま
10. とうきょう
11. かなざわ
12. たかやま
13. よこはま
14. ふじさん
15. ぎふ
16. なごや
17. びわこ
18. きょうと
19. ひめじ
20. おおさか
21. こうべ
22. なら
23. おかやま
24. たかまつ
25. ひろしま
26. こうち
27. まつやま
28. せとないかい
29. きたきゅうしゅう
30. ふくおか
31. べっぷ
32. おおむた
33. くまもと
34. ながさき
35. かごしま
36. おきなわ

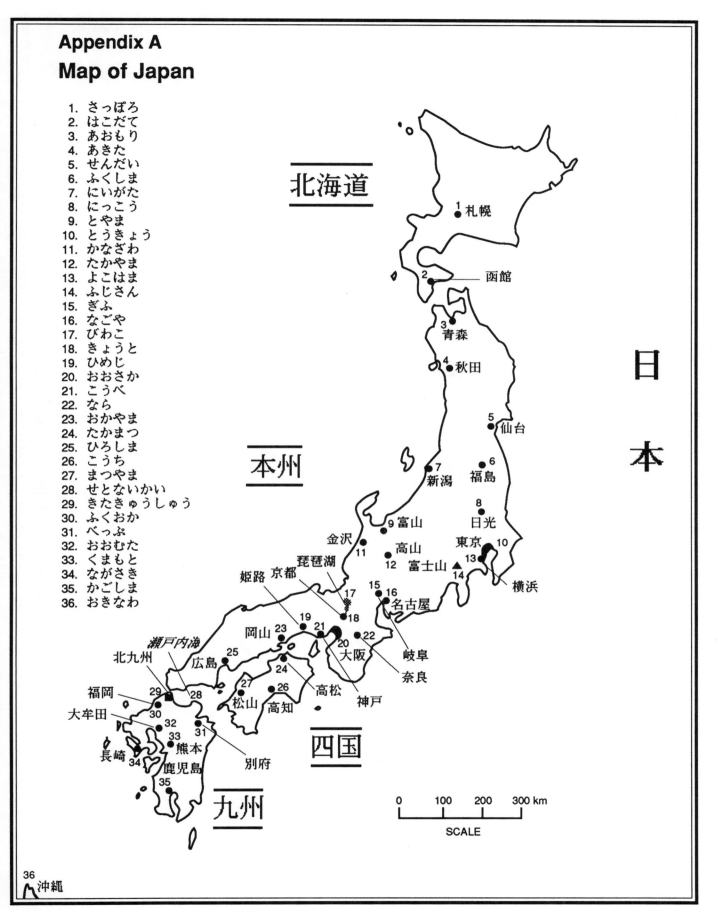

日本

北海道

1 札幌

2 函館

3 青森

4 秋田

5 仙台

本州

7 新潟

6 福島

8 日光

9 富山

金沢
11

高山

12 富士山

東京
10
13
14

横浜

15
16 名古屋

17
18

琵琶湖
姫路 京都

岡山 23
19
21

瀬戸内海
北九州 25
広島

20 大阪
22

岐阜

奈良

福岡
29 28
27 24
26

神戸

高松

松山 高知

高知

四国

大牟田
30
32
31

33
別府

長崎 熊本
34
鹿児島
35

九州

0   100   200   300 km

SCALE

36
沖縄

あ a	い i	う u	え e	お o
か ka	き ki	く ku	け ke	こ ko
さ sa	し shi	す su	せ se	そ so
た ta	ち chi	つ tsu	て te	と to
な na	に ni	ぬ nu	ね ne	の no
は ha	ひ hi	ふ fu	へ he	ほ ho
ま ma	み mi	む mu	め me	も mo
や ya		ゆ yu		よ yo
ら ra	り ri	る ru	れ re	ろ ro

わ wa	を o
ん n	

Appendix C
Katakana Chart

ア a	イ i	ウ u	エ e	オ o
カ ka	キ ki	ク ku	ケ ke	コ ko
サ sa	シ shi	ス su	セ se	ソ so
タ ta	チ chi	ツ tsu	テ te	ト to
ナ na	ニ ni	ヌ nu	ネ ne	ノ no
ハ ha	ヒ hi	フ fu	ヘ he	ホ ho
マ ma	ミ mi	ム mu	メ me	モ mo
ヤ ya		ユ yu		ヨ yo
ラ ra	リ ri	ル ru	レ re	ロ ro

ワ wa	ヲ o
ン n	

Appendix D

A summary of verb-endings of selected verbs

This chart lists a selection of each type of verb.

Ichidan Verbs

English	Japanese stem	Stem + ない	Stem + ます	Stem + る	te-form	ta-form
Be, exist	い-	いない	います	いる	いて	いた
Be born	うまれ-	うまれない	うまれます	うまれる	うまれて	うまれた
Begin	はじめ-	はじめない	はじめます	はじめる	はじめて	はじめた
Can do	でき-	できない	できます	できる	できて	できた
Consider	かんがえ-	かんがえない	かんがえます	かんがえる	かんがえて	かんがえた
Eat	たべ-	たべない	たべます	たべる	たべて	たべた
Fall	おち-	おちない	おちます	おちる	おちて	おちた
Forget	わすれ-	わすれない	わすれます	わすれる	わすれて	わすれた
Gather	あつめ-	あつめない	あつめます	あつめる	あつめて	あつめた
Get up	おき-	おきない	おきます	おきる	おきて	おきた
Go out	でかけ-	でかけない	でかけます	でかける	でかけて	でかけた
Help	たすけ-	たすけない	たすけます	たすける	たすけて	たすけた
Leave	で-	でない	でます	でる	でて	でた
Look	み-	みない	みます	みる	みて	みた
Open	あけ-	あけない	あけます	あける	あけて	あけた
Put in	いれ-	いれない	いれます	いれる	いれて	いれた
Remember	おぼえ-	おぼえない	おぼえます	おぼえる	おぼえて	おぼえた
Reply	こたえ-	こたえない	こたえます	こたえる	こたえて	こたえた
Show	みせ-	みせない	みせます	みせる	みせて	みせた
Sleep	ね-	ねない	ねます	ねる	ねて	ねた
Start	はじめ-	はじめない	はじめます	はじめる	はじめて	はじめた
Teach	おしえ-	おしえない	おしえます	おしえる	おしえて	おしえた
Visit	たずね-	たずねない	たずねます	たずねる	たずねて	たずねた
Wear	き-	きない	きます	きる	きて	きた

Godan Verbs

(いく and する are considered regular godan verbs even though the forms asterisked** are irregular.)

English	Japanese stem	Base 1 A あ	Base 2 I い	Base 3 U う	te-form	ta- form
(a)						
Arrive	つ-	つかない	つきます	つく	ついて	ついた
Catch cold	ひ-	ひかない	ひきます	ひく	ひいて	ひいた
Go	い-	いかない	いきます	いく	いって**	いった**
Hold event	ひら-	ひらかない	ひらきます	ひらく	ひらいて	ひらいた
Listen	き-	きかない	ききます	きく	きいて	きいた
Play (piano)	ひ-	ひかない	ひきます	ひく	ひいて	ひいた
Walk	ある-	あるかない	あるきます	あるく	あるいて	あるいた
Wear (on feet)	は-	はかない	はきます	はく	はいて	はいた
Work	はたら-	はたらかない	はたらきます	はたらく	はたらいて	はたらいた
Write	か-	かかない	かきます	かく	かいて	かいた
(b)						
Speak	はな-	はなさない	はなします	はなす	はなして	はなした
Spend time	すご-	すごさない	すごします	すごす	すごして	すごした
Take out, post	だ-	ださない	だします	だす	だして	だした

English	Japanese stem	Base 1 A あ	Base 2 I い	Base 3 U う	te-form	ta-form
(c)						
Hold	も -	もたない	もちます	もつ	もって	もった
Wait	また -	またない	まちます	まつ	まって	まった
Stand	たた -	たたない	たちます	たつ	たって	たった
(d)						
Die	し -	しなない	しにます	しぬ	しんで	しんだ
(e)						
Drink	の -	のまない	のみます	のむ	のんで	のんだ
Read	よ -	よまない	よみます	よむ	よんで	よんだ
Rest	やす -	やすまない	やすみます	やすむ	やすんで	やすんだ
(f)	Note verbs asterisked *. Their Base 3 form looks as if it is an ichidan verb. However, they are all godan verbs.					
Be, exist	あ -	ない **	あります	ある	あって	あった
Cross street	わた -	わたらない	わたります	わたる	わたって	わたった
Cut *	き -	きらない	きります	きる	きって	きった
Display	かざ -	かざらない	かざります	かざる	かざって	かざった
Enter *	はい -	はいらない	はいります	はいる	はいって	はいった
Finish	おわ -	おわらない	おわります	おわる	おわって	おわった
Make	つく -	つくらない	つくります	つくる	つくって	つくった
Need *	い -	いらない	いります	いる	いって	いった
Rain	ふ -	ふらない	ふります	ふる	ふって	ふった
Return *	かえ -	かえらない	かえります	かえる	かえって	かえった
Ride	の -	のらない	のります	のる	のって	のった
Run *	はし -	はしらない	はしります	はしる	はしって	はしった
Sell	う -	うらない	うります	うる	うって	うった
Sit	すわ -	すわらない	すわります	すわる	すわって	すわった
Stop	とま -	とまらない	とまります	とまる	とまって	とまった
Take	と -	とらない	とります	とる	とって	とった
Know*	し -	しらない	しっています (commonly used form)	しる	しって	しった
(g)						
Buy	か -	かわない	かいます	かう	かって	かった
Celebrate	いわ -	いわわない	いわいます	いわう	いわって	いわった
Differ	ちが -	ちがわない	ちがいます	ちがう	ちがって	ちがった
Learn	なら -	ならわない	ならいます	ならう	ならって	ならった
Meet	あ -	あわない	あいます	あう	あって	あった
Say	い -	いわない	いいます	いう	いって	いった
Sing	うた -	うたわない	うたいます	うたう	うたって	うたった
Think	おも -	おもわない	おもいます	おもう	おもって	おもった
Use	つか -	つかわない	つかいます	つかう	つかって	つかった
Wash	あら -	あらわない	あらいます	あらう	あらって	あらった
(h)						
Hurry	いそ -	いそがない	いそぎます	いそぐ	いそいで	いそいだ

English	Japanese stem	Base 1 A あ	Base 2 I い	Base 1 U う	te - form	ta - form
(i) Fly Learn Play	と - - まな - - あそ -	とばない まなばない あそばない	とびます まなびます あそびます	とぶ まなぶ あそぶ	とんで まなんで あそんで	とんだ まなんだ あそんだ
Irregular Come Do		こない しない	きます します	くる する	きて して	きた した
Some verbs which follow the する *pattern* Visit Start school Invite		ほうもん しない にゅうがく しない しょうたい しない	ほうもん します にゅうがく します しょうたい します	ほうもん する にゅうがく する しょうたい する	ほうもん して にゅうがく して しょうたい して	ほうもん した にゅうがく した しょうたい した

Kinkakuji, Kyoto

Glossary Japanese – English

あ

Japanese	English	Page
あ、そうか	I see!	14
あいさつ	Greetings	16
あいだ [間]	During	16
アイロンだい	Ironing board	21
あおい [青い]	Blue	14
あかい [赤い]	Red	14
あかげ [赤げ]	Red hair	14
あかにく [赤にく]	Red meat	20
あかるい	Light, bright	21
あき [秋]	Autumn	15
あく（あいている）	To be opened, open (v.)	16
あける	To open (v.)	17
あさ [朝]	Morning	15,19
あさがお	Morning glory	15
あし [足]	Leg, foot	20
あしくび [足くび]	Ankle	20
あじさい	Hydrangea	15
あしもと [足元]	Step (gait)	22
アスパラガス	Asparagus	21
アスピリン	Aspirin	20
あたたかい	Warm	15
あたま [頭]	Head	20
あたらしい [新しい]	New, fresh	13
あっち	Over there, that direction	21
あっちがわ	That side over there	21
あつい	Hot	15
あつめる	To gather, collect (v.)	19
あに	Older brother	13
あね	Older sister	13
あの	That (over there) (adjective)	15
アパート	Apartment	20
あひる	Duck	18
あぶない	Dangerous	15
あまい	Sweet, sugary	17
あまり ... ません	Not very (much)	16
あめ [雨]	Rain	15
あれ、みて [あれ、見て]	Look at that	14
あるく	To walk (v.)	21
アルミの　あついなべ	Deep aluminium saucepan	22
あんしん [安しん]	Peace of mind, relief	21
あんしんする [安しんする]	To be relieved, free from worry (v.)	17
あんぜん [安ぜん]	Safe	18
アンテナ	TV antenna	21
アンドルー	Andrew	13
あわせて	Altogether, the sum	13

い

Japanese	English	Page
イースター	Easter	15
いえ [家]	House	19
いう [言う]	To say, call, name (v.)	13,15
いか	Squid	20
いかがですか	How is it?	20
いけぶくろ [池袋]	Suburb of Tokyo	22
いけません	Must not do	16
いこう [行こう]	I will go (volitional form of 行く)	20
いしゃ	Doctor	13
いっしょうけんめい（に）	With all one's might	21
いそがしい	Busy	16
いたい	Hurting, painful (adjective)	20
いたみ	A pain, an ache (noun)	20
いためる	To stir fry (v.)	22
いったん	Once (e.g. "Once you've stopped")	21
いちがつ [一月]	January	15
いちご	Strawberry	14
いちにちじゅう [一日中]	For/During one day	20
いちねんじゅう [一年中]	Throughout the year	19
いちばん [一ばん]	Number one	17
いちまん [一まん]	Ten thousand	19
いつか [五日]	Fifth (day of the month)	15
いつごろ	About when?	19
いっとう [一とう]	First class	19
いとこ	Cousin	13
いなりずし	Rice wrapped in fried bean curd	22
いっぱく [一泊]	One night's stay	22
インフルエンザ	Influenza	20
いみ	Meaning	13
いもうと（さん）	Younger sister	13
いや（な）	Awful	15
いらっしゃい	Welcome	22
いる	To want, to need, to require (v.)	20
いれる [入れる]	To put in, insert (v.)	22
いろ [色]	Colour	14
いろいろ（な）	Various, all kinds of, many	16
いんこ	Macaw	18
いわう	To celebrate (v.)	15
いわれている [言われている]	Is called (v.)	19

う

Japanese	English	Page
ウインドーショッピングを　する	To window shop (v.)	17
うえ [上]	On top of, above	21
ウエートレス	Waitress	13
うかがう	To call (on a person at the person's house), visit (v.)	22
うけつけ	Receptionist	13
うさぎ	Rabbit	18
うし	Cow	18
うしろ	Behind	21
うた	Song	16
うたう	To sing (v.)	21
うつくしい [美しい]	Beautiful	14
うで	Arm	20
うま [馬]	Horse	18
うまにのる [馬にのる]	To ride a horse (v.)	17
うまれる	To be born (v.)	15
うめ	Plum	15
うりば [売ば]	Counter (with cash register)	16
うる [売る]	To sell (v.)	16,17
うるさい	Noisy, annoying	16
うれしい	Happy	16
うん	Yes, all right. Okay	14

さる	Monkey	18
ざる	Bamboo plate	22
（ざるに）あげる	To put on (a bamboo plate) (v.)	22
さるやま	Monkey Mountain	18
サロンパス	Liniment-treated stick-on bandages used to relieve muscular pain	20
…さんに よろしく	Give my regards to …	21
さんかする	To participate (in) (v.)	16
さんがつ [三月]	March	15
サンドイッチ	Sandwich	13
さんぽ	Stroll, walk (noun)	14

し

し [市]	City	19
しっ	Hush! Shh!	14
シーズン	Season	17
ジーンズ	Jeans	14
しか	Deer	18
しか…ません	Only	19
しかし	However	21
しかた [し方]	Way of doing	22
しかたがない [し方が ない]	It can't be helped	22
しがつ [四月]	April	15
じかん [時間]	Time	16
しく	To make, lay out a bed (a futon) (v.)	22
じこくひょう [時こく ひょう]	Timetable	22
しごと	Job, work	17
しずけさ	Silence, tranquillity, serenity	17
した [下]	Under, underneath	21
しちがつ [七月]	July	15
シチュー	Stew	22
しつもん	Question	13
しつれいします	Excuse me	13
じつは	As a matter of fact	21
シドニー	Sydney	16
しば [芝]	Suburb of Tokyo	19
しまう	To put away (v.)	22
じむいん	Clerk, office worker	13
じむしつ	Office	17
しゃしんを とる	To take a photograph (v.)	18
しゃしんやさん [しゃし ん屋さん]	Owner/manager of a camera shop	18
しゃしょう [車しょう]	Conductor, guard (of a train)	22
しゃちょう	Company director, head of a firm	13
シャツ	Singlet or casual shirt with no buttons, T-shirt	17
しゃもじ	Large wooden spoon	21
ジャカランダ	Jacaranda	14
ジャル	Japan Air Lines (JAL)	15
じゆうせき [自由席]	Unrestricted seating	19
じゅういちがつ [十一 月]	November	15
しゅうがくりょうこう [しゅう学りょう行]	School excursion	17
じゅうがつ [十月]	October	15

しゅうしゅうを する	To collect (v.)	19
しゅうてん	Terminus, terminal	22
じゅうにがつ [十二月]	December	15
じゅく	Cram school	13
じゅぎょう	Lesson, class	17
しゅじん [しゅ人]	Husband	13
しゅっぱつする	To depart (v.)	22
しゅふ	Housewife	13
しゅみ	Hobby, interest	17
しょうかいする	To introduce oneself (v.)	16
しょうぎを さす	To play chess (shoogi) (v.)	19
しょうしょう	A little, a bit, a moment	17
しょうしょうおまちくだ さい [しょうしょうお 待ちください]	Please wait a moment	22
じょうず [上手]（な）	Skilful	16
しょうたいする	To invite (v.)	15
じょうだんでしょう？	You don't mean it? You're joking! (for females)	14
じょうだんだろう？	You don't mean it? (for males)	14
じょうばを する [じょう馬を する]	To ride a horse (v.)	19
しょうゆ	Soy sauce	21
しょっきだな	Kitchen cupboard	21
しょくぎょう	Occupation	13
しらが [白が]	White (grey) haired	14
しらたき	Clear Japanese noodles	22
しらべる [調べる]	To investigate, to look into (v.)	14
しる [知る]	To know (v.)	21,22
しる	Juices, broth	22
しろい [白い]	White	14
しろくま [白くま]	Polar bear	18
しんごう	Traffic lights	21
しんじゅく [新宿]	Suburb of Tokyo	22
しんせつ（な）	Kind, considerate	13
しんぞう	Heart	20
しんぱいしないでくだ さい	Please don't worry	18
しんぶん [新聞]	Newspaper	17
シンボル	Symbol	19

す

すいえい	Swimming	16
すいか	Watermelon	14
スイス	Switzerland	22
スーツ	Suit	17
スーツケース	Suitcase	17
スーパー（マー ケット）	Supermarket	14
すばらしい	Wonderful	16
すごく	Extremely	18
すごす	To spend (time) (v.)	20
すごすことが できる [すごすことが 出来る]	To be able to spend one's time (v.)	16
スカート	Skirt	17
スカーフ	Scarf	17
すき [好き]（な）	Like	17
スキー	Ski	16
すくない	Not many, not much, few, little	16
スケート	Skate (ice skate)	16
スケートボードを する	To skate (board) (v.)	19

Glossary 333

ねつが　ある	Have a fever	20
ねむい	Sleepy	18
ねむり	Sleep, nap (noun)	20
ねる	To sleep (v.)	17
ねん [年]	Year	15
...ねんまえに [...年前に]	... years ago	21
ねんがじょう [年がじょう]	New Year's greeting card	16

の

の	One (thing), used as a noun nominaliser	17
のう	Traditional theatre with highly stylised acting, wooden masks and elaborate costumes	17
のうぎょう	Agriculture	21
ノート	Notebook	16
のこっている	To remain behind (v.)	14
のこり	Remainder, rest	13
のこる	To be left over (v.)	22
のせる	To place (a thing) on (v.)	22
のち [後]	Future, after	15
のど	Throat	20
のぼる	To climb (v.)	19
のむ [飲む]	To drink (v.)	16
のりかえる	To change trains (v.)	19

は

は	Teeth	20
パーティーを　ひらく	To hold a party (v.)	19
パーティーを　する	To have a party (v.)	15
はいる [入る]	To enter (v.)	17
パイナップル	Pineapple	21
パイナップルジュース	Pineapple juice	16
はがきしゅうしゅう	Postcard collecting	19
はぎ	Bush clover	15
はっきり	Clearly	16
はく	To vomit (v.)	20
はく	To wear on one's feet (v.)	16
はく [泊]	Counter for night's stay	22
はくぶつかん	Museum	16
バッグ	Bag	17
バケツ	Bucket	21
はげ（あたま）	Bald-headed	14
はし	Chopsticks	17
はじめに	Firstly	22
はじめて	First time	21
はしる	To run (v.)	16
はしりまわる [はしり回る]	To run about (around) (v.)	14
はす	Lotus	15
パス	Pass (a season ticket, e.g. a JR rail pass)	19
バスタオル	Bath towel	21
パスポート	Passport	19
はたけ	Field or farm	13
はたらいている	To be working (v.)	13
はちがつ [八月]	August	15

パチンコ	Japanese pinball	17
はつか [二十日]	Twentieth (day of the month)	15
はな [花]	Flower	14
はな	Nose	18
はなが　でる [はなが出る]	To have a runny nose (v.)	20
はなしょうぶ	Iris (flower)	15
はなび [花火]	Fireworks	15
はなびを　する [花火をする]	To let off fireworks (v.)	15
はは [母]	Mother	13
はブラシ	Toothbrush	21
はみがき	Toothpaste	21
ハム	Ham	21
ハムサンド	Ham sandwich	16
はやい	Fast (adjective)	18
はやく	Quickly	18
ばら	Rose (flower)	14
はらじゅく [原宿]	Suburb of Tokyo	22
はれです	It is fine	15
はる [春]	Spring	15
はれます	It will be fine	15
はれています	It is fine	15
はん	Half	19
ばんおどり	Bon Festival dance	22
ばんごう	Number	22
パンダ	Panda	18
バンド　エイド	Bandaid	20
はんとし [はん年]	Six months (half a year)	19
ハンドバッグ	Handbag	17
はんぶん	Half	22

ひ

ひにかける [火にかける]	To put on the fire/heat/stove (v.)	22
ピアノ	Piano	16
PTAいいん	Member of Parent-Teacher Association	13
ピーナツ	Peanuts	18
ビール	Beer	16
ひかり	The bullet train that is faster than the Kodama because it stops at fewer stations	19
ひき	Counter for small animals	18
ひく	To play (the piano, guitar, violin) (v.)	17
ひくい	Low	14
ピンク（いろ [色]）（の）	Pink	14
ピクニック	Picnic	15
びっくりした	I'm surprised! You surprised me!	14
びっくりしました	You surprised me. I am surprised.	18
ひざ	Knee	20
ピザ	Pizza	19
ひじ	Elbow	20
ひしょ	(Private) secretary (to Director)	13
ビタミン	Vitamin	20
ひだりがわ [左がわ]	Left side	21
ひつじ	Sheep	18

まいねん [まい年]	Every year	19
まえ [前]	In front of, before	21
まがる	To turn, go around (v.)	21
マッサージ	Massage	20
マシュー	Matthew	13
まっすぐ	Straight up	21
まぜる	To stir, mix, blend (v.)	22
まつ [待つ]	To wait (v.)	17
まつり	Festival	15
まつやデパート	Matsuya department store	21
まだ	Still, yet	13
まないた	Chopping board	22
まなぶ [学ぶ]	To learn (v.)	16
マネージャー	Manager	13
まもなく	Soon	22
マリア	Maria	13
まる	Circle	20
まるぜん	The name of a large bookstore which stocks many books written in English	16
まんが	Comics	13
マンション	Apartment ("mansion")	21
まんぞく (な)	Contented, satisfied, satisfying	17

み

みちにまよいました	I'm lost	21
みえる [見える]	Can see (v.)	19
みっか [三日]	Third (day of the month)	15
みぎがわ [右がわ]	Right side	21
みこし	Portable shrine	22
みじかい	Short	14
みずぼうそう [水ぼうそう] (に なる)	(To have) chickenpox	20
みっつめ [三つ目] (の)	The third (in a sequence)	21
みどり (の)	Green	14
みどりのひ [みどりの日]	Green Day (29 April)	15
みにくい	Ugly	18
みね	Summit	19
みみ [耳]	Ear	20
ミリ	Millimetre	18
みる [見る]	To see (v.)	17
ミルク	Milk	13

む

むいか [六日]	Sixth (day of the month)	15
むかいがわ	Across the street	21
むぎちゃ	Barley tea, a popular drink served cold in summer	13
むこう	Other (or opposite) side	21
むしあつい	Humid	15
むすこ (さん)	Son	13
むすめ (さん)	Daughter	13
むね	Chest (of the body)	20
むらさき (の)	Purple	14

み

め [目]	Eye	14
めいしを だす [めいしを 出す]	To give one's name card (v.)	22
メートル	Metre	19
メキシコ	Mexico	21
めずらしい	Rare, uncommon, unusual	18
めのまえに [目の前に]	Right in front of your eyes	21

も

もくはんが	Woodblock print	17
もうすこし	A little more	21
もういちまい [もう一まい]	One more (flat thing)	20
…（と）もうします	I am called …	13
もうちょう	Appendix	20
もうちょう (に なる)	(To have) appendicitis (v.)	20
もし	If	22
もつ	To hold (in one's hand) (v.)	20
もってくる [もって来る]	To bring (v.)	16
もの	Thing	17
ものがたり	Tale, story	22
もも	Peach	14
もりつける	To dish up, dish out (v.)	22
もん	Gate	21

や

やおや [八百屋]	Greengrocer, vegetable shop	22
やぎ	Goat	18
やきもの [やき物]	Pottery, earthenware	17
やっきょく [薬局]	Pharmacy	13,20
やさい	Vegetables	20
やさしい	Gentle, kind-hearted	16
やさしい	Easy, simple	22
やすみ [休み]	Holiday	16
やすみの あいだ [休みの 間] （に）	During the holidays	19
やすみちゅう [休み中] （に）	During the holidays	19
やせている	To be thin (v.)	14
やね	Roof	21
やめる	Not do, to cancel (v.)	22
やる	To play, act, perform, do (v.)	22
やわらか （な）	Tender, soft	22

ゆ

ゆうがた	Evening, nightfall	19
ユーカリ	Eucalyptus tree	18

English – Japanese

A

About (a specific time)	ごろ	19
About how long?	どのぐらい	19
About when?	いつごろ	19
Above	うえ [上]	17
Ache (noun)	いたみ	20
Across the street	むかいがわ	21
Act (v.)	やる	22
Adonis, a pheasant's eye (flower)	ふくじゅそう	15
Adult	おとな [大人]	13
After	のち [後]	15
After graduation	そつぎょうご	13
Airmail	こうくうびんで [こうく便で]	21
Airpot/Vacuum flask filled with hot or cold drink	ポット	21
All (in all)	ぜんぶで	13
All kinds of	いろいろ（な）	16
All right	だいじょうぶ [大じょうぶ]	21
Alligator	わに	18
Altogether	あわせて	13
Altogether	ぜんぶで	13
Andrew	アンドルー	13
Ankle	あしくび [足くび]	20
Annoying	うるさい	16
Annoying	おっくう（な）	18
Answer (v.)	こたえる	13
Antenna (TV)	アンテナ	21
Anything	なんでも [何でも]	13
Apartment	アパート	20
Apartment ("mansion")	マンション	21
Appendicitis (have) (v.)	もうちょう（に　なる）	20
Appendix	もうちょう	20
April	しがつ [四月]	15
Area	へん	18
Arm	うで	20
Arrival	とうちゃく	17
As a matter of fact	じつは	21
Asparagus	アスパラガス	21
Aspirin	アスピリン	20
Assist someone with their work (v.)	てつだう [手つだう]	21
Asthma	ぜんそく	20
Asthma attack (seized by an …) (v.)	ぜんそくの　ほっさ（を　おこす）	20
Asthma attack (have an …) (v.)	ぜんそくの　ほっさが　ある	20
Athletics	うんどう	16
Athletics carnival	たいいくさい	15
August	はちがつ [八月]	15
Aunty	おば（さん）	13
Australia	オーストラリア	13
Autographs (collecting)	サインしゅうしゅう	19
Autumn	あき [秋]	15
Awful	いや（な）	15

B

Back	せ	14
Back	せなか	20
Bad	わるい	20
Bag	バッグ	17
Bald-headed	はげ（あたま）	14
Balloon	ふうせん	14
Bamboo plate	ざる	22
Bandaid	バンド　エイド	20
Bank	ぎんこう [銀行]	13,21
Bank clerk	ぎんこういん [銀行いん]	22
Barking	なきごえ	19
Barley tea, a popular drink served cold in summer	むぎちゃ	13
Bath towel	バスタオル	21
Bathroom	せんめんじょ [せんめん所]	21
Bean Throwing Festival	せつぶん	15
Beautiful	うつくしい [美しい]	14
Become (v.)	なる	13
Beef	ぎゅうにく	22
Beer	ビール	16
Before	まえ [前]	21
Behind	うしろ	21
Belly	おなか	20
Belongings left behind	おわすれもの	22
Belt	ベルト	17
Besides this	それに	15
Birds	とり	18
Bite (won't bite) (v.)	かむ（かまない）	18
Bitter	きびしい	15
Black	くろい [黒い]	14
Black hair	くろかみ [黒かみ]	14
Blend (v.)	まぜる	22
Blond hair	きんぱつ	14
Bloom (v.)	さく	15
Blouse	ブラウス	17
Blow (v.)	ふく	15
Blue	あおい [青い]	14
Body	からだ	20
Boil (v.)	にる	22
Bon Festival dance	ばんおどり	22
Bone	ほね	20
Book (v.)	よやくする	22
Bookcase	ほんばこ [本ばこ]	21
Bookshop	ほんや [本屋]	21
Boring	つまらない	17
Born (to be …) (v.)	うまれる	15
Bound for	ゆき [行き]	19
Bowl (deep …)	どんぶり	22
Break (a bone) (v.)	おれる	20
Bright	あかるい	21
Bring (v.)	もってくる [もって来る]	16
Broken (v.)	こわれている	20
Broth	しる	22
Brother (older)	あに、おにいさん	13
Brother (younger)	おとうと（さん）	13
Brothers and sisters	きょうだい	13
Brown	ちゃいろ [ちゃ色]（い）	14
Bucket	バケツ	21
Building	たてもの [たて物]	16
… building	…だて	16
Built (was …)	できました [出来ました]	19
Bush clover	はぎ	15
Busy	いそがしい	16

Eye	め [目]	14

F

Face	かお	13
Fact, used as a noun nominaliser	こと	17
Fairly	かなり	16
Fall (v.)	おちる	20
Fall ill	おこす	20
Farm (with livestock)	ぼくじょう	18
Farmer	ひゃくしょう	13
Fast (adjective)	はやい	18
Fat (v.)	ふとっている	14
Father	おとうさん (ちち [父])	13
February	にがつ [二月]	15
Feel sick (out of sorts)	きもちが わるいです [気もちが わるいです]	20
Fence	へい	21
Fermented beans	なっとう	18
Festival	まつり	15
Festival of Ancestral Souls	おぼん	15
Fever (have a …)	ねつが ある	20
Few	すくない	16
Field or farm	はたけ	13
Fifth (day of the month)	いつか [五日]	15
Fill in (the blanks) (v.)	きにゅうする	20
Film	フィルム	18
Film (colour)	カラーフィルム	18
Fine (it is …)	はれています	15
Fine (it will be …)	はれます	15
Finger	ゆび	20
Finish (v.)	おわる	22
Finished (to be …) (v.)	できる [出来る]	16
Fireworks	はなび [花火]	15
First (day of the month)	ついたち [一日]	15
First (in a sequence)	ひとつめ [一つ目] (の)	21
First basement	ちかいっかい [ちか一階]	16
First class	いっとう [一とう]	19
First time	はじめて	21
Firstly	はじめに	22
Fish	さかな	14
Flamingo	フラミンゴ	18
Flower	はな [花]	14
Fly away (v.)	とんでしまう	14
Fold (v.)	おる	22
Food scraps	たべもの くず [食べ物くず]	18
Foot	あし [足]	20
For/During one day	いちにちじゅう [一日中]	20
Foreigner	がいじん、がいこくじん [外人、外国人]	16
Forget (v.)	わすれる	16
Fork	フォーク	19
Form (blank)	ようし	20
Four-storeyed building	よんかいだての たてもの [四階だてのたて物]	16
Fourth (day of the month)	よっか [四日]	15
Fowl	にわとり	18
Fresh	あたらしい [新しい]	13
Frightened	こわい	18
Frog	かえる	22
From now on	これから	17
Front of (in …)	まえ [前]	21
Frying pan	フライパン	21

Funny	おかしい	22
Future	のち [後]	15

G

Gas stove	ガスレンジ	21
Gate	もん	21
Gather (v.)	あつめる	19
Gentle	やさしい	16
Get down from (v.)	おりる	22
Get off (v.)	おりる	22
Ghost	ゆうれい	18
Ginza line	ぎんざせん	19
Giraffe	きりん	18
Girl	おんなのこ [女の子]	15
Give my regards to …	…さんに よろしく	21
Glass	ガラス	19
Go (Japanese board game using black and white stones)	ご	16
Go out (v.)	でかける [出かける]	20
Go sightseeing in (v.)	けんぶつに いく [見ぶつに 行く]	19
Goat	やぎ	18
Golf	ゴルフ	16
Good	よい、いい	20
Good idea	よいかんがえ	18
Gradually	だんだん	15
Gram	グラム	21
Grandfather	おじいさん、そふ	13
Grandmother	おばあさん、そば	13
Grapes	ぶどう	14
Grass	くさ	14
Great	すてき (な)	16
Green	みどり (の)	14
Green Day (29 April)	みどりのひ [みどりの日]	15
Greengrocer	やおや [八百屋]	22
Greetings	あいさつ	16
Guard (of a train)	しゃしょう [車しょう]	22
Guitar	ギター	16
Give one's name card (v.)	めいしを だす [めいしを 出す]	22

H

Hair	かみ (のけ)	14
Hair brush	ヘアブラシ	21
Half	はん	19
Half	はんぶん	22
Hall	ホール	16
Ham	ハム	21
Ham sandwich	ハムサンド	16
Hand	て [手]	20
Handbag	ハンドバッグ	17
Happy	うれしい	16
Harajuku (suburb of Tokyo)	はらじゅく [原宿]	22
Have a cold (v.)	かぜを ひいている	20
Have a party (v.)	パーティーを する	15
Have the experience	…ことが ある	21
He	かれ	21
Head	あたま [頭]	20
Healthy	げんき [元気] (な)	18

Hear (be able to) (v.)	きこえる [聞こえる]	19
Heart	こころ	16
Heart (medical term)	しんぞう	20
Heavy	おもい	19
Height	たかさ [高さ]	19
Help (v.)	てつだう [手つだう]	21
Help me (I'm in danger!)	たすけて　ください	16
Help someone who is in trouble (v.)	たすける	22
Hen	にわとり	18
Here, this direction	こっち	21
Hibiya (suburb of Tokyo)	ひびや [日比谷]	19
High	たかい [高い]	14
High school	こうこう	14
Hikari (the bullet train that is faster than the Kodama because it stops at fewer stations)	ひかり	19
Hippopotamus	かば	18
Hobby	しゅみ	17
Hold (an event) (v.)	ひらく	15
Hold (in one's hand) (v.)	もつ	20
Hold a party (v.)	パーティーを　ひらく	19
Holiday	やすみ [休み]	16
Home (your)	おうち	13
Hong Kong	ホンコン	19
Horse	うま [馬]	18
Hospital	びょういん [病院]	13
Host family	ホスト　ファミリー	13
Hot	あつい	15
Hot chips	フライドポテト	16
Hotel	ホテル	20
House	いえ [家]	19
Housewife	しゅふ	13
Housing development (high rise)	だんち	21
How can I help you?	ごようけんを　どうぞ	20
How is it?	いかがですか	20
How many days?	なんにち [何日]	20
How many floors? Which floor?	なんかい [何階]	16
How many hours?	なんじかん [何時間]	19
How many minutes?	なんぷん [何ぷん]	19
How many months?	なんかげつ [何か月]	20
How many nights?	なんぱく [何泊]	22
How many times?	なんかい [何回]	21
How many weeks?	なんしゅうかん [何しゅう間]	19
How many years?	なんねんかん [何年間]	19
How to	かた [方]	22
However	けど	15
However	けれども	17
However	しかし	21
However	それでも	19
However (less formal than keredomo)	けれど	21
Huh?	ええ？	14
Humid	むしあつい	15
Hurting (adjective)	いたい	20
Husband	しゅじん [しゅ人]	13
Husband (my)	おっと	13
Hush!	しっ	14
Hydrangea	あじさい	15

I

I am called …	…（と）もうします	13
I had an enjoyable time	たのしく　すごしました	20
I think that is so	そうだとおもいます [そうだと思います]	17
If	もし	22
Ikebukuro (suburb in Tokyo)	池袋	22
Illustration	え	13
Important	たいせつ [大せつ](な)	16
In	なか [中]	21
Inconvenient	ふべん（な）	18
Influenza	インフルエンザ、かぜ	20
Ingredients	ざいりょう	22
Insert (v.)	いれる [入れる]	22
Inside	なか [中]	21
Intelligent	りこう（な）	18
Interest in (have an) (v.)	きょうみを　もつ	19
Interested in (to be …) (v.)	きょうみが　ある	13
International	こくさい [国さい]（の）	22
Interpreter	つうやく	13
Introduce oneself	しょうかいする	16
Investigate (v.)	しらべる [調べる]	14
Invite (v.)	しょうたいする	15
Iris (flower)	はなしょうぶ	15
Iron (metal)	てつ	19
Ironing board	アイロンだい	21
It can't be helped	しかたがない [し方がない]	22
It was awful	たいへん　でした	17
Itchy	かゆい	20

J

Jacaranda	ジャカランダ	14
January	いちがつ [一月]	15
Japan	にほん [日本]	13
Japan Air Lines (JAL)	ジャル	15
Japan Alps	にほんアルプス [日本アルプス]	15
Japanese cooking	にほんりょうり [日本りょうり]	17
Jeans	ジーンズ	14
Job	しごと	17
Juices	しる	22
July	しちがつ [七月]	15
June	ろくがつ [六月]	15
Junior high school student	ちゅうがくせい [中学生]	15

K

Kangaroo	カンガルー	18
Karaoke (form of nightclub entertainment)	カラオケ	17
Kilometre	キロ	20
Kind	しんせつ（な）	22
Kind-hearted	やさしい	16
Kitchen	だいどころ [だい所]	21
Kitchen cupboard	しょっきだな	21
Kitchen knife	ほうちょう	22
Knee	ひざ	20
Knife	ナイフ	19
Know (v.)	しる [知る]	21,22

My spouse	おっと	13

N

Name (v.)	いう [言う]	13,15
Nap (noun)	ねむり	20
Narita airport	なりた　くうこう	15
Narrow, pokey, confined	せまい	21
Nearby	ちかい [近い]	21
Nearby	ちかく [近く] （の）	16
Necessary	ひつよう（な）	17
Neck	くび	20
Necktie	ネクタイ	19
Need (v.)	いる	20
Neighbourhood	きんじょ [近所]	21
Never	けっして … ません	16
New	あたらしい [新しい]	13
New Year	おしょうがつ [おしょう月]	15
New Year's Day food (special)	おせちりょうり	15
New Year's Eve	おおみそか	15
New Year's greeting card	ねんがじょう [年がじょう]	16
News	ニュース	17
Newspaper	しんぶん [新聞]	17
Next	つぎ	13
Next door, next door neighbour's house	となり	21
Next month	らいげつ [来月]	15
Next to, beside	そば	21
Nightfall	ゆうがた	19
Ninth (day of the month)	ここのか [九日]	15
Noisy	うるさい	16
Nonetheless	それでも	19
Noo (theatre with highly stylised acting)	のう	17
Nose	はな	18
Not at all	ぜんぜん … ません	16
Not do (v.)	やめる	22
Not many, not much	すくない	16
Not very (much)	あまり … ません	16
Notebook	ノート	16
November	じゅういちがつ [十一月]	15
Number	ばんごう	22
Number one	いちばん [一ばん]	17
Numerous	おおい	14
Nurse	かんごふ	13

O

Occupation	しょくぎょう	13
October	じゅうがつ [十月]	15
Office	じむしつ	17
Office worker	じむいん	13
Oh!	わあ！	14
Oh! I'm surprised (at such a magnificent sight)!	わあ　おどろいた！	14
Okay	だいじょうぶ [大じょうぶ]	21
Okay	よろしい	17

Old (not used for people)	ふるい	16
On doing that	すると	21
On the same side	ならび	21
On this day	そのひ [その日]	15
One (thing), used as a noun nominaliser	の	17
One hundred	ひゃく [百]	15
One more (flat thing)	もういちまい [もう一]	20
One night's stay	いっぱく [一泊]	22
One person	ひとり [一人]	13
One-piece dress	ワンピース	17
One thousand	せん [千]	15
One way	かたみち	19
Only	しか…ません	19
Only	だけ	20
Open (v.)	あける	17
Opened, open (v.)	あく（あいている）	16
Orange (coloured)	オレンジ（いろ [色]）（の）	14
Orange juice	オレンジジュース	16
Other (or opposite) side	むこう	21
Outside	そと [外]	21
Over there, that direction	あっち	21
Overcoat	オーバー	17
Owner/manager of a camera shop	しゃしんやさん [しゃしん屋さん]	18

P

Package (noun)	こづつみ	21
Pain (noun)	いたみ	20
Painful (adjective)	いたい	20
Panda	パンダ	18
Pants, trousers	ズボン	17
Paper	かみ [紙]	14
Paper folding	おりがみ	17
Paper money	さつ	20
Parent-Teacher Association (member of)	PTAいいん	13
Parents	りょうしん	13
Participate (in) (v.)	さんかする	16
Pass (a season ticket, e.g. a JR rail pass)	パス	19
Passport	パスポート	19
Peace of mind, relief	あんしん [安しん]	21
Peach	もも	14
Peacock	くじゃく	18
Peanuts	ピーナツ	18
Pear (Japanese)	なし	14
Pedestrian crossing	ほどうきょう	21
Penguin	ペンギン	18
Perform (v.)	やる	22
Perhaps	たぶん	20
Persevere (v.)	がんばる	16
Persimmon	かき	14
Personal effects (one's)	おてまわりひん [お手回りひん]	22
Pharmacy	くすりや [薬屋]	13
Pharmacy	やっきょく [薬局]	13,20
Physique	たいかく	14
Physique (have an excellent …)	たいかくが　いい	14
Piano	ピアノ	16
Picnic	ピクニック	15
Picture	え	13

Pig	ぶた	18
Pinball	パチンコ	17
Pineapple	パイナップル	21
Pineapple juice	パイナップルジュース	16
Pink	ピンク（いろ [色]）（の）	14
Pizza	ピザ	19
Place	ところ [所]	16,22
Place (a thing) on (*v.*)	のせる	22
Plants	き [木]	14
Plates	さら	21
Platform	ホーム	19
Platypus	かものはし	18
Play (the piano, guitar, violin) (*v.*)	ひく	17
Play (*v.*)	やる	22
Play chess (shoogi) (*v.*)	しょうぎを　さす	19
Playground, school oval	グランド	16
Playing cards	トランプ	16
Please don't worry	しんぱいしないでくだ	18
Please don't …	… ないでください	20
Please help me! (I'm in danger!)	てつだってください	13
Please wait	おまちください	17
Please wait a moment	しょうしょうおまち ください [しょうしょ うお待ちください]	22
Plum	うめ	15
Polar bear	しろくま [白くま]	18
Polite	ていねい（な）	16
Portable shrine	みこし	22
Post (*v.*)	だす [出す]	21
Post office	ゆうびんきょく [郵便 局]	21
Post box (a red-orange colour)	ポスト	21
Postcard collecting	はがきしゅうしゅう	19
Pottery	やきもの [やき物]	17
Pour on (*v.*)	かける	22
Principal	こうちょう（せんせい [先生]）	13
Programme, schedule, plan	よてい	19
Programme, e.g. television programme	プログラム	17
Proper	ただしい	21
Pupil (of the eye)	ひとみ	14
Purple	むらさき（の）	14
Put away (*v.*)	しまう	22
Put in (*v.*)	いれる [入れる]	22
Put on (a bamboo plate)	（ざるに）　あげる	22
Put on the fire/heat/ stove (*v.*)	ひにかける [火にかけ る]	22

Q

Question	しつもん	13
Quickly	はやく	18

R

Rabbit	うさぎ	18
Radish	だいこん	14

Rain	あめ [雨]	15
Rain (*v.*)	ふる	15
Raincoat	レインコート	17
Rainy season	つゆ	15
Rare	めずらしい	18
Razor	かみそり	21
Read (*v.*)	よむ [読む]	17
Ready (to be …) (*v.*)	できる [出来る]	16
Really	ほんとうに	13
Really?	ええ?	14
Reason	わけ	22
Receptionist	うけつけ	13
Record	レコード	17
Red	あかい [赤い]	14
Red hair	あかげ [赤げ]	14
Red meat	あかにく [赤にく]	20
Refrigerator	れいぞうこ	21
Relieved, free from worry (to be …) (*v.*)	あんしんする [安しん する]	17
Remainder	のこり	13
Request (*v.*)	おねがう	19
Require (*v.*)	いる	20
Research (*v.*)	けんきゅうする	17
Rest	のこり	13
Return/round trip	おうふく	19
Rhinoceros	さい	18
Rice cakes	おもち	15
Rice cakes made for Otsukimi	つきみだんご	15
Rice planting	たうえ	15
Ride a horse (*v.*)	うまにのる [馬にのる]	17
Ride a horse (*v.*)	じょうばを　する	19
Ride on a train	でんしゃに　のる [電車 に　のる]	19
Right, correct	ただしい	21
Right in front of your eyes	めのまえに [目の前に]	21
Right side	みぎがわ [右がわ]	21
Ring, telephone (*v.*)	でんわを　かける [電話を　かける]	17
Road	とおり	21
Rollerskate (*v.*)	ローラースケートを　する	19
Roof	やね	21
Room	へや	21
Roots	ね	22
Ropeway	ロープウェイ	20
Rose (flower)	ばら	14
Rugby	ラグビー	16
Rules	きそく	16
Run (*v.*)	はしる	16
Run about	はしりまわる [はしり 回る]	14
Runny nose (have a) (*v.*)	はなが　でる [はなが 出る]	20

S

Safe	あんぜん [安ぜん]	18
Salad	サラダ	16
Salary man (white-collar worker)	サラリーマン	17
Salesperson	てんいん	13
Same	おなじ	21
Sandwich	サンドイッチ	13
Sasanqua (camellia)	さざんか	15
Satisfied, satisfying	まんぞく（な）	17

English	Japanese	Ch.
Saucepan	なべ	21
Sausage	ソーセージ	21
Say (*v.*)	いう [言う]	13,15
Scared	こわい	18
Scarf	スカーフ	17
Scenery	けしき	20
School dance	ダンスパーティー	15
School excursion	しゅうがくりょうこう [しゅう学りょう行]	17
School uniform	せいふく	13
Science	かがく	17
Scribble	らくがき	16
Seamail (by …)	ふなびんで [ふな便で]	21
Season	きせつ	15
Second (day of the month)	ふつか [二日]	15
Second (in a sequence)	ふたつめ [二つ目] (の)	21
Second basement	ちかにかい [ちか二階]	16
Second class	にとう [二とう]	19
Secretary, private (to Director)	ひしょ	13
See (*v.*)	みる [見る]	17
Seized with	おこす	20
Sell (*v.*)	うる [売る]	16,17
Send (*v.*)	おくる	16
Senior high school student	こうこうせい	15
September	くがつ [九月]	15
Serenity	しずけさ	17
Seventh (day of the month)	なのか [七日]	15
Severe, strict	きびしい	15
Sew (*v.*)	ぬいものを する	19
She	かのじょ [かの女]	14
Sheep	ひつじ	18
Shelf	たな	21
Shh!	しっ	14
Shiba (suburb of Tokyo)	しば [芝]	19
Shinjuku (suburb of Tokyo)	しんじゅく [新宿]	22
Shoe shop	くつや	13
Shop assistant	てんいん	13
Short	みじかい	14
Shoulder	かた	20
Sick	びょうき [病気]	14
Sick bay, rest room	きゅうけいしつ	14
Side	がわ、よこ	21
Sightsee/see the sights (*v.*)	けんぶつする [見ぶつする]	19
Sightseeing (*v.*)	かんこうする	19
Sightseeing tour (to go on a …) (*v.*)	かんこうりょこう [かんこうりょ行] （する）	19
Sign	ひょうしき	22
Sign (*v.*)	サインする	20
Signpost	ひょうしき	22
Silence, serenity	しずけさ	17
Simple, easy	やさしい	22
Sing (*v.*)	うたう	21
Single (one-way)	かたみち	19
Singlet or casual shirt with no buttons, T-shirt	シャツ	17
Sink (in the kitchen)	ながし	21
Sister (older)	おねえさん、あね	13
Sister (younger)	いもうと（さん）	13
Six months (half a year)	はんとし [はん年]	19
Sixth (day of the month)	むいか [六日]	15
Skate (board) (*v.*)	スケートボードをする	19
Skate (ice skate)	スケート	16
Ski	スキー	16
Skilful	じょうず [上手] （な）	16
Skirt	スカート	17
Sky	そら	14
Slacks	スラックス	17
Sleep (*noun*)	ねむり	20
Sleep (*v.*)	ねる	17
Sleepy	ねむい	18
Slender	ほそい	22
Slow	おそい	18
Smelly (awful), stinking	くさい	18
Smoking (no …)	きんえん	22
Snake	へび	18
Snow (*noun*)	ゆき	15
Snow (*v.*)	ふる	15
Snowman	ゆきだるま	15
Soba (clear Japanese noodles)	しらたき	22
Soft	やわらか（な）	22
Soft tennis	ソフトテニス	22
Something	なにか [何か]	18
Son	むすこ（さん）	13
Song	うた	16
Sony building	ソニービル	21
Soon	まもなく	22
Soon, before long	さきに	21
Souvenir	おみやげ	20
Soy sauce	しょうゆ	21
Spa (hot)	おんせん	19
Spaghetti	スパゲッティ	19
Spend (time) (*v.*)	すごす	20
Spend one's time (be able to …) (*v.*)	すごすことが できる [すごすことが 出来る]	16
Spoon	さじ	22
Spoon	スプーン	19
Sports Day	たいいくのひ [たいいくの日]	15
Sports festival	うんどうかい	15
Spread out, unfold (*v.*)	ひろげる [広げる]	22
Spring (season)	はる [春]	15
Square cloth used to wrap goods	ふろしき	20
Squid	いか	20
Stairs	かいだん [階だん]	22
Stamp collecting	きってしゅうしゅう	19
Star Festival	たなばた	15
Start school (*v.*)	にゅうがくする [入学する]	15
Station master	えきちょう [駅ちょう]	22
Stay (at a place) (*v.*)	たいざいする	22
Stay (*v.*)	とまる [泊まる]	19
Steamed egg custard	ちゃわんむし	22
Steel	てつ	19
Step (gait)	あしもと [足元]	22
Stew	シチュー	22
Still	まだ	13
Stir fry (*v.*)	いためる	22
Stir (*v.*)	まぜる	22
Stomach	おなか	20
Stop (*v.*)	とまる [止る]	21
Story, tale	ものがたり	22
Straight up	まっすぐ	21
Strange	おかしい	22
Strange	へん（な）	18
Strawberry	いちご	14
Street	とおり	18
Stroke order	かきじゅん	13
Stroll (*noun*)	さんぽ	14
Strong (*adjective*)	つよい [強い]	15
Strongly (*adverb*)	つよく [強く]	15

Student	がくせい [学生]	16
Subject (school)	かもく	17
Sugar	さとう	22
Sugary	あまい	17
Suit	スーツ	17
Suitcase	スーツケース	17
Summer	なつ [夏]	15
Summit	みね	19
Sunflower	ひまわり	15
Superb	すてき（な）	16
Supermarket	スーパー（マーケット）	14
Surely (very likely)	きっと	20
Surf (v.)	サーフィンを　する	19
(I'm) surprised! You surprised me!	びっくりした	14
(You) surprised me. I am surprised.	びっくりしました	18
Sweater	セーター	17
Sweep (a house) (v.)	そうじする	17
Sweet	あまい	17
Swimming	すいえい	16
Switzerland	スイス	22
Sydney	シドニー	16
Symbol	シンボル	19

T

Table	テーブル	19
Tablespoon	おおさじ [大さじ]	22
Take (a length of time) (v.)	かかる	19
Take a photograph (v.)	しゃしんを　とる	18
Take off (jacket) (v.)	ぬぐ	22
Take pleasure in (v.)	たのしむ	16
Tale	ものがたり	22
Tall	たかい [高い]	14
Tatami mat shop	たたみや [たたみ屋]	21
Tea ceremony	ちゃのゆ	17
Tea ceremony (study of …)	さどう	17
Teach (v.)	おしえる [教える]	13,16
Teacher (used when talking about self)	きょうし [教し]	13
Teeth	は	20
Telephone (v.)	かける	17
Telephone number	でんわばんごう [電話ばんごう]	17
Television (colour)	カラーテレビ	16
Ten thousand	いちまん [一まん]	19
Tender	やわらか（な）	22
Tennis	テニス	17
Tenth (day of the month)	とおか [十日]	15
Terminal	しゅうてん	22
Terminus	しゅうてん	22
Terrific	りっぱ（な）	13
That (adjective)	その	15
That (over there) (adjective)	あの	15
That kind of …	そんな	18
That side	そっちがわ	21
That side over there	あっちがわ	21
That's a good idea	それは　よい　かんがえですね	18
The fact that I could come	これたこと	16
There, that direction	そっち	21
Therefore	それで	15

Thin	ほそい	22
Thin (to be …) (v.)	やせている	14
Thing	もの	17
Things	こと	16
Think (v.)	おもう [思う]	13,14,17
Think about (v.)	かんがえる	16
Third (day of the month)	みっか [三日]	15
Third (in a sequence)	みっつめ [三つ目]（の）	21
This (adjective)	この	15
This kind of …	こんな	18
This month	こんげつ [今月]	15
This morning	けさ [今朝]	20
Throat	のど	20
Throughout the year	いちねんじゅう [一年中]	19
Ticket	きっぷ	19
Ticket wicket	かいさつぐち	19
Tie up (a furoshiki) (v.)	つつむ	22
Tiger	とら	18
Time	じかん [時間]	16
Time (free …)	ひま	18
Timetable	じこくひょう [時こくひょう]	22
Tired (to be …) (v.)	つかれる	19
Title for young people	…ちゃん	13
Toaster	トースター	16
Toilet paper	トイレットペーパー	21
Tomato	トマト	16
Tomato sandwich	トマトサンド	16
Tonsillitis	へんとうせんえん	20
Tonsils	へんとうせん	20
Toothbrush	はブラシ	21
Toothpaste	はみがき	21
Top of	うえ [上]	21
Towel	てぬぐい [手ぬぐい]	21
Towel rack	ふきんかけ	21
Traffic lights	しんごう	21
Tranquillity	しずけさ	17
Travel (v.)	りょこうする [りょ行する]	17
Travel around Japan	にほんじゅうりょこうする [日本中りょ行する]	22
Travel the world (v.)	せかいじゅうりょこうする [せかい中りょ行する]	22
Traveller's cheques	トラベラーズチェック	20
Trees	き [木]	14
Troublesome	おっくう（な）	18
Trousers	ズボン	17
True, truth	ほんとう	15
Turn (v.)	まがる	21
Turn off (v.)	けす	22
Twentieth (day of the month)	はつか [二十日]	15
Two people	ふたり [二人]	13
Typhoon	たいふう	15

U

Ugly	みにくい	18
Um, let me see	ええと	19
Uncle	おじ（さん）	13
Uncommon, rare	めずらしい	18
Under, underneath	した [下]	21

Understand (v.)	わかる [分かる]	15
Unfortunately, it is unfortunate	ざんねんですが ...	21
University	だいがく [大学]	13
University student	だいがくせい [大学生]	14
Unlikeable	きらい（な）	17
Unrestricted seating	じゆうせき [自由席]	19
Unusual, rare	めずらしい	18
Urgent business	きゅうよう	20
Use (v.)	つかう	16
Utensils	どうぐ	22

V

Vacuum cleaner	そうじき	21
Various	いろいろ（な）	16
Vegetable shop	やおや [八百屋]	22
Vegetables	やさい	20
Very	とても	14
Vice (Deputy) principal	ふくこうちょう(せんせい) [先生]	13
Video	ビデオ	22
Violet (flower)	すみれ	14
Visit (v.)	うかがう	13
Visit (v.)	たずねる	19
Visit (v.)	ほうもんする	20
Vitamin	ビタミン	20
Voice	こえ	16
Vomit (v.)	はく	20

W

Wait (v.)	まつ [待つ]	17
Waitress	ウエートレス	21
Walk (noun)	さんぽ	14
Walk (v.)	あるく	21
Want (adjective)	ほしい	20
Want (v.)	いる	20
Want (third person) (v.)	ほしがっている	20
Want to ... (I)	...たいです	13
Wants (someone else)	...たがっている	20
Warm	あたたかい	15
Washing machine	せんたくき	22
Waste paper basket	くずかご	21
Water temperature, bath	ゆかげん	19
Watermelon	すいか	14
Way of doing	しかた [し方]	22
Wear (v.)	きる	15
Wear on one's feet (v.)	はく	16
Weather	てんき [天気]	15
Weather report	てんきよほう [天気よほう]	19
Welcome	いらっしゃい	22
Welcome, we are glad that you have come	ようこそ いらっしゃいました	22
Well, healthy	げんき [元気]（な）	18
Well, skilful	よく	19
Well then	ところで	17
Well, in that case	それでは	22
Western food	せいようりょうり [西洋料理]	16
What	なに [何]	13
What?	えっ？ええ？	14

What day?	なんにち [何日]	15
What do you think about it?	...どうおもいますか [...どう思いますか]	17
What kind of ... ?	どんな	18
What month?	なんがつ [何月]	15
What number?	なんばん [何ばん]	17
What to do	どうする	22
What track number?	なんばんせん [何ばんせん]	19
What's happened?	どうしたんですか	20
What? Really? Are you sure?	へえ？	14
When you've done that, then	そうすると	21
Where does it hurt?	どこが いたいんですか	20
Whereupon	すると	21
Which (one)?	どの	15
Which one(s)?	どちら	14
Whining, barking	なきごえ	19
White	しろい [白い]	14
White (grey) haired	しらが [白が]	14
Why?	なぜ	19
Wide	ひろい [広い]	18
Wife	おくさん、かない	13
Wife, my spouse	つま	13
Wind	かぜ	15
Window shop (v.)	ウインドーショッピングを する	17
Winter	ふゆ [冬]	15
Wish to have (1st, 2nd person) (v.)	ほしい	20
Wish to have (3rd person) (v.)	ほしがっている	20
Wisteria	ふじ	15
Won't you please ...	...くださいませんか	13
Wonderful	すばらしい、すてき（な）	16
Woodblock print	もくはんが	17
Wooden	きの [木の]	19
Wooden bowl	おわん	21
Wooden spoon (large)	しゃもじ	21
Word processor	ワープロ	14
Work	しごと	17
Working (to be ...) (v.)	はたらいている	13
World (in the)	せかいで	19
Wrap (a furoshiki) (v.)	つつむ	22
Wrist	てくび [手くび]	20
Written (to be ...) (v.)	かいてある [書いてある]	22
... written in Japanese	にほんごで かいてある [日本語で 書いてある]	21

Y

Year	ねん [年]	15
... years ago	...ねんまえに [...年前に]	21
Yellow	きいろ [き色]（い）	14
Yet	まだ	13
Your kindness	ごしんせつ（な）	16
Youth hostel	ユースホステル	21

Z

| Zero | ゼロ | 16 |
| Zoo | どうぶつえん [動物園] | 18 |